A Life of Soolivan

A Life of Soolivan

Based on the Recollections of John MacLeod, Gael, Traveller, Rebel, Convict and Raconteur

CALUM FERGUSON

This edition first
published in 2004 by
Birlinn Limited
West Newington House
10 Newington Road
Edinburgh EH9 1QS

www.birlinn.co.uk

ISBN 1 84158 328 6

British Library Cataloguing-in-Publication Data
A catalogue record for this book is available
from the British Library

Designed and typeset in Sabon
by Mark Blackadder, Edinburgh

Printed and bound by GraphyCems, Spain

CONTENTS

Acknowledgements

I am grateful to the large number of friends who helped me to write this book.

Aiginis & Garrabost – Donald Alasdair MacDonald, Duncan MacLeod, Sandy MacLeod, Nan S. MacLeod. *Aird* – Donnie (Dhòmhnaill Eòghainn) Martin, Anna Màiri Martin, Peggy MacLeod. *An Cnoc* – Jack Nicolson, Tarmod (Chaluim Chuileim) MacLeod. *East Kilbride* – Peggy A. Darroch. *Pabail Iarach* –Kenneth (Curro) MacLeod, Angusan MacLeod, John (Hoddan) MacDonald, Dòmhnall Iain a' Chànrain MacLeod. *Pabail Uarach* – Calum Murray, Donald J. MacKenzie. *Port Mholair* – Murchadh (Bhob) Ferguson, Iain Eachann Ferguson, Iain (Nomy) Campbell, Calum E.MacKenzie. *Port nan Giùran* – Iain (an t-Saighdeir) MacDonald, Angus Campbell, Iain (Dhoilidh) Campbell, Murdo Dan (Sheumais) MacDonald. *Seisiadar* – John MacAulay, Cailean Iain MacDonald, Norman MacDonald, Nora Tharmoid Uilleim. *Siadar* – Calum Iain Murray. *Steòrnabhagh* – Sheriff Colin S. MacKenzie, Iain (Ghràidein) MacAskill, Maggie MacKay, Iain (Louis) MacLeod, John (Shondan) MacLeod, Joanne MacKenzie. *Suardail* – John Murdo MacLeod, Kenneth (Cully) MacLeod. *Edinburgh* – Kenneth ('Ain Dowdall) MacLeod. *Liverpool* – Andrew MacLeod. *Red Deer, Alberta* – Doug MacLay. *Sasunn* – Dr Màiri Sterland. *Norway* – Geir Ottesen, Ian Wood.

For permission to reproduce photographs from their archives, thanks to the Scottish Fisheries Museum; National Trust for Scotland; Scottish Ethnological Archive; Shetland Museum and Leabharlann Steòrnabhaigh; for supplementary landscape photography and computing support, Kenneth Ferguson; and for aerial photography, Bristow Helicopters and, particularly, the late Bob Alderson of Bristow's.

I am grateful for the enthusiasm and advice of Bridget Mackenzie of Dornoch, whose specialist knowledge of Norse proved invaluable in the interpretation of many of the place-names. Ciad mìle taing also to Iain MacDonald of Eilean Ghriomsaigh, who proof-read the text and advised on orthography and presentation. Extra-special thanks to my wife, Sandra, for her continuous support and patience during my hours of research and writing.

Introduction

The world of my childhood was Port Mholair, a small crofting township at the tip of the peninsula called the Rubha, on the Isle of Lewis. Most of the eighteen families in the township were closely related to each other through more than a century of intermarriage. In short, the people of Port Mholair lived and worked together as a clan and provided a stimulating environment in which to spend one's formative years.

Unlike the clans of yore, our clan was not led by just one chieftain. Port Mholair had eighteen chieftains, namely the tenants of the township's eighteen crofts. The local ruling body was called the Grazings Committee, a forum in which the biggest egos and the loudest voices prevailed.

Except for six weeks in the summer when the township was invaded by Glasgow Highlanders, the language of my childhood was exclusively Gaelic. The 'invaders' were the children of local men and women who had long since migrated to Glasgow in search of employment and had returned to their native heath, seeking short-lived respite from the polluted air and raucous sounds of the shipyards and city streets. The extrovert city-bred children quickly shed their pallor and bloomed in the fresh, clean breezes of the seaside. They always arrived in the Rubha at the same time as another extrovert summer visitor – the corncrake. In July and August, the declamatory cries of both children and bird resounded with bright, carefree echoes in the sunlit crofts and craggy hills. Heather moors slowly turned to rose and romances blossomed.

The Minch is the sea channel separating the Outer Hebrides from the mainland of Scotland. It is some thirty miles wide and dominates the lives of the people living along its shores. The serrated mountain chain on the distant horizon, stretching from Cape Wrath in Sutherland to the Coolin Hills of Skye, is a translucent frieze behind which the sun rises. It is enchantingly beautiful and, to the mind of the Lewis child, is forever beckoning. Beyond that frieze is the far-off, intangible world which grown-ups call 'Away'.

In my young days, few folk from 'Away' could speak Gaelic (or cared not to) and so were called 'strangers'. In the heat of the late summer when the air was crystal clear, the atmospheric conditions

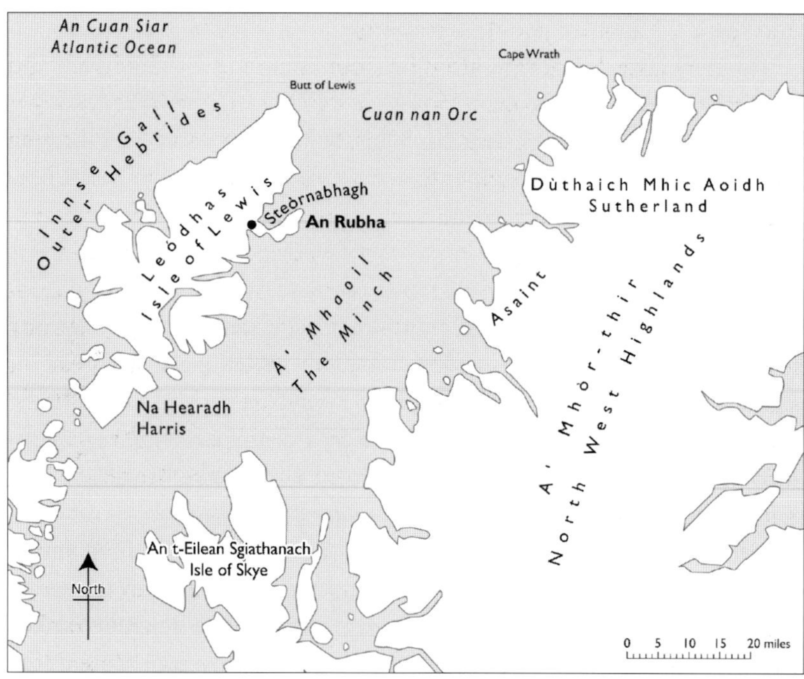

produced mirages and one could sometimes discern buildings on the mainland. In those magical moments the imagination was excited and made one yearn to touch what was seemingly intangible.

The Minch itself was mysterious, alive with fish shoals, seabirds, basking sharks and many varieties of sea mammals – otters, seals, dolphins and whales. As a child I could imagine that in the tide-torn depths of the Minch the sea monsters of legend lurked, unseen since the days of the Féinne!

Beneath the visible world in which I was privileged to awaken was the nether world of the *Sìthichean* – the Little Folk – who haunted the minds of old men and women and excited hours of discussion in the ceilidh house. To the child of the 1930s, the *Sìthichean* were as real as the rage of the north wind or the glory of the summer sunset!

Located two miles from my home was an august institution called *Sgoil na h-Àirde* (otherwise Àird Public School) at which one learned a foreign language called English. All teaching was through the medium of that language so that, at first, most monoglot infants found their introduction to the Three Rs as bewildering as it was nerve-racking. As crofters' children, the pupils had a far more interesting form of education at home. While still infants, they helped their parents and grandparents to look after sheep, cattle and poultry. They learned how to read the weather and the tides. By the time they were twelve years old, they knew scores of Gaelic songs, proverbs and psalms; knew how to work the plough, the harrow, the scythe and the peat-cutter. Perhaps more importantly, they learned the importance of family loyalty and the need for family unity. They learned manners

Lewis lies some thirty miles west of the Scottish mainland

and respect for other people's property.

Shortly after I began to attend school, a man called Soolivan who had been away was 'brought home' to No. 11. The phrase 'brought home' suggested that the man who had been away had been suffering from some kind of incapacity, the nature of which was left to titillate the imagination. Adults seemed to know the cause of Soolivan's misfortune but never spoke of it in the presence of children. In due course, a small, felt-roofed cottage known as Taigh Shuileabhain (Soolivan's House) was built by the roadside, halfway between my home and school. For months, neither my school pals nor I caught sight of its reclusive occupant but, from fireside gossip, we gathered that women were dismissive of him as a *truaghan**, a person of neither worth nor substance. By contrast, men seemed to regard him with muted admiration.

It was nearly a year before we caught a sight of the Soolivan, a fresh-faced, broad-shouldered man with a square jaw and a ready smile. He was poorly clad, spoke Gaelic spiced with Yankee expressions and had a habit of gesticulating with half-closed fists which were disproportionately large.

'Howdy, young fella! Bheil sibh gu math air Ceann a' Loch? Sure is a good day to be alive, eh!'

After he settled into his new home, Soolivan acquired a wife called Shonag, a local woman who was the mother of his child, born many years previously. Like most of the middle-aged women in our district, Shonag was good-humoured and stout, and generally wore a floral overall and calf-length wellington boots. Owing to an accident suffered during the carting home of the annual supply of peats, she had lost her left eye. Coincidentally, her husband likewise had lost his left eye, but that had happened in circumstances which, according to himself, were 'best left unsaid and, in any case, were beside the point!'

'Two right eyes is OK, now that none on the left is left!'

In the years before the Second World War, the House of Soolivan was a magnet for all the young bachelors of the district. Alas, it was emptied of its ceilidh-makers as soon as Britain declared war on Hitler's Germany in 1939. In that year, the slow tempo of life in the Western Isles quickly changed, as did the scenery and the people around us. Within a month of war being declared, all the able-bodied men and women in the community departed on the mail-steamer from Steòrnabhagh (Stornoway), many of them never to return. Simultaneously, uniformed warriors transporting an assortment of weaponry and other unfamiliar hardware appeared all around us. Camouflaged trucks, laden with soldiers and airmen, roared along the

* A poor wretch.

roads. Concrete pillboxes snuggled into the cliffs. Throughout the Rubha, clusters of Nissenhuts surrounded by tunnel upon tunnel of barbed wire were built overnight to house some of the thousands of military personnel swelling what remained of our Hebridean population. The peacetime drifters and trawlers and tramps sailing through the panorama of the Minch gave way to convoys of ponderous, grey merchantmen overhung with barrage balloons and escorted by fast-moving destroyers, frigates or corvettes. The tall pyramids of radar aerials began to dominate the skyline. As the war progressed, we came to recognise the unsteady drone of the occasional German aircraft. The restrained throb of Whitley bombers, which seemed to move across the sky at walking pace, was gradually replaced by Anson bombers and Sunderland flying-boats of Coastal Command. Then came the waspish Spitfires and Hurricanes waltzing over moors and skimming across stretches of water, as if high-flying were denied them. As the war progressed and the tide began to turn in favour of the Allies, those aircraft, in turn, were replaced by new generations of bombers and fighters, the most spectacular of which were the Super Fortresses that migrated in from the far side of the Atlantic to roost briefly on the Machair at Mealabost, before flying off to active theatres of war.

The BBC's news bulletins were crucial to our understanding of the progress of the war. The language of the 'wireless' was English. Everybody listened even to the German radio station which poured forth Lord Haw-Haw's torrent of anti-British propaganda. Everybody listened, but not everybody understood. Young minds quickly learned the meaning of expressions such as 'Blitzkrieg', 'strafing', 'Resistance', 'Scorched Earth', 'Stalags' and 'Third Column', and translated them for the old. It was at that time that the English language took a grip that it has never relinquished.

Uniformed Geordies, Cockneys, Yanks, Newfoundlanders, Poles and Free French mingled with civilians on the streets of Steòrnabhagh. For a brief period, even Italian POWs, who were intended to live inconspicuously in the sylvan environs of the Lews Castle grounds, mingled with the throng. Their idyll ended after a 'civil disturbance' – the result of their persistently courting the sisters and girlfriends of lads who were fighting Italians and Germans in the deserts of North Africa.

After their demob, ex-servicemen felt compelled to return to our village carrying various forms of obsolete, though yet lethal, weaponry, including revolvers, jungle-knives and hand-grenades. Our father arrived home armed not only with a Lee Enfield rifle of First World War vintage but also with several thousand rounds of armour-piercing bullets, a tiny fraction of the huge consignment which the

Admiralty had instructed him to dump in the Atlantic.

In 1946, half a dozen veterans of the 1914–15 Somme and Gallipoli campaigns spent many happy hours behind the hills teaching youngsters the art of rifle shooting. Among the veterans was the one-eyed Soolivan, who, owing to the fact that he was unable to 'get a bead on the sights', was unable to contribute much to the youngsters' instruction. Without reference to the military authorities or coastguards, explosive mines which had broken free from their moorings and drifted close to our shores were promptly sunk by unauthorised rifle-fire. The sinking of the mines gave a semblance of respectability to the unlicensed arsenal under our parents' bed. As soon as the supply of ammunition was spent, the rifle was committed to the deep.

Even by the time I graduated from the University of Aberdeen at the age of twenty-two, my travels had not extended much beyond the bounds of Scotland. Rationing of food and clothing had only just ended, money was scarce and, so far as crofter folk were concerned, holidays abroad were unheard of. University education had opened my eyes to the extent of my own ignorance and made me crave for an opportunity of visiting foreign lands and, through first-hand experience, discovering the outside world.

During my vacations, I spent much of my time in the company of the older generation of Gaels in the Rubha – gentle, unassuming men and women steeped in our oral tradition and ever ready to draw on their extensive repertoire of songs, poetry, proverbs and stories. In peacetime, most of them had earned their living by following the herring fishing round the British Isles at ports such as Lerwick, Wick, Fraserburgh, Lowestoft and Yarmouth. A number of the women had been 'in service' in grand houses and hotels in the cities of the south and had acquired some of the genteel polish required of them by their urban employers. Some of the men had been through the carnage of the Somme or Gallipoli or had served in the Royal Navy during the First World War. To a degree, all of those men and women were religious – all, that is, except for the one called Soolivan. In the closing years of his life, I spent many hours in Soolivan's company. The more I listened to his tales, the more I realised that, in his heyday, he was an undisciplined rascal, intelligent, strong-willed and rebellious. Considering the poverty of his childhood and the harsh social conditions that he endured throughout his adolescence, his behaviour is understandable if not entirely excusable.

'A bhalaich, come in and chat to old Soolivan here, a man edicated in the Academy of Hard Knocks – the University of Life – in which the professors were brute ignorant and you earned your degree by your bodily strength and your cunning.'

Soolivan's attitude to life and death was unique among the Gaels of his generation. He did not repent his hell-raising past; nor did he appear to be unduly concerned about his fate in the hereafter. His were tales of personal conflicts mainly, but also of love, betrayal, and dramatic escapes from perilous situations in places as far apart as Australia, Patagonia, Fiji, Mexico, Canada, Turkey and, not least, the 'Old US of A'.

The following collection of stories, translated from Gaelic, was first published in 1983 in *Suileabhan,* a book which in the following year won the literary award at the National Mod. Although the stories are in chronological order, they are by no means intended as a biography. I offer them as recounted to me a few years after the Second World War and cannot guarantee their accuracy in detail or in substance. When telling yarns through the medium of English, Soolivan did so with a slight American drawl, occasionally interjecting a Gaelic phrase or proverb which seemed to him more expressive of his thoughts. His was a forthright style, humorous and robust, and, in the austere surroundings of the living room of the House of Soolivan, the storyteller held his listeners spellbound.

Like many men and women of his generation, Soolivan had a talent for composing poetry. Towards the end of his life, he was happiest when seated in the open air, viewing the grassy, rounded hills of his native Port Mholair. When last I saw him, he was composing a snatch of *bàrdachd* in praise of his homeland – 'the most beautiful place in God's creation!' His Crimean shirt was unbuttoned at the throat and his cap, as usual, was slightly askew on his head. He lifted his gnarled right hand to the hills and peered through his one eye.

'I'm glad that, at the end of my life, I am sitting here in my forefathers' village and able to look upon my Cnuic an Aigh – my Hills of Joy!'

Foitealar, Goitealar Tom an Fhithich's an t-Siùmpan!
Nam biodh cothrom coiseachd agam, dheighinn fhathast unnta.
'S iomadh latha muladach a dh'fhuiling mi gan ionndrainn;
Ach thog iad mi gu sunnd nuair a thill mi nan còir.

[Foitealar, Goitealar, the Raven's Hill and the Siùmpan!
If my legs could carry me, I'd walk those knolls once more.
In foreign lands, I dreamed of them and of the freedom there
to roam;
And when at last I returned to them, on wings my spirit soared.]

Chapter One
Temptations Galore

Schools Black and White

My mother and father got what little schooling they had in the *Sgoil Cheap*, the Turf School, an earthen bothy on Iain Beag's croft at Lot No. 7. The children in the Turf School were taught in Gaelic. Those were the days of the Great Bible Thumpers. Religion had taken over people's lives everywhere, so that the children had to memorise whole chunks of the psalms. They were also taught to read and write and do arithmetic and a certain amount of English, which they learned as if they were parrots. As soon as I was born, they passed an Act of Parliament saying that every child in Great Britain had to get their education through the English language. That made life very difficult for me and all other Gaelic children. We were taught through a foreign language.

Just before I came on the scene, the authorities built a new school at Druim Oidealar in the Aird, about a mile from my home at No. 11 Port Mholair. It was officially called Àird Public School – a whitewashed building with big windows, chimneys, slates on the roof and a wooden floor. Each classroom had benches to sit on, desks and a sort of pulpit and high chair for the teacher. They demolished the old Turf School at No. 7, which was an awful pity. The only good thing that came out of that English-only education act was that the *riasg* (raw peat) from the old Turf School provided three months' fuel for the family of Iain Beag.

Wasn't I the toff when I started going to school and got my first book. I was as proud as a cockatoo. Unfortunately, it wasn't long before I took a terrible dislike to the school and all who taught there. Talk of tyranny! Some of the teachers were no kinder to the pupils than the jailers of Jacksonville Penitentiary were to convicts doing hard labour. *'S mi a bha thall 's a dh'fhairich!** Although the majority of the teachers were brutal, there was one of them who was particularly so – a fellow from Sutherland whose English name I never knew. Everyone out of his hearing just called him the Caoidheach, which is the Gaelic for 'a man from Sutherland'. A big, handsome fellow he

* I am one who can vouch for that.

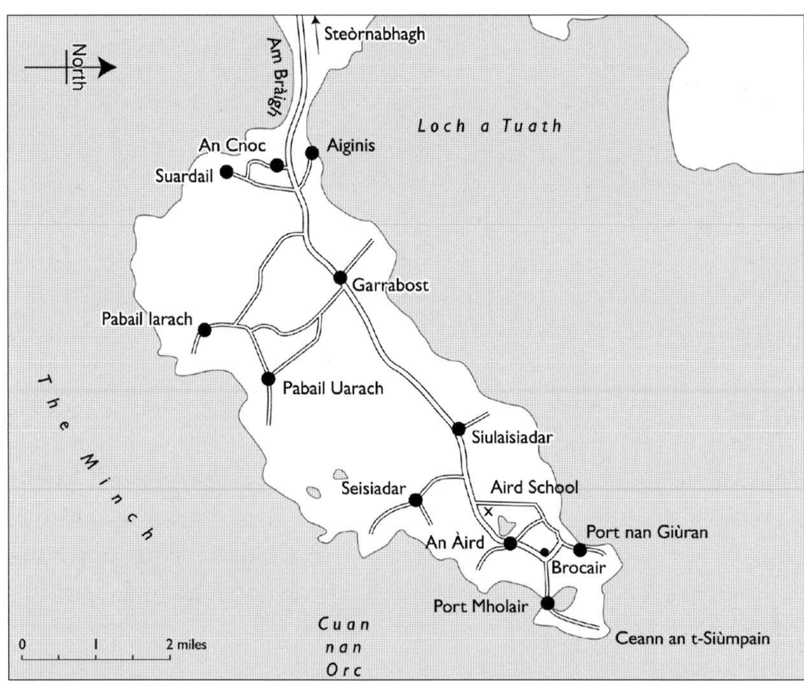

was, fair-haired, with a crisp ginger moustache on him drooping over his top lip. When the man was in a lather of anger, bubbles of foam rained in all directions from the tufts at the corners of his moustache. The Caoidheach was a Christian. On Sundays he would go to church as meek and mealy-mouthed as a lamb. By George, though, come Monday, there was not much of his Christian goodwill to be seen in his behaviour. He was a raging bull, shouting sarcastic comments and threatening us with the tawse. That was the method of teaching in those days – education through fear. If you weren't shaking in your boots listening to your teacher, it was assumed that you were not taking in any of the 'sùbhags' [strawberries] he was after spreading out in front of you. Mind you, English aside, our heads were already so full of Gaelic rabbits and Gaelic cuddies that there wasn't a great deal of room for anything else!

I was about twelve years old when I was promoted to the Caoidheach's class. It was a promotion that neither he nor I welcomed. I was a sturdy boy for my age, and I had grown that strong that I wasn't scared of any other *brogach* [lad] going to Druim Oidealar. Not a day went by that didn't see me in a scrape with somebody. Though it is myself that's saying it, I was pretty good with my fists. That's as I remember it anyway. But I was scared of the Caoidheach all right. He was bigger than me and he had two types of tawse, each able to inflict a different degree of agony. As if that wasn't enough, he had the School Board on his side and there was no power but the Lord more powerful than the School Board.

Port Mholair, at the outmost tip of An Rubha, is about ten miles from the isthmus of Am Bràigh

One winter's morning, my mother got me out of bed. I looked out of the window – a miserable morning, with a scatter of sleety snow on the wind and a thin plate of ice on the puddles. I ate my porridge and off I went on my bare feet as usual, with my three schoolbooks bound with the leather strap I had stolen from Innis Uilleim's stable. Oh, I remember the morning well, a dull twilighty day with that strong, searching wind you get when it comes at you out of the Broad Bay. My mother came to the door after me and gave me an old coat of hers, which I placed over my head. And off I went.

I was up by Loch an Dùin when I realised that I had not taken my *fàd,** with me for the classroom fire. No problem! I stole one from 'Slingeam's peat-stack and, with my books and my purloined *fàd* under my arms, I went on my way. 'Slingeam', you see, was a really good Christian, a close relative of my father, and if he had seen me taking the peat, he would not have minded. That was the way of it in those days. All the families were either poor or very poor, and there was a great sense of fellowship among them and a willingness to share.

I heard the bell while I was on the open road on Druim Oidealar moor. The playground gradually fell silent and I began to panic a little, but my feet were so cold that they would not run for me. I entered the classroom with my books and my *fàd* under my arm, and my mother's coat around my head.

The pupils, sitting in rows on the benches, were as quiet as mice. The Caoidheach had his head in the attendance-register, so I tried to tiptoe silently past him. Suddenly, out of the blue came a noise like a terrible clap of thunder and a searing pain burned through my calves. On turning round, I saw Himself glowering over me with a squall on his face, and I realised that he had given me a skelp with the tawse. *A Chruthaigheir,* although I was numb with the cold, my temper caught fire. Dropping my *fàd,* I threw the coat off my head and I let hang the books I was carrying bound together by Innes Uilleim's leather thong.

'What's your excuse this time, boy?'

I had no voice to answer him but stood there before him, measuring him for an almighty wallop if he should attack me again. When he saw this obvious act of defiance, he returned to his high chair, closed the attendance register, opened his desk and substituted for the broad four-fingered tawse with which he had struck me a two-finger heavy-duty tawse. The Caoidheach advanced on me, snarling like Tarmod Iomhair's crazy bitch. When he was nearly at me, I swung my books, aiming them at his head. The blow landed on him four-square and he fell backwards and moaned as his shoulder hit the corner of the cupboard. The Caoidheach was upset, to say the least!

* A block of peat dried by wind and sun.

What man wearing a cravat would not have been? He gathered himself together, left the strap behind him on the floor and made for me again, determined to punish me with his bare hands. But if he did, I was ready for him. As he approached, so did I advance on him. It was now a full-blown scrap. Every man-jack in the class rose on his or her feet in support of me. I heard them behind me, like the Highland Light Infantry in a charge, with their war-cries ringing in the rafters! I got my arms around the teacher's waist and I started to squeeze so that the wind was emptying out of his chest. Oh, I was fairly going at him and I was quite surprised that someone who had terrorised me for so long could be so weak in my bear-hug.

'Gabh dha!' [Let him have it!] shouted the class.

Right enough, on that morning, I got a lot of coaxing. And did I give them a soiree, holding the merciless ruler of our class in my grasp. I believe that the Caoidheach was near to fainting. His two eyes were like two seagull's eggs about to fall out of his red face. But then, did he not catch a glimpse of my two purple feet, firmly planted under him on the floor. He had on him a pair of tackety boots and did *Mac an Diabhail** not lift his booted foot, and put all his strength into pressing it on my already numb, bare *spàg* [foot]! Och, I let go my hold on him at once and fell to the floor writhing. And was it a surprise that that brutal *tràill* [villain] won? Numb as it had been with the wind and ice, my foot now swelled under me till it was the size of a pan-loaf! Holding on to my *spàg,* I looked up and saw the Caoidheach towering over me. Wounded though I was, he made me stand before him.

'Now,' he began – (oh, he wouldn't speak anything but English) – 'you insolent, unspeakable wretch: I'm going to give you a choice. Are you going to take your punishment for your conduct from me? Or shall I send you to the headmaster?'

I knew only too well that if I was sent to the headmaster, my mother would be summoned by the School Board, and I did not wish for that. Yet I felt angry and defiant and, with as firm a voice as I could master, I says, 'I'll take my punishment, so long as you don't stamp on my bare foot again.'

Well, talk about punishment! That grown-up fella dressed to kill – bow-tie an' all – made me stand on a seat and then gave me five lashes of the heavy-duty tawse to my calves and my buttocks. Strangely enough, I never felt any pain after the first two lashes.

Before returning to the register, the Caoidheach, sweating like a pig, growled at the class, 'I shall deal with you later!'

The looks on the faces of the boys and girls sitting on the benches

* Devil's son.

told him, as they told me, that the events of that morning could not be erased from their memory. The teacher had won the morning's battle with Soolivan but his pupils had lost their last ounce of respect for him. Not even the tawse would win that back for him. And as events were to show before the winter was over, the children had even lost their fear of him. Not for the first time, I hobbled down the road like an old man after the school skailed. I swore that day, as I fought back my tears, that I would never again accept such a beating from the Man from Sutherland – School Board or no School Board.

In the weeks following the classroom brawl, the Caoidheach withdrew into himself. Maybe, at last, his conscience was bothering him. Anyhow, I never forgave him for the pounding he dished out to me that day, and, although I feel a wee bit guilty about it now, I confess that I tried to make his life as miserable for him as I could. I continued to arrive at class later than I should, and at every ebb-tide skulked away from school to sit eating dulse in Geodha Mhór Sheisiadair. *A Charaid ort*, those were the Good Old Days. No wonder I grew up to be such a gentleman.

THE TEACHER'S ROAD-BOAT

One night, after a particularly heavy fall of snow, the villages went to sleep under a beautiful white sheet. During the night, the thaw came and messed it all up. In the morning, when we put our *piullagan* [ragged clothes] on to go to school, we discovered that the gravel roads were clear but the snowdrifts were still deep in the ditches. As always, I walked the mile to Druim Oidealar on my bare feet. And I wasn't the only one. A lot of the children did not have shoes but that

Soolivan's favourite edible seaweeds: dulse (left), *mircean* and *daoithean*

didn't seem to bother us too much in those days. At least, that's the way I remember it.

Anyway, I spent another long day at school, miserable and impatiently waiting for the final bell to ring. As ever, the Caoidheach was his raging self, lashing the kids with his tongue and with his tawse.

Now, although I had no great love for him, I have to admit that, in his own way, he was a clever fellow. He had put together an invention that became the talk of the Rubha. Well, perhaps you couldn't really call the thing 'an invention'. It was more a contraption – a kind of road-boat that was made by adding bits and pieces to a bicycle. It had an upright mast sticking straight up above the front wheel, and then tied on to that there was a sail hung from it like a curtain. To the lugs of the sail the Caoidheach had attached two ropes, which he held in his hands as he grasped the handlebars. By those ropes, he controlled the trim of the sail just the same as a fisherman out of Port nan Giùran would use the 'sheets' on a *sgoth* – an open-decked boat. I don't tell a word of a lie, but before you could get a thing like that to work properly, he would have had to have a five-man crew aboard the bicycle.

The road-boat had two faults. In the first place, the rider couldn't

Left.
'. . . desperately pulling on his brakes . . .'

Opposite.
Tangles hung with dulse are easily accessible at low tide

see the road very well because the sail was before him. Most sensible people would agree that anyone riding a bike of any sort must have a clear view of the road ahead. As well as that, you should also have some way of stopping the vehicle in an emergency. Well, as things turned out, the brakes on the Caoidheach's road-boat weren't up to much. They couldn't have been, you see! The wind billowing in the sail made it hard for the rider to stop. But, being a religious man, maybe the fellow was relying on the Almighty to guide him as he whirred along the Druim Oidealar Road which, after four o'clock, was always swarming with school-weary, hang-dog kids. In due time, us home-bound children learned to stand well off the road until the tall, billowing sail of the teacher and the braying horn passed us by. In my childhood, I could name several *cailleachan* [old women] between here and Druim Oidealar who were as deaf as a post – as, indeed, was Iain Beag's mare! If any of them had been on the road at quarter past four, they would have been at risk, but as Fate would have it, the *cailleachan* and Iain Beag's mare had enough savvy to stay indoors or behind the peat-stacks until the whirring contraption carrying the teacher passed by.

For many weeks, everyone in our class quietly prayed for the fall of the tyrant. When you think of it, we were wicked little buggers! The Caoidheach himself had told us, over and over, that those who took Holy Communion were 'God's elect'. The fellow imagined that, since he was a regular church-goer, God was his mate. None of his pupils really believed that. We knew in our heart of hearts that God was on our side and, with a little help from us, He would arrange one day for our oppressor to come a cropper. Och, we all knew it in our bones, right enough. And one day, it happened!

It was about quarter past four and we were traipsing down the road, but were still within sight of the school. Looking back to Druim Oidealar, we watched the well-groomed figure of the teacher mount his *eathar-rothaid*, his road-boat. There was a good strong wind from the south-west and it quickly filled the sail. Soon the Caoidheach was a goose feather floating on the breeze. As usual, he began to sound his horn and the children scattered out of his path. Before he had reached the bend at Loch an Dùin, he was moving as fast as a hawk chasing a sparrow. There was a crowd of us boys just off the road at Loch an Dùin, a hundred yards before you came to the homes of the 'Bloody' and Tarmod Dhòmh'll 'Ic Dhòmhnaill. I can't remember who said something along the lines that, if the Caoidheach were a hawk, you could bring it down with the throw of a stone. Oh, you can see that Satan was at us again! Well, I could never make up my mind whether it was Satan or the other fellow – but whichever it was, the idea was a good one. All the boys began to look for suitable missiles.

Now, you have to believe that in my generation and in the generations before that, Highland boys were first-class stone-throwers. Older boys than me – the likes of 'Bigg' and Tarmod Chailein – could remove the handle off a china chamber pot from a distance of fifty yards. No doubt about that, for I have seen them both do it. When those two fellas were around, none of the housewives would put out a sparkling clean chamber-pot on the thatch.

On that special afternoon, the wind billowing in his sail made it hard for the teacher to stop at all, though you could see that he was desperately pulling on his brakes. As he was on the point of coming level with us, everyone prepared to let fly. Well, the missiles we threw arrived on target just after the road-boat had passed us. Not one actually hit the man, nor indeed were they intended to.

They arrived in the poke of his sail – a hail of *oileagan**, snowballs and hard chunks of ice. Och, it wasn't out of the ordinary marks-manship at all!

The poor landlubber, wobbling on the road-boat, tried to let go of the two ropes he was holding on his handlebars. Amidst all the hurly-burly, didn't the front wheel suddenly leave the road and the whole vehicle do a somersault, out of sight. By George, the Caoidheach was nowhere to be seen, not even a leg of him! There was dead silence.

'O Lord!' says somebody. 'I bet we'll all get flogged – especially if we've killed him!'

Right enough – I dreaded the thought that our deed might bring the wrath of the School Board down on our parents' heads in a few days' time. I can honestly say that I wanted my poor mother never to suffer on my account.

We went over to where the teacher had vanished – the big boys and all the infants who had been congregating at the edge of the road. There the Caoidheach lay in the ditch with his eyes blinking and himself, poor fellow, wishing that he wasn't where he was. You wouldn't be far wrong if you said he was looking poorly, sprawling like that in the trenchful of slushy snow. When he managed to get to his feet, he looked as uncomfortable as a wet shirt on a clothes-line. Freezing cold he was and his teeth were chattering out of control.

Och, you just had to pity the man! When he managed to collect himself, he fair spat with temper. And it didn't help the situation when we offered to carry him home. *Cha robh taing an taig a sheanar*! That was the kind of man he was, not an ounce of gratitude in him.

The Caoidheach tried to lift his contraption on his own but he failed, so he trudged off down the road with water squelching in his trousers and in his brogues.

* Fist-sized stones.

That was the last sight we ever saw of the tyrant teacher. So far as I know, he never again entered the school precincts. Served him right, in my opinion. He had made my life, and the life of every other child trapped under his authority, so sour that we had turned out like himself – like savages. I am not going to say that the children who were under him were genteel and polite by nature. No, sir! They were like generations of crofters' children who had gone before them, scarcely able to survive in a world of oppression and poverty. My generation had to suffer a school system that was part-punishment, part-bullshit. Our masters seemed determined to break our spirit or to rid the country of us all together. If the Caoidheach and the other teachers had shown us a glimmer of compassion instead of continuously bullying us, maybe it would have made life easier for them and for us.

The wreck of the Caoidheach's road-boat soon rusted in the roadside *dìg* [ditch] opposite Loch an Dùin. None of us touched it. It just lay there disintegrating, a symbol of one man's oppressive authority that was shattered and could never be mended.

The Tinker's Burial

There were two John MacLeods in my class. I was one and Shony Nàsan was the other. Shony was an upright citizen from the start – one who rose in education so high that, in the end, he became a university professor. But on one particular day, being in the company of Soolivan (as I came to be known), he went and blotted his conduct-sheet good and proper.

I suppose that we were about nine or ten years of age at the time, and Shony and I were sitting beside each other in the classroom – two John MacLeods as fond of each other as *dà cheann each* – the two horses' heads of the proverb.* For some reason that I couldn't understand, Shony had a terrible interest in what the teacher was trying to teach us. If I ever had a couple of books, my friend would have three times as many. An honest, bright young fellow he was, born into a community of Gaelic urchins. He was so bright and honest that he sometimes fell foul of the school bullies. Well, I saw to it that anyone who tried to bully Shony Nàsan had to answer to me. Right enough, I fancied myself in those days. A bleeding nose or a black eye or a torn jersey – or all three – never bothered me. That's why they called me Soolivan after the great John L. Sullivan, who, in my day, was the invincible World Heavyweight Boxing Champion.

* Evoking the image of two horses in harness, ploughing or reaping.

Hard as nails and full of vim I was. That's how I saw myself anyway. Damn fool I must have been, for I remember taking quite a few poundings.

You ask me why I never became a university professor? Well, there were many reasons for that, including the obvious one, that I didn't have the necessary grey-matter. To a large extent, I blame my rebellious nature for the way my life turned out. But, above all, I blame the School Board who saw to it that we were confined indoors at a stage in our lives when all we wanted was the open air of the hills. My generation was born to run in the heather, to fish and wrestle – not to sit on hard seats for hours on end listening to the one rasping voice preaching endlessly and throwing the occasional question at us weary children. I grant you that the work of the teacher was hard in those days, but if it was, then life for the children was ten times harder.

As I said, schooling wasn't hard for Shony Nàsan. He soaked up his education like a sponge. I have not got the faintest idea why it was that Shony ended up in my company during our dinner-break on one particular day. But I vividly remember skulking with him in the peat-banks of the Mòinteach Mhór, so that the teachers wouldn't see us from the school windows at Druim Oidealar.

'Come on up to Cnoc Chùsbaig,' says I. 'The funeral of one of the tinkers is going to be in the Siadar camp today.'

Shony had no wish to go among the tinkers, for he was wearing his new pair of trousers that were barely a week old. He didn't want them to get ruined in a wild adventure. Fair enough, I agreed, but then all of a sudden, the solution to Shony's problem came to me. Oh, the Sàtan himself had a field-day in my head that morning.

'We'll take our trousers off,' says I, 'and we'll hide them in a peat-stack. If we go to the funeral without any trousers, the tinkers will think that we belong to their clan.'

It must have been about the end of August for there were scores of peat-stacks lining both sides of the main road, ready to be carted home. We took off our trousers, and Shony couldn't stop laughing, We hid our trousers under peats in the Griogalach's *cruach* [peat-stack] at the end of the Seisiadar road, a quarter mile from the tinkers' camp at Cnoc Chùsbaig. We pulled our jerseys down to our knees like frocks and rubbed wet peat on our legs and faces, so that we wouldn't look normal. It was drizzly anyway, and before we reached the tinkers' camp we looked like two scrawny chickens!

We heard the hubbub of the camp long before we reached it. There were three pipers standing well apart from one another, each playing a different lament. At the same time, half a dozen young boys with chanters were each playing any tune that came into their heads. What a beehive. There was an assortment of half-clad infants wandering around the tents, some of them squalling like lambs looking for their mothers in a fank. At the doorway of one of the tents, there was a heavyweight *cailleach* [old woman], singing to herself a sorrowful Gaelic lament. In her lap she nursed a piggy of whisky. As soon as she saw us, she called us over and hung her head to one side to show how sad she felt.

'Ochan-ochan, isn't the very day itself weeping for Seumas mac Dhòmhnaill Sheumais!' she said. She took a swig from the piggy and then took a hold of Shony, who by this time was shivering with fright and cold.

''Ille!' says she, 'who is it you said you belong to?'

Being unpractised in the art of telling lies, Shony stood dumb. Says I, 'We're just the grandsons of Alasdair Mór from Ceann nam Buailtean.'

News of who we were distressed the *cailleach* no end.

'It's yourselves that are the grandsons of the great man! I say that though my own husband, God rest his soul, thought Alasdair Mór was a world-beating *trustar* [filthy wretch].'

She took another swig from the piggy. 'Of course, that was because the piebald horse he sold him died before a quarter year was out.'

She told us in confidence that Alasdair Mór was in favour with her personally, but out of favour with a lot of the others present.

As we had no idea who Alasdair Mór was, I felt that it was pointless to try to explain away the matter of the piebald horse. Suddenly, the *cailleach* was overcome with a bout of weeping: 'Och, no wonder my heart is sore. Isn't the very day itself weeping salt tears.'

After she recovered, the *cailleach* uttered the very words that I wanted to hear, 'Come along now till you get a *strùpag* [swig] out of my piggy!'

Cha b' e ruith ach leum! Now you're talking, lady! She gave the piggy to Shony first, and as soon as the firewater touched his tongue, he began to spit and splutter as if he had been scalded. The *cailleach* laughed as she watched Shony's antics. When she handed the piggy to me, the expression on her face slowly changed to a scowl as I drank a long, healthy *slugan* out of it.

'Enough!' she cries, as I clung to the piggy. 'Gléidh mi! Give me back my uisge-beatha!'

Although my head began to reel, I danced a little jig while holding the tails of my jersey. That pleased her a lot and she rolled about with laughter. And no wonder, for I had forgotten that my trousers were lying hidden in the Griogalach's peatstack, and without realising it, I had treated her to an exhibition of my most precious possessions.

Out of a hut men appeared with the remains, which were in a kist made of thin white board, just like a kipper-box. On their heel several women appeared, all of them wailing. The last to appear was a good-looking young woman who carried a child in her arms. She threw herself on the kist, sobbing and resisting the gentle efforts of the men to remove her.

'I will not allow you to do the burial,' she cried, 'unless my child is allowed to see her dead grandfather!'

At that, the toothless *cailleach,* still clinging to her piggy, stood up from her seat, looking very wild. 'If the daughter of Alasdair Dhòmhnaill's child is allowed to see the bodach, then every grandchild must also be allowed a keek!'

What a lot of grandchildren there were, from tiny little babies to big strapping youths. What a kerfuffle. Shony and I joined the throng and after a while managed to have a dekko at the fellow lying snug on his back in the kist. As we were crowding round, my eye caught sight of two teenage boys staring at me.

'Come on!' Shony whispers under his breath. 'These fellows know that we're not blood!'

The two boys, about fifteen years old, bore down on us. Big, broad-shouldered *brogaich* they were, with stacks of reddish hair and freckles on their faces.

'Leigibh dhaibh! Leave them alone!' shouts the *cailleach*. 'They are of ourselves. Alasdair Mór of Ceann nam Buailtean sent them instead of himself. He didn't dare come to Cnoc Chùsbaig because of the piebald horse that had the tacket! But that was a while ago, although I'm sure he's still a crooked bastard.'

She laughed heartily and distracted the boys by offering them a *slugan* out of her piggy. Shony and I shot off, and I swear that a sheepdog would have had difficulty catching up with us. Near the Griogalach's peat-stack, we washed ourselves in the ditch by the roadside, and then went to retrieve our trousers. We couldn't believe our eyes. There was not a sign of the trousers. Not a thread, not a button could we find.

We had demolished half the stack, looking for our clothes, when we heard a woman approaching with a creaking creel on her back, piled high with peats. She was knitting a long woollen stocking.

'You two blackguards, why have you demolished the peat-stack of the poor Griogalach. Shame on you, you rascals! What vandals you are!'

Right enough, there were peats lying all over the place. *A bhalaich ort*, we were in a right pickle. Standing aghast, the woman was running out of things to call us. For myself, insults were nothing new, but Shony became quite upset.

'Please don't call us that!' he bleated with his face white as a sheet. 'We hid our trousers in the stack, and we cannot find them.'

'There's a good reason for that,' replies the woman. She suddenly belly-laughed and a couple of peats fell off the top of her load. 'This morning, I saw a cow chewing items of clothing on this very spot. What a shame that I didn't know that she was eating your trousers!'

She continued to laugh as she surveyed our plight, but then set off with her creaking creel. As she went, she shouted back, 'Your four trouser-legs are now in a cow's belly walking home to Seisiadar. Funny cow-pats she will be delivering in the morning!'

Shony and I skulked off homewards, crouching along the peat banks until we reached near to the Breun-loch. We stayed in hiding there in an *iodhlann chàil** until the sun touched Beinn Bharabhais.

When I reached home, my mother was waiting for me with my father's shaving-strap dangling from her wrist. As my buttocks were bare, access to my backside was not going to be a problem for her. But in spite of the waving of the leather shaving-strap, physical punishment was not my mother's style. She specialised in something far more unpleasant – an hour of shouting, bawling and huffing! She ignored my news that a cow from Seisiadar had eaten my trousers. Nor was she upset or surprised when I admitted that I had been playing truant from school. What really upset her was that the Sàtan had made her believe that I had lost my life on the cliffs of the terrible Geodha Mhór Sheisiadair, one of my favourite playgrounds.

That evening, Shony Nàsan fared better than I, but his day of reckoning was yet to come. In those olden days, parents couldn't afford to buy more than one pair of trousers per son, per annum. They bought the trousers in the autumn, just at the end of the herring fishing. From the beginning of the summer, the trousers of most boys in the island were held together by patches, safety-pins and sometimes (in my own case) even by two-inch nails. O, I don't tell a word of a lie! I swear that when I lost the buttons off the rim of my trousers, I used to insert two-inch nails in the cloth and attach the loops of my braces to them. It was an excellent invention. Of course, I cannot claim that I had invented it. For it had been in use long before my time.

What the Seisiadar cow had done amounted to swallowing Shony Nàsan's annual quota of trousers! Shony had a serious problem all right, but like the intelligent fellow he was, he found a solution to it. When he arrived home, he discovered that his parents were out at their usual mid-week prayer-meeting. Unlike my mother, the Nàsan parents believed that the Sàtan could never lead their son from the straight and narrow. They didn't have to worry if their son was late coming home from school because he would never dream of taking

* A moor-land nursery built with high turf walls and surrounded by a moat; used for growing cabbage seedlings.

the crooked path that led to the terrible cliffs of Geodha Mhór Sheisiadair.

Poor Shony was quite desperate. He went up to the *cùlaist* [bedroom] and, with the 'shissor', he cut the legs off the first pair of adult trousers he met with in the clothes-chest. Perfectly content he was, tailoring at his leisure, not realising that he was de-legging his father's only good trousers – his Sunday best! After an hour or so, he heard the worshippers coming along the road, nattering solemnly about the highlights of the prayer session. Having pulled on the abbreviated trousers, Shony rushed off with the detached leggings and hid them as a bundle, in a dark corner beside the peats-bunker. When his parents entered the living room, their son – the apple of their eye – was in his usual place at the table doing his homework by the light of the paraffin oil lamp.

Like almost all the houses in Lewis, the inside of the Nàsan home was very dark. That's why the old thatched dwellings were called black-houses. It was to my friend's advantage that his mother couldn't see properly for, as sure as guns, she would have noticed that the garment on her son's lower half was not his. Of course, you have to remember also that the woman considered her son to be so moral that he could never be involved in any kind of conspiracy. For a few days, Shony was on edge – and no wonder, for his mother was very angry that the hem of what she assumed was her son's new trousers had come adrift. She threatened that she would box the ears of Fat John, the Cromwell Street draper, if only the Lord would allow her, but one more time, to visit the town of Steòrnabhagh. She even called in two of her neighbours so that they could see the disgraceful quality of Fat John's wares.

Sunday came, and Nàsan's wife couldn't find the old man's good trousers anywhere. Without them, Himself the Elder couldn't go to church – something that was bound to bring their whole household into disrepute. The family was agog. Who could have stolen the trousers of Nàsan's Sunday suit, leaving the doublet and waistcoat behind? Nàsan angrily searched in every corner, and even Shony had to pretend to be searching under beds and under the living-room *beingean* [benches].

On the following day, Shony discovered the meaning of the phrase 'Di-Luain a' Bhreabain' – which is a kind of Gaelic Judgement Day. What happened was this: while Nàsan was repairing a herring-net, what did he find enmeshed in it but the legs of his Sunday-best trousers. The game was up.

Nàsan was waiting for him at the door when Shony arrived home from school. In his hands the Old Man held the two cylinders of serge cloth which, at one time, had been part of his best suit. For the first,

Prof. John MacLeod (Shony Nàsan)

and probably the only time in his life, Shony got a hiding – if only a verbal one. The lesson he learned from that terrible, guilt-ridden week affected him for the rest of his days. And in later life, when he was writing his scholarly papers,* Shony's mind probably drew weighty conclusions from that limited experience of law-breaking and guilt. I'd bet my bottom dollar that that was Shony's only departure from the straight and narrow. Poor fellow. Unlike myself, he suffered from an over-active conscience. The only lesson I learned from our adventure was that it's not wise for boys to hide their trousers in the Griogalach's peat-stack when four-legged comedians from Seisiadar are in search of garments to chew.

Those were the days when I was daring and I was rebellious. No point in denying it! I just didn't have the gumption to toe the line. When I became an adult, I learned the hard way that going about with a bleeding nose and a black eye is inclined to give a fellow a bad name.

* In 1912, Shony Nàsan, alias John MacLeod of No. 12 Àird, graduated from the University of Glasgow with First Class Honours in Mental Philosophy. During his illustrious career, he held a number of senior posts in different countries and, finally, that of Professor of Divinity at the University of Aberdeen.

Diamond Days

Diamond wasn't just a mongrel collie. He was boy-dog, a big, hairy, multi-coloured daftie who had a mind of his own and was as intelligent as he was crafty. At times he was under the influence of *caithris na h-oidhche*, that wild unreasoning urge that takes hold of the young male as soon as night falls. The result of Diamond's night-time labours was to be seen in every litter born this side of Allt na Muilne in Garrabost. But if Diamond was a charmer among the bitches, he had an even bigger reputation among us boys, for he was an ace rabbit-hunter. In the evening, when nose-twitching rabbits came out to graze, Diamond often lay in wait nearby, hidden on a heathery tussock. If any ventured more than a few yards away from its burrow, he would shoot after it like an arrow. Every rabbit between Geàrraidh Foitealar and the back of the Siùmpan was a nervous wreck!

One day we went to the Siùmpan with him. I would have been about twelve years old, and a crowd of boys, mostly younger, were in tow. I promised them that Diamond would catch us a rabbit, hopefully one that would not be so badly mauled that she couldn't be brought round and imprisoned in a hutch. We all loved the thought of having a pet rabbit. None of us ever got one.

The dog showed a lot of interest in a burrow near the coastguard station at the top of the Siùmpan. Scraping and whimpering as he went, he advanced through the peat like an October threshing-mill, the whole gang of us boys helping to break up the spongy ground before him with our heels. The more work he did, the more excited Diamond became, scratching away, slavering and occasionally stopping to yowl.

We spent most of the day at the burrow, all of us filthy with the damp *riasg*. The dog was still scrabbling, scraping, slavering, and cursing under his breath. Oh, he wasn't the only one who was impatient! I suppose that after three hours or so, Diamond had excavated about seven or eight yards. The ribbon of loose earth in his wake on the hillside suggested that the burrow he was digging was leading directly to the door of the coastguard station. Our enterprise seemed doomed to failure.

'Let's go home,' I said to the dog wearily. 'Come on, Diamond.'

I got hold of his collar but Diamond wasn't listening. He struggled, warning me to let go, and, with short barks, told us that he was within smelling distance of a whole platoon of rabbits with their backs against the wall. Desperate the fellow was with excitement, his claws and teeth opening the den until, in the end, he came right up to the door of the building.

It was well known to us that coastguards came on duty to the Siùmpan station for only three months in the winter and that the building was left unattended for the rest of the year. As there wasn't a soul about but ourselves, we allowed Diamond to continue his diggings, expecting him to admit defeat as soon as his claws hit concrete. Well, it was a big surprise to us that he did no such thing. The concrete walls of the building were a foot thick but the foundation under the door was supported only by wooden two-by-twos which were so decayed by wet-rot that they were like pulp.

While building the Siùmpain lighthouse, one of the engineers of Aitken & Frew who was staying in the village had taught young Hector Ferguson how to discover the secret hoard of honey belonging to a moorland bee, known to us as a *còinneachan.** What Hector had to do was to kill one bee and extract its honey-sac. After capturing a second bee under his cap, he would deposit the contents of the honey-sac all over its wings. The creature would splutter and buzz for a while, trying to figure out what had happened to him. Once he managed to take off, it seems that all he wanted to do was make a beeline for home, to tell his mother of his strange experience.

The poor *truaghan* couldn't fly faster than we could run, and so, in the end, we were able to find the mossy little *somag* in which he and his clan had hidden their honeycomb. The larder which the *còinneachan* had spent weeks of his time stocking up for the winter

* In his book, *A Hundred Years in the Highlands*, Osgood MacKenzie states that, when he was young, bees were so plentiful in Lewis that boys used to collect large quantities of honey which they drained from the combs into bottles and sold on market days in Steòrnabhagh. 'Hunting for wild bees', he claims, 'was one of the great ploys of boys in the autumn.'

Looking south from Ceann an t-Siùmpain

was soon ransacked by a bunch of hungry urchins. We had no mercy in those days. I remember that we followed one *còinneachan* all the way from where Diamond was undermining the doorway of coastguard station to an abandoned rabbit burrow near the old quarry. Hector quickly dismantled the nest, and after each of us got a mouthful of the honeycomb, we returned to see Diamond's progress. At the top of the hill, there was no sign of the dog to be seen but we could hear him, still yelping and scrabbling in the darkness of the foundations. Under the building, we could see the white tuft on the end of his tail waggling this way and that. We tried to get the fool out, but he wouldn't listen. Now, as we peered into the hole that Diamond had dug, we could see the floor-boards above us. By pushing up on the nearest two, we could see the legs of a table and chairs above us, inside the kitchen. Well, we pushed and we pushed and, after a bit, we managed to heave ourselves up on to the floor. Before long we were quite at home, relaxing in the coastguards' swivel chairs. You bet we were happy as Larry! We examined everything. I remember there was a log-book telling the names and countries of origin of all the ships that had sailed in daylight round Ceann an t-Siùmpain during the three months of the winter. But the most eye-catching thing in the station was a telephone contraption, part of which was a beautiful bell screwed on to the wall. I couldn't take my eyes off the bell. It was bigger than the size Tarmod Sàra has on his bicycle and it was made of a metal like gold. Because it belonged to His Majesty's Coastguards, I had it in my head that it was indeed made of gold. By turning it anti-clockwise, it was easy to screw it off the wall. I started hitting it with a teaspoon that I had found on the table and the sound it made was like music. It was a sweeter sound than anything I had ever heard in my whole life.

'I think I shall take the bell home with me!' says I to the boys.

Iain Torachan thought that I shouldn't. He said, 'The coastguards' telephone will be jiggered without a bell!'

Co-dhiù, I figured that that was a shame right enough, but I didn't want to be parted from the bell. So I said, 'I am taking the bell home!' And that was that.

Off we went, leaving poor Diamond in the darkness mining away under the building. And I have to tell you that the fellow didn't return to his home port for three days. When he did, he was so huffy and tired that he wouldn't let anyone speak to him. He could be a grumpy old bugger at times!

Anyway, we four boys reached the houses at Ceann a' loch, with me up front playing ding-dong with my teaspoon and bell. Who was there at the end of Murdo Campbell's house but Shony, Innis Mór's son who had just graduated from the police college in Glasgow. John

Campbell was his name in the book, but to us he was Shony the son of Innis Mór – just one of our own.

'How I envy you your bare feet running about on the heather!' he cries, friendly-like. He approached us smiling – a tall handsome fellow who had a good opinion of himself. Black Son of the Devil he was, though I did not know it at the time! If only I had realised that the smile on his face was a policeman's smile. But that's the problem with being young, you see: you're what they call in the United States a 'greenhorn', but you don't know you are.

'What have you there?'

We showed him the bell and I played him a tune on it with the teaspoon. Now, I must tell you the honest truth. In my state of perfect innocence, it had not occurred to me that taking the bell was wrong. And the fellow who was quizzing me certainly didn't advise me to put it back where I had found it. Instead, he joked with us and we went on our way. On Monday morning, I went to school with the golden bell in my pocket, my most prized possession. But my backside hadn't even warmed my seat before I was summoned to the headmaster's

Steòrnabhagh, of a century ago

office. One of the older pupils escorted me – a lamb being led to the slaughterhouse!

In the headmaster's office, I was introduced to a uniformed policeman who came straight to the point. 'Did you, along with a gang of boys, break into the Siùmpain coastguard premises and steal property from there? Speak up, boy, I can't hear you!'

I took the bell and the teaspoon from my pocket and gave them to him. Well, the next thing is, he tells me that he is going to my mother with a summons. That miserable no-good, son-of-a-gun – Innis Mòr Campbell's son – had reported me to the authorities. Well, by George, I'll never forget how upset my mother was when I reached home. She was only a poor widow and when she told me that she had to take me to the court in Steòrnabhagh on the following Monday, she was very, very upset. For my own part, I wasn't bothered for myself, but I have to say that my heart was really sad for my mother.

Steòrnabhagh was ten miles from our home at No. 11 and I had never been there before. The island's herring-fleet was based there and I had heard that there were public houses there and streets lined with shops. In Port Mholair, there were only two shops and no public houses at all. *Co-dhiù*, I was glad as a cucumber to be given the opportunity to see the town, even if it meant that I might be drawn and quartered while I was there.

Of all the millions of trousers in the world, Soolivan owned only one pair, and that was in a mighty state of disrepair. On the Saturday before the court case, my mother noticed that there was a *caithtean* on the buttocks of them – that is to say, the seat of them had worn so thin that they were as see-through as muslin.

'I had better fix that caithtean!' says my mother, and she cuts a square patch from an empty flour bag and sews that fair and square on the seat of my trousers. White flour-bag patches were all the rage when I was young.

Well, weren't we the toffs, myself and my mother, when we left on our trek to Steòrnabhagh. She was dressed entirely in black with a crocheted shawl over her head and me on my bare feet with 140 Pounds Net stated in bold pink on a white background on my *tòin* [backside]. Today, people would probably laugh at you if you dressed like that. But in 1903, everybody was poor and not being dressed in smart clothes was the least of their worries.

The boys of my generation were notorious for throwing stones. There was not a seagull, cat or strange dog who would enter the village without it hearing a stone whirring by its ears. In Sanndabhaig, some of the house had lots of trees in their front gardens – trees that were full of birds. Now, as a boy, I always carried a supply of stones in my pockets in case I should come across challenging targets. Well,

South Beach Street, Steòrnabhagh as Soolivan first saw it

I can tell you that there wasn't that many birds left sitting in the Sanndabhaig trees by the time Soolivan had passed by. When we reached Steòrnabhagh and I saw the streets, I got a shock. I could never have believed that there were that many people living in the whole world. I tried to break away from my mother but, by following the writing on my backside, she kept a beady eye on every move I made.

In the Court, I was questioned in detail. My defence was to put the blame entirely on my dog. Nobody believed my line of reasoning and I was told so more than once. I had led young boys into mischief, they said, had broken into premises belonging to His Majesty and had stolen HM's bell. The sheriff ordered that I be punished immediately, with seven lashes of the *cuip** applied to my bare *manachanan* [buttocks]. After being ushered into a small room at the back of the Court, a scarf was placed round my eyes, so that I couldn't see who was hitting me. While two hands held my wrists firmly I felt my braces being unbuttoned and my trousers fall to half mast. Then came some very sharp stings on my rear.

After justice had been administered, an older voice said, 'We're sorry we had to do this, son!'

As soon as the hands that held me down relaxed, I pulled the scarf from my eyes so that I was able to see the three officials who were giving me my desserts. They quickly replaced the scarf over my eyes and informed me that I had no right to look. Well, although I was nothing but a young boy, I thought it strange that they did not wish me to be able to identify them. Maybe they were feeling ashamed for

* The *cuip* was a rod made of birch twigs. It is likely that Soolivan was punished, not only for stealing 'HM's bell' but also for malicious mischief (nowadays, vandalism).

Cromwell Street as Soolivan first saw it

having beaten me.

When I was let out to meet my mother, she was weeping but her spirits lifted when she saw that I wasn't crying. We went for a walk along Cromwell Street and then along the quays. After that, we headed off back home. This time I did not feel like running, and the Sanndabhaig birds sat smugly on their roosts smiling because of the way I walked. They might have sensed that the homeward-bound Soolivan had nothing left in his arsenal. We walked the ten miles back through the villages of the Rubha quite slowly, but in better spirits than we had been in the morning.

When we arrived home, Diamond was lying on his side by the door and gave a dejected wag of his tail by way of greeting. He knew very well that his pal Soolivan had been in serious trouble that day. Tarmod Iomhair, our neighbour, was also there to tell us that he had 'a big feed' waiting for us at No. 15. *Cha b' e ruith ach leum!* [Invitation enthusiastically accepted!]

When I tried to sit at the table, I found it difficult to do so because of the swelling, heat and pain in my rear. I ate my thick mutton broth while leaning against the dresser. For two days and nights, I was not without pain except when lying down. The 140 Pounds Net advertised on my backside seemed just about right, for my trousers felt every bit as full as a bag of flour. Those were hard days for old Soolivan. But every dog has his day. By a strange coincidence, I came face to face a few years later with the very fellow who had been in command during my leathering. I had not forgotten his bulging blue eyes and his shiny pate, for he had made quite an impression on me – in more ways than one. I had grown to manhood by then and my shoulders were broad and my limbs well muscled. Fate arranged for me to meet the brave fellow alone in a locked-up shop. But that's another story.

Adventures in the Daras Beag

In our day, myself and my mates climbed some of the most difficult cliffs in the Rubha – two or three of them as far to the south from here as Seisiadar and Pabail Uarach. Goodness only knows why we wanted to climb cliffs and put our lives in danger. It was just a tradition among boys of that time – just like stone-throwing, playing truant from school and stealing turnips from Innis Uilleim's gardens. My Granny Màiread lived in Pabail Iarach and that gave our family a base there. It so happened that my Aunt Kirsty, my mother's sister, was married at No. 23 Seisiadar. That was a lucky stroke for us, for we could also visit Seisiadar any time we wanted. Kirsty was married to Tarmod Uilleim and they lived in the Daras Beag, a small bunch of houses out in the far end of the village. The Seisiadar people were different from other folk in those days and perhaps the reason for that is that the village was isolated. It was famous for two reasons. Firstly, it had the biggest men in the Rubha. Iain Mór was by far the biggest man in the parish and his sons were young versions of the same. In fact, a cobbler in Steòrnabhagh claimed that he needed the leather from half a cow to make the Sunday boots for some of the Seisiadar fellas. Now, there was another reason why Seisiadar was famous, and that was because the wittiest people in Lewis lived there. They'd make up a *rabhd* [rhyme] about you in just the twinkling of an eye. Big, sharp, witty men, and every second woman was a comedian as well.

As I said, Tarmod Uilleim's croft was out in the Daras Beag. Whenever I visited there, I was given a great welcome. Many's a time when I was a truant from school I'd play possum in the Geodha Mhór. Once or twice, I even skulked all the way out to hide in the refuge-cave at Geodha Mille Gruaman.* Now that's a right scary place for a young lad. But sooner or later, hunger would force me into the open and I would nip over to the Daras Beag for a slab of *aran coirc* [oaten bread]. I fancy that I can still hear Tarmod's greeting whenever I burst in on the family and me pretending that my mother had sent me on some errand or other.

'Seadh, a bhalaich! What's your news from the Ceann Shìos [Lower End]? I'm sure you have another important piece of news to give us today but, until you draw breath, sit down while Kirsty is putting lots of butter and crowdie on a piece of the aran coirc for you.'

* According to a local historian, sailors who had deserted from a naval vessel in the 1860s or 1870s took refuge in this cave. Discovered by village boys, Murdo MacAulay of No. 20, a devout Christian, provided the fugitives with food. Someone reported the matter to the authorities with the result that Mr MacAulay had to appear in court and was fined five shillings. It is said that a number of the fugitives managed to escape – some to the mainland in a rowing-boat. See *Geodha Mille Gruaman*, p. 258.

'My mother sent me up, just to say that she is well and the hens are laying eggs every day and she wonders if there is any work that you would like me to do while I am here.'

'That is very Christian of your mother, Iain,' Kirsty would say, 'but should you not be at school instead of looking for work in Seisiadar?'

'Well, you see, there is the piocas [chickenpox] raging among the Port nan Giùran children and the teine-dé [shingles] as well, and my mother doesn't want me to catch any.'

Usually my excuses were scary stories about an infectious disease that was raging among people in faraway places like Col Uarach or Cùl nan Cnoc. But one day, I appeared at the Daras Beag with news of a real disease that had broken out in Port Mholair – a disease that was killing off hens by the barrowload. A big disaster it was. Only four of my mother's hens survived the epidemic but the cock didn't, poor fella. He went under like most of his harem. Without a cock to frolic with the hens, the eggs would not produce chickens, you see. When I was wee, eggs were an important part of everybody's diet. Eggs, potatoes and fish was our bread and butter, you might say.

As soon as Tharmoid Uilleim and Kirsty heard of our family's misfortune, they decided to make a gift to our family. Kirsty walked all the way from Seisiadar with a half-grown brown cock imprisoned in the sack which she carried in a creel on her back. Oh, aye, in those days the families were concerned for each other and were always ready to lend a helping hand.

When the school was shut for the summer holidays, I got another genuine reason for going to Seisiadar. Iomhar Nèill [Evander MacRae], a near neighbour of ours from No. 8, had come to my

In shadow on the left, the spooky cave of Geodha Mille Gruaman

mother with a gift of half a dozen fat edible crabs and an enormous lobster. Iomhar was the owner of a successful fishing-boat called *Tuskar* and he and the other fishermen often gave gifts of fish to widows who had young families – and in those days there were lots of them in the district. Lots of poor people!

As the saying goes: one good deed deserves another. As soon as my mother saw the lobster, she said right away, 'Iain, you will take this giant lobster up to Tarmod Uilleim in the Daras Beag. Kirsty was telling me that himself would eat lobsters until the cows come home! You can carry the creature in the sack in which Kirsty brought the coileach. Ask them if they have any odd jobs they want you to do. Sleep with them for a couple of nights if they invite you. You can also tell Kirsty that the cock is already acting as sultan among our hens!'

No sooner said than done! I set off with the lobster and followed the Main Road up through the Àird until I was near the school at Druim Oidealar. That's where I met two brothers who were cousins of mine – rough tough characters known as the 'Bloody' and his brother 'Gayis'. These two fellas were very well built for their age and were afraid of nobody. In fact, they were quite a handful when they grew up and regularly fought with one another if they ran out of opponents. I grew up in an age when fighting with your fists was

Off to the moor for another load of peats

nothing out of the ordinary. I tell you, you had to be tough to survive. My cousins were about my own age – eleven or thereabouts – and there was no quarrel between us. The Bloody was leading a collie on a piece of string. The animal was a young bitch – a beauty: black all over but with a white muzzle and apron on her. I tell you she was a lovely animal – friendly-like – and as I knelt down beside her, she put her front paws on my shoulders and licked my face.

'What are you carrying in that sack?' says Gayis.

'Och,' says I, 'it's just a lobster that my mother is after sending up to Tarmod Uilleim out in the Daras Beag.'

'Let's have a look at the lobster then!' demands the Bloody.

I opened the sack and let the two brothers peer within.

'A Thighearna,' says the Bloody, 'I have never seen a giomach as big as that. It's a monster.'

Gayis agreed.

'Tell you what,' says the Bloody, 'we'll give you the collie in exchange for the giomach. It so happens that Tarmod Uilleim's family have lost their dog and they would be very pleased to get a beautiful animal like this.'

Looking into the pleading eyes of the collie, it took me no time at all to decide. With my right hand I accepted the makeshift dog-leash, and with the other I handed over the *giomach*. After that I couldn't take my eyes off the collie. She and I walked all the way to Seisiadar, the best of pals. When I reached the Daras Beag and introduced the collie, everyone in the Tarmod Uilleim household was overjoyed.

'A ghràidh, where did you find our dog?' cried Kirsty, and, all at once, the youngsters in the family rushed to the dog with hugs and kisses.

'Our beautiful Dìleas has been missing for nearly a month now,' says Tarmod Uilleim. 'We were afraid that we had seen the last of her.'

'My mother will be pleased,' says I. 'She sent me up with a present to you.'

I thought it wise not to tell the way I was tricked into exchanging the lobster for Tarmod Uilleim's own bitch. As it happened, everything turned out in my favour, for I spent three days living in style in the Daras Beag. It was as if I had gone on holiday to a hotel. News of my living-conditions at the Daras Beag must have travelled on the wind. On the second day, Uilleam, my younger brother, appeared unexpectedly and asked Kirsty if he also could stay.

'Of course you can,' says she, and, before I could raise any objections, Uilleam (better known as 'Kellan') was added to the guest-list. If I tell you the truth, I wasn't too pleased that my little brother was to be with me day and night.

One evening, Tarmod Uilleim gave each of us a *bunag-slait,* a

bamboo fishing-rod about eight feet long. He had asked a lad in his late teens from that end of the village to take us fishing to a gully called Ligh Bilidh. Now I cannot remember the name of the lad who took us, but I sure do remember the name of the fella who was fishing at Ligh Bilidh when we arrived there. The man was Dòmhnall Dall, a blind man who, without anybody to guide him, was able to walk from his home (at No. 17 Seisiadar) to Ligh Bilidh. It must have been at least half a mile along the clifftops. What is almost unbelievable is that he was able to make his way to and from Ligh Bilidh, day or night.* It didn't matter to him, so long as the weather was fair and the state of the tide was right for the fishing.

When you think on it, there really were some very unusual people in Seisiadar when I was young. There was even a woman who used to feed her children on a porridge made of nettles and cuddies. Mind you, you'll eat anything if you're hungry! In my growing-up time, I knew a lot about being hungry. I'd eat anything – including cuddies-and-nettles porridge!

Co-dhiù, when Kellan and I came home from our short holiday in the Daras Beag, we couldn't get Dòmhnall Dall out of our heads. We started to go about with our eyes closed, trying to find our way in Port Mholair. I remember the two of us walking down the croft like that,

An Daras Beag, Seisiadar, photographed in 2001

* One night, having settled himself by the water's edge at Ligh Bilidh, Dòmhnall Dall heard cries for help coming from somewhere to landward of him. He abandoned his rod and climbed in the direction from which the cries were coming. In due course, he discovered a lad who had fallen some hours previously and was lying injured on the gully floor. Dòmhnall Dall helped Norman Montgomery (Tarmod Chaluim Alasdair) to climb the side of Ligh Bilidh and to walk to his home at No. 8 Seisiadar. Sadly, at the age of thirty-nine, Norman lost his life in the *Iolaire* disaster, 1 January 1919. Dòmhnall Dall [Donald MacKay] died in 1904, aged seventy-four.

trying to find our way to Cnoc nan Arbh just to see how we would get on if we were suddenly struck blind. Time after time, we fell flat on our faces in the drains. The neighbours must have been thinking that we had caught *galair nan cearc* [fowl pest].

Shortly after we came home, the Bloody and Gayis arrived in Port Mholair, demanding that I give them their dog back. I laughed myself so hard that I nearly peed in my breeks. The lobster that I gave them – the present that I was on my way to deliver to Tarmod Uilleim – turned out to be a monster all right. Nobody could eat it, for its meat was so tough that even their cow wouldn't look at it. And that was strange, for their cow was famous for eating all sorts of inedible things. In fact, it was well known that that *trustar* had gone up to Cnoc Chùsbaig one day and eaten all the nappies off the tinkers' clothes-line. *Dia tha fhios* what kind of milk she had.

Admiral Jack

The Tiumpanhead Lighthouse was opened in 1900 when I was eleven years old. On the day of the opening, the Steòrnabhagh police were out in force. All the toffs from the town were down here, including the Provost and gentry from away. In Port Mholair, there was a lot of excitement but, of all the people living in the Rubha, only Innis Uilleim the merchant and the church ministers were invited to the 'soo-haree' (soirée). Of course, that didn't keep the children of Port Mholair, the Àird and Port nan Giùran from enjoying the shenanigans at the Siùmpan. We were all gathered in a heap on the hill overlooking the palaver. By George, you should have seen all the horse-drawn carriages that went out the clay road to the opening. There must have been nearly a dozen of them rumbling down the Sràid and up to the lighthouse. For nearly an hour they rolled up with all the sheepdogs barking at them and the children running about in the roadside ditches and waving. You have never seen so many gentlefolk in the one place. The men had their good suits on and their top hats. All the women wore white gloves and wide hats with nets over their faces. But it was their frocks that I remember most because, when the women came off the coaches, some of their frocks came right down to the ground and the lower half of them was as big as a *tocasaid* [hogshead]. I'm only surprised that nobody told them before they came out like that that they looked *suathaid* [ridiculous].

When the speeches were done and everybody had inspected this and that, all the carriages and horses rolled back up to town. After that, anybody who wanted to could go out to the lighthouse and see the station – but only from outside the boundary wall. And no doubt about it, the lighthouse station was a sight worth seeing. The wall and the houses and the lighthouse tower itself were whitewashed and gleamed in the sun. So far as we were concerned, the Tiumpanhead Lighthouse Station was the most important building in the whole island of Lewis. A spick an' span place, as clean as a whistle – a special place and you had to be a special fella to be allowed inside its gates – a wee bit like Heaven, you might say.

Now, the people who were in charge of the lighthouse wore uniforms. They were important people, so they had to have a uniform, you see. The top man was known to us as the Caiptean and his sidekick, his second in command, was known as the Mate – *An Caiptean agus am Meit*. That is what we called them and that is how they wanted to be known. Both were married but only the Captain had children. We got to know the Captain's children, for they had to go to Sgoil na h-Àirde, and before you knew it, it was Gaelic they were talking, though, like everybody else, they weren't allowed to utter one word of it inside the school gates.

But this story is not about the Captain or the Mate – or even the Captain's children. It is about a third gentleman who was working for a short time at the lighthouse. I believe that he was there for just six weeks in 1900, but during that time he made a big impression on Port Mholair folk even though he didn't have a uniform to wear. He was a tall, tall man wearing a cravat all the time and spoke English with the kind of accent that the military officers have – unsmiling and stiff as a post. His name was Jack, and because he always went about looking as if he was Admiral of the Fleet, he became known in the village as Admiral Jack. And he played the part. He looked like a man who wouldn't stand any nonsense from nobody – so everybody kept well out of his way. That was the way it was in those days – the locals here kept clear of men wearing cravats or neckties, especially if they spoke only English.

I cannot say what the Admiral's trade was, but the Lighthouse authorities were after giving him the task of finding an underground spring that would provide the families living at the lighthouse with a reliable supply of clean water. Well, I can tell you first-hand that the fella took weeks to find what he was looking for. Walking about like an *amadan* [fool] with two twigs held out in front of him, the Admiral divined here and then he divined over there. All over Port Mholair he walked, holding those two twigs before him and shaking his head everywhere he went until, at last, he went to Na Fleisearan. When he came to Calum Iain's potato-field at No. 5 Na Fleisearan, he points to the ground and says, 'Sink the well here!'

Next day, the pick-and-shovel boys arrived and started to dig, and when they reached about six feet down in the clay, there was a gush of water that filled the hole and then flowed on to Calum Iain's newly planted potatoes and became a small river that carried the newly sprouted potatoes right down to the shore. *Thighearna*, it was like something out of the Old Testament. As you know, the Lighthouse authorities employed specialists to plug the water and make a properly built well there with a pump on it. That pump was a wonderful thing. Everybody in Na Fleisearan got their drinking water from 'Pumpa Chaluim Iain'. So you see, the Admiral was a mighty important fella and it's a pity that he had to go and spoil his reputation.

It was the Captain that told Iomhar Neill that Admiral Jack was only a bull-shitter. What I'm telling you is the truth now! Nobody in the village knew what kind of a job a bull-shitter did inside the lighthouse tower, but we assumed it had to be something to do with the workings of the engine. Of course, in those days, everybody here spoke only Gaelic and those with a few words of English had never before come across a technical name like 'bull-shitter'. I should tell you here and now that in America a fella who is called a bull-shitter here would be called a horse-shitter over there. Oh, aye, horse-shitters are ten to the penny in America – especially south of the Mason-Dixon Line.

It seems that when he was working his boat at the lobster-pots close to the base of the cliff of Mac Ille Dhuilich, Iomhar Nèill noticed half a dozen of his own ewes grazing close to the cliff edge and, as you know, Mac Ille Dhuilich, is a mighty dangerous cliff (see p. 241) which has claimed the lives of many a beast. As soon as he got ashore, Iomhar took his dog and walked out to Mac Ille Dhuilich which is only a few yards from the wall of the lighthouse station. Well, you'll never guess what happened when he got out there and started to round up his ewes. Who comes striding out of the station gates but Admiral Jack wearing a Campbell tartan cravat.

'What do you think you're doing?' shouts Jack. 'Who gave you authority to set foot between the station and the cliff?'

Iomhar Nèill, who was a village constable* of our township at the time, was not the kind of fella to be put upon by any man – especially when he was on his own turf. He became angry and gave the fella such a Gaelic mouthful that his ears were scorched. The Admiral goes wild, claiming that the ground between the lighthouse station and the cliff edge belonged to the Commissioners of Northern Lighthouses. Iomhar then told him that without the Royal Scots with fixed

* The Estate Factor delegated the management of each township to the local crofters who were required to meet annually to elect a Grazings Committee. Also appointed were two Constables who were required to enforce the Estate's 'Rules and Regulations'.

bayonets and a gunboat to back them up, the grazing of the Port Mholair common would continue to be controlled by the local crofters.* Anyways, Iomhar got his ewes away from Mac Ille Dhuilich and brought them home to No. 8. but the Admiral was after raising a hornets' nest among the crofters, some of whom had been in prison in Edinburgh because they rioted at Aiginis a few years earlier. A meeting of crofters was hastily called and the Northern Light people in Edinburgh were notified. Before you knew it, the Captain came to Iomhair to apologise. He told him that Jack was acting beyond his authority and explained that the fella was nothing more than a bull-shitter first-class. The long and the short of it was that the Admiral lost face. He soon lost his hoity-toity accent as well, for he was really a man from Drumnadrochait or Dundee or somewhere ordinary like that though he wanted people to believe that he was a well-bred Sasunnach.

One day, when me and my pals were over at Port nan Giùran meeting the boats coming in from the great-lines, who sidles up to us but the deflated Admiral. He says, 'Innis Uilleim has promised me that, if I can find myself a crew, I can take his cobble out to fish for pollacks, over by Sgeir Iomhair.'

Understandably, the fishermen of Port Mholair and of Port nan Giùran had refused to give the Admiral a berth in any of their boats. Well, it stands to reason when you look at it. Those were real fishermen earning a living for their families and they didn't want no

For taking part in the Aiginis Riot, 1888, Iain mac Uilleim spent nine months in Calton Jail

* During the 'land disturbances' of the 1880s, Marines and gunboats were sent against crofters in the Inner and Outer Hebrides rebelling against the conditions imposed on them by their landlords. The Aiginis Riot took place in 1888, some twelve years before this contretemps.

lighthouse bull-shitter in their boats telling them where or how they should fish. That was the way they saw him, you see. The long and the short of it is that the fella was so pathetic-looking that me and Tuileasdar and Calum an Rùid felt sorry for him and said that we would meet him on the shore on the following day with our fishing-tackle.

When the Admiral came to fish out of Port nan Giùran, he came dressed to kill. He came fully kitted out with knee-length leather boots – beautiful they were and polished to the hilt. He had a deerstalker hat on and a herring-bone tweed suit that must have cost him ten quid, at the least. He also had a *druimeag* [small knapsack] on his back and a cigar in his mouth. What a toff he was, going fishing to Sgeir Iomhair with three bare-foot *brogaich*, dressed in short trousers and a home-knit jersey.

'Have you brought sandwiches?' says he.

Sandwiches? *B'eòlach mo sheanair orra!* Sandwiches were not part of a crofter's diet in those days. Shortly after we left the Shingle, Calum an Rùid says, 'Where is this Sgeir Iomhair?'

In fact, none of us boys knew where Sgeir Iomhair was and had no idea what we were letting ourselves in for. Sitting royally in the stern of the boat, Jack took a small chart from his *druimeag* and, after a moment or two peering at it, he holds it up and points to a place near the middle of the Loch a Tuath.

'It's over there,' he says, 'just a mile or two to the west, between here and Am Bac. Now, I have the chart and a compass and you have nothing to worry about. Just row the ship as I direct you and we shall come to the best place in the North Atlantic for fishing for pollacks.'

The weather was in our favour. There was a gentle swell coming into the loch and the tide was on the turn – nothing at all to worry about. Right enough, there was a bank of fog lying to the east of us,

A *liùth* is a Gaelic pollack not less than two feet long; *sgleòtag* is one smaller

stretching from Rubha Tholastaidh and out into the sea. It had been there all morning without moving this way or that.

I suppose it took us a good half an hour of hard rowing to get over to where our Admiral said the pollacks were waiting for us. Tuileasdar was on the oars and the rest of us were getting our tackle ready to pay out. As soon as the boat came to a halt and our leads went to the bottom, the fish were for us. Right away, they were there – not pollacks but big fat silvery haddock. We were hauling them up as fast as we could – all three of us. Tuileasdar was midships just sitting patiently watching and hoping that the Admiral would soon give him the order to ship the oars and start fishing.

All of a sudden, Admiral Jack started to yell that he had a heavy weight on his line. He was ordering Tuileasdar to row this way and then that way because he was unable to pull the fish up to the surface. It didn't take long for the rest of us to realise that what he had on the end of his line was not an almighty fish but Sgeir Iomhair herself!

The Admiral spent a long time trying to lift Sgeir Iomhair from where the *Cruthaighear* had put her! By the time the line went slack and he had surrendered his tackle to the tangles below, the fog had crept in on us and we were lost in the middle of it. Och, he kept telling us there was nothing to worry about. He had lost his tackle in Sgeir Iomhair but he seemed happy enough. We watched as he took from his *druimeag* a compass, and then a pack of six Havana cigars. He leisurely withdrew one cigar, then lit it with a match. Full of the envy, me and my two pals sat sharing the Admiral's pleasure. We breathed in the drifting smoke and imagined what it would be like to be holding that thick stick of sweet tobacco between our teeth. O, how we wished then that we were grown up and could have cigars like that and sit in a boat with flunkies at our beck and call.

'Now, lads,' says the Admiral, 'you have nothing to worry about. Just enjoy this beautiful haar. As well as being a water-diviner, I'm a fully qualified Master Mariner. I took the bearings as soon as we arrived at Sgeir Iomhair and I will have you back on the Shingle at Port nan Giùran in half an hour – no bother.'

To do the donkey-work of rowing to our home port, he promoted Calum an Rùid and me to the oars. Tuileasdar had to sit in the prow. Himself was in the stern smoking and allowing his cigar-smoke to drift with our wake, across the Loch a Tuath. In no time, Calum an Rùid and me had the boat moving sweetly. The fog continued, thick as treacle. But there was nothing to worry about – so the man told us. So we just did as we were told. With his compass in his hand, Admiral Jack kept shouting instructions, 'A point and a half to port there' or 'Ease her slightly to starboard, Iain'. Us boys pulled on the oars without a care in the world. Tuileasdar started humming a wee Gaelic *port* [tune] to make him forget that our feet were a couple of inches deep in cold sea-water. Half an hour passed and no Port nan Giùran! Three quarters of an hour passed and the master mariner was beginning to look worried. As a matter of fact, as time was passing with no land in sight, the Admiral was starting to panic.

Calum an Rùid was enjoying himself. 'The night is falling, sir. We should be at Kyle of Lochalsh by daybreak!'

Of a sudden, we heard a weird sound coming at us from up ahead – something that was eerie because it was so unexpected. We stopped rowing and the sound approached as we were carried forward on the swell. The three of us lads were looking aft and could see Jack's face as pale as a boiled spud. He rose from the thwart with terror on his face.

'Look, there's a white pillar dead ahead of us. My god, what thing is it?' Calm as a cucumber, Tuileasdar says, 'Och, it's a waterfall. We are at the bloody Stalla waterfall in Garrabost. You are three miles off course, skipper!'

Admiral Jack suddenly decides that he needs to relieve himself big time, so we follow the shore a bit and put him ashore. As soon as he got his feet on dry land and started to climb the rocks, didn't that son-of-a-gun shout to us, 'Now boys, you row the boat back to Port nan Giùran. I'll meet you on the shingle there.'

Mac an Diabhail was so scared that, at that moment, he wasn't interested in the *druimeag* that he was after leaving behind him on the aft thwart. Us boys were as hungry as winter wolves and, as soon as he was out of sight, we fell on his sandwiches and scoffed the lot. Cold we were, but happy as could be – three youngsters left in charge of one of Innis Uilleim's fancy rowing-boats. Calum an Rùid and I turned the boat round and, with a song in our hearts, pulled on the oars, happy to be rid of the Admiral. Long before we reached the shingle at Port nan Giùran, a breeze started to blow in from the east and the fog lifted before we reached Sgeir nan Ràmh. Jack wasn't on the shingle to meet us. Not that we expected him to be! The man was no more a Master Mariner than he was a gentleman. The proof of that was that he had tried to make a beeline between Sgeir Iomhair and Port nan Giùran, never thinking of the action of the flowing tide.

He had jumped ship and then had to walk the four miles from the Stalla to the Siùmpan in the fog. You've got to laugh. The fella really was a blusterer, right enough – and a bull-shitter first class!

Jack didn't come looking for his *druimeag* or for his share of the fish either. I never saw him again. Down there by Càrn a' Bhonaich, I smoked the last of his Havana cigars. In fact, I'm sure that it was through smoking his cigars down by Càrn a' Bhonaich that I learned how to be a gentleman!

Chancing His Arm

A Sabbath Bonanza

During the summer months, we used to spend most of the day and much of the night working, fishing or playing in the rocks or on the hills. Of course, everywhere you went you had to be careful not to break the rules and regulations laid down by your elders. Well, that was the general idea. On the village common, you had to be careful not to damage the turf or the constables would be on your tail. I remember once using a spade to carve my initials in the side of Foitealar, and Eòghann down at Port went wild, trying to find out which of the dozen JMLs in the village had defaced the grazing.

The girls were not allowed to whistle because the adults said that that was forbidden in the Bible. When a hen crowed like a cock, which the occasional one of them did, she was bound to end up in a soup-pot on the following Sunday. Bad medicine, you see! Hens were supposed to behave like hens and cocks like cocks and there was no room for negotiation. The Sabbath Day was the Lord's Day and you were taught to respect that. No shouting, crying or swearing; no loud noises or rushing about. God Himself was watching every move you made and, since Himself was not on hand to give you a telling-off in the here-and-now, Eòghann and 'Ain Chaluim were backwards and forwards, rigged out in their Sunday best to keep you in line.

I never fancied being an Eòghann 'ic Anndra or an 'Ain Chaluim. I never even wanted to be a village *conastapal*. I was quite content to be on the other side and to enjoy carrying out a wee sin here and another sin there. I could never see myself as a sour-faced son-of-a-gun spending my life dishing out telling-offs to my fellow creatures. As I told you before, I wasn't keen on toeing the line. Now, my father – he was different. He died young but I remember that he believed in the palaver of going on your knees to pray for our forgiveness because we were so sinful. He was never done apologising to God for something that Adam did in the dim and distant past. And by gum, he made our whole family feel guilty along with himself!

When the Bodach was saying the Books in the evening, we had to be quiet as mice. First of all, he says a wee prayer, with all of us kids having our hands clasped and our eyes tight shut. Then he sings a few verses of a psalm with all the family joined in. We all liked singing the psalms, for we had good singing voices. After the singing, the Bodach opens the Bible and pretends to be reading a long passage from it. We all knew that he was pretending, for he could neither read nor write. He had memorised this long passage from the Old Testament when he was a child and he enjoyed reciting it every evening. My own reading and writing are very poor and I have long since forgotten what I learnt of the psalms when I was a *brogach*. There's nothing in my head now but memories of how things were and the battles I fought with the Sàtan – the battles that I lost every time.

We lived in a remote place, but hardly a week went by during the Yellow Months but strangers appeared in Port Mholair from away. I admired the families who came to live in the lighthouse, for they were decent folk and were highly respected by everybody. There were other visitors from away who earned their living by wandering from village to village, selling their wares. You couldn't really classify the tinkers as strangers, for they were regularly backwards and forwards selling things – Stewarts, MacDonalds and Drummonds. These fellows were skilful at making things out of tin. I guess that was why they were called tinkers.

From time to time, evangelists visited us. There were preachers called 'Pilgrims' who lived in tents and spent hours in remote villages, explaining the Gospel to anybody who had the patience to stand in the open to listen to them preaching through a megaphone and singing hymns with one of their number banging a wee tambourine. The problem was that they spoke only English. Most of the listeners couldn't understand more than a few words.

Then there was 'Bodachan Sàbhaig' [The Old Sawman], who for years visited houses with a barrowload of sharpening tools. And he was good at it. He sharpened knives, scissors, scythes, sickles and razors at a ha' penny farthing a piece. He was a first-rate barber and would give a man a haircut and shave for a ha' penny. Children's hair he wasn't keen on. He would do them for free on condition that he was given his dinner and that the children weren't lousy.

One day – must have been a Saturday – I got a haircut from this Bodachan Sàbhaig. I'm sure that he had examined my mop and couldn't find a single louse. If there was one, there sure wasn't any by the time he finished. He sheared off the lot except a wee *dosan* at the front. That's the way I liked it. You could identify the dunces at school by the scarcity of hair on their heads. We left as little as possible for the teacher to get hold of when he was in a foaming rage. Of course, the brainy ones had 'cliop a' bhóbhla'* – with only the sides shorn and a *cràic* [stack] of hair on top.

Anyways, I was pleased with Bodachan Sàbhaig's handiwork that day, for he had not only shorn off my hair but had shaved it as well and put cod-liver oil on it because, he said, that was good for the

* A specially shaped bowl was placed over the head to cover the hair to within an inch above the eyes. All the hair then showing was clipped. The resulting 'Bowl Clip' resembled the hairstyle of a medieval pageboy.

In the foreground, Foitealar (hill) with the Sràid overlooking Bàgh Phort Mholair in the mid-distance

scalp. It certainly stank plenty, so that I became a big attraction for the houseflies.

A great shoal of herring came into Bàgh Phort Mholair about that time, probably around 1903. I remember that it was a calm Sunday – a lovely day. When the tide went out, all the rock-pools between Bilidh Bheag and Clach na Muilne were full of the silver darlings. That day, every seagull in Lewis came over to Port Mholair and just swam about aimlessly in the inner bay, unable to take flight because their stomachs were so full of herring. Gannets, porpoises and seals were everywhere and all the local men in their Sunday best before going to church wishing that the day was Monday! The Sàtan told me to go home and get a sack and fill it with herring which the good Lord had laid out for me, free for the taking. To be honest, I didn't really consider whether what I was doing was right or wrong. Myself never went to church after I was past the age of Sunday school and saw nothing wrong with going down and helping myself to a share of the bonanza. After all, the shoal was bound to disappear as soon as the tide came in and filled up the Cladach. It took no time at all to fill my sack. The herring were in their thousands in the rock-pools or skittering about on the bladder-wrack. All the churchgoers disappeared into their houses to collect their Bibles and the bachelor-buttons that they ate during the sermon. I walked up the road with the bulging sack on my back. In for a sheep, in for a lamb, I thought! I started to gut the herring at the end of our barn, just as the black-coated, Bible-carrying brigade moseyed off up the road to church.

Believe it or not, none of our neighbours would accept the basinful of herring that I offered them at their doors in the late evening. *Ochan, ochan,* they said, what shame my sinfulness was after

bringing on my late father's house that day and how easily I had yielded to the Sàtan's temptation. My mother was black-affronted and so were my sisters – not because of my sinfulness but because I had given the neighbours a reason to think that I had not been raised in a God-fearing home. I laughed at my mother when she told me she had a mind to put me 'over her knee'. Fat chance! I was long past the age of correction, for I was a big strong lad by the time I was twelve or thirteen.

When I heard that my Sabbath-breaking was discussed at length by the elders at the Prayer Meeting on Wednesday, I told my mother that I was going off to my grandparents in Pabail Iarach. She seemed pleased to let me 'get out of her sight'.

Wonderful how fast news travels *air an tuath.** Though he was living five miles to the south of Port Mholair, my *seanair* [grandfather] greeted me with a broad grin: 'Have you brought us any of your Sunday herring?'

Cladach Phort Mholair at low tide with rock-pools and bladder-wrack

* In rural areas.

When he saw that I was feeling in the dumps, he says, 'Put the whole episode out of your mind, Iain. If accepting a gift from God is the worst crime you'll commit in your lifetime, you'll probably go straight to Glory when the time comes.'

After a day or two, more news came to my grandparents from Port Mholair. My mother didn't want to throw all that beautiful herring out on the midden for the cats and seagulls to eat. Strangers came to the house, asking if they could have some. The Bodachan Sàbhaig took some. More pleasing still, the Pilgrims came and were grateful to be given a share of Soolivan's Sabbath bonanza.

Hunger at Hógaraid

My *seanair* owned about forty sheep. It so happened that I arrived as all the neighbours were preparing to go off to *Faing a' Bhearraidh* [shearing fank] on the Lewis Moor. That's when the crofter folk go to the fank at Hógaraid to shear their sheep and bring home the fleeces that, in those days, were sold for the Harris Tweed.

After a mighty breakfast of boiled eggs, barley bread and buttermilk, I set off with Sandy Phàdraig, one of the local lads, about seven in the morning. We went barefoot and lightly dressed – a pair of trousers, a hand-knitted gansey and my seanair's cap. Both Sandy and myself carried a *druimeag* – a kind of home-made knapsack – on our backs. That was the handiest way of carrying shears and the empty sacks for carrying the wool. Most important of all, our *druimeagan* contained stacks of *aran-coirc* and flask of milk which were supposed to sustain us through the long hours of traipsing to and from Hógaraid – a place that was six or seven miles from Pabail Iarach. We started off about seven in the morning, cutting across the moor to Aiginis, where we joined the main road going to Steòrnabhagh. At Aiginis, we joined a crowd of Rubhaich travelling briskly towards the town. Most of them were on foot but there must also have been eight or ten cart-loads of passengers – mostly women and *bodaich*. Lean collie-dogs everywhere, heading for Hógaraid.

The people on foot cut along the back of the Bràigh to Stèinis and out by Lacasdal to the Lewis Moor. By the time we arrived within sight of the fank, there was a big throng of people already there. Far out on the hills, we could see the shepherds with their dogs gathering in the flocks. The first of them would not reach the enclosure at Hógaraid for an hour or more, so, before crossing the broad stream that barred our way to the fank, Sandy and I decided it was time for lunch. We were starving even though the time was no later than nine or ten in the morning.

The carts arrived and a few of the men began to carry the women across the stream on their backs. While we were scoffing our 'pieces', we enjoyed watching a doddery, old *bodach* wading the stream with a woman on his back. He made it to the far bank without toppling, which spoiled our ploy! Sandy and I finished off the remainder of our *aran-coirc* before the work of shearing began. When the shepherds and the dogs managed to corral all the sheep in the fank, the people plunged into the crush of bleating animals and started to haul out their own, one by one.*

What a noise there was! The ewes were going crazy calling for their lambs. Dog-fights erupted here and there, and some of the men, arguing so loudly above the din, were so red-faced and sweaty that I thought they might come to blows. No such luck, but it was great fun to see the carry-on! Between us, Sandy and I managed to shear more than a dozen sheep. Neighbours of my grandparents sheared the rest of my seanair's flock. The wool-sacks were loaded on to the carts. Those belonging to each croft was easy enough to identify. My seanair's sacks, for example, had green and red yarn sewn in their sides.

As Sandy and I were leaving the moor and approaching the first of the Lacasdal houses, a cart passed us. A shepherd jumped off the cart and said to me, 'You'd better go back there a half mile and get one of your seanair's old ewes that hasn't been shorn. She wouldn't budge for the dogs but should be easy enough to catch. The fleece is beginning to peel off her.'

Before resuming his homeward journey on the cart, the shepherd threw us a length of rope. 'You'll need that,' he cries.

In less than a quarter hour, we sighted the ewe in a dip and she immediately knew the purpose of our visit. Old she might have been, but she was as lively as a pollack on a hook, jinking this way and that in the ditches until all three of us were exhausted. At last, Sandy lunged and clung on to her till I got the piece of rope round her neck. Even then, she fought us, me hauling and Sandy pushing her along the road to where we had left our *druimeagan* containing our shears.

I had been aware of a man watching us from some distance down the cart-track. He was leaning against the wall of the first *taigh-dubh* [black-house] you come to, where the village of Lacasdal merged on to the moor. Still shoving and pushing the ewe, we suddenly found the man beside us.

'What an old scrag you have there, boys!' says he. 'Let me help

* Each crofter was able to identify his own sheep by three different forms of marking: different patterns of dye, called 'keel', on the fleece; ear-markings cut into the animals' ears shortly after its birth; and croft initials burned into the horns when the animal reached adulthood.

you to drag her to our house there. You can tie her to the cart-wheel and she'll be secure enough there.'

Sandy and I were too tired to refuse the man's offer. But what a surprise was waiting for us once we had managed to tie the ewe to the cart-wheel. The stranger invited us into the house, and as soon as we entered we were hit by a wonderful gust of roasting meat – *fàileadh feòla ri ròstadh*.

The woman of the house said, 'You have come at a good time.'

Tied to the *being* [bench] was a mangy old collie bitch that was going crazy at the sight of us strangers. The man shouted, 'Fanny, bi sàmhach!' and the animal retreated under the *being*. When that kerfuffle was over and it was safe for us to come in, the woman smiled and said, 'You'll eat with us, I hope.'

Nothing surer, lady! We were starving. The man sat us at the table and the woman busied herself by the fire. After a few minutes, she came carrying a big tray on which there were two tureens – one stacked up with jacket-potatoes and the other with fried mutton chops.

She says, 'Now, lads, after the man of the house says the grace, you can dig in. Here we eat with our fingers. You can put your *smodal* [refuse] in this little basin.'

The man took his cap off and put it over his face. He then started muttering the longest grace that God ever had to listen to. On and on he went – mutter, mutter, mutter – so that I was tempted to take a couple of mutton chops and join the mangy dog under the *being*. Man, it was torture. We hadn't eaten since about half past ten and our stomachs were groaning. Sandy suddenly sneezed loudly and the man got such a fright that he stopped the grace abruptly and asked, 'A

The wide open acres of the Lewis Moor where Rubhach sheep grazed in summer bheil dad ceàrr?' [Is there something wrong?]

We said, 'No.'

'Now, boys,' he says, 'the Lord has been pleased to bring us together at this table. Eat as much as you wish. I'm sure that the woman of the house has more chops on the fry-pan if you need them.'

When the eating was done, the man and his wife wanted us to stay and chat with them, but we refused, saying that we had to shear the rogue sheep waiting for us by the cart-wheel. We made ready to leave, and as soon as the man opened the outside door, Fanny the bitch dashed out. When the ewe saw her coming, she got such a fright that she ran full pelt, broke the rope and made off into the moor.

'Go fetch, Fanny!' cries the man.

The old collie followed the ewe on short, podgy legs and was out of puff after his first fifty yards.

'Don't worry, lads,' says the man. 'Fanny will bring the ewe back to us within the hour. Now come on in and have a drink of buttermilk. It's good for the stomach after a meal.'

Needless to say, we didn't hang about. We started trudging the long miles back to the Rubha and were halfway to Pabail Iarach before we remembered that our *druimeagan* were still lying by the cart-track beyond Lacasdal. I decided not to show my face at Pabail Iarach but continued to follow the road to Port Mholair. The sun was low in the sky before I reached home. I was so tired that I just slumped into my bed. I'll always remember that day as the hungriest, most tiring of my growing-up time. Having said that, it was the kind of day that I used to recall when I was thousands of miles from Hógaraid and wishing that I could go there one more time.

My First Pay-packet

German measles closed the school at the start of the summer and the children were allowed to run riot – spots or no spots. For myself, child diseases didn't bother me. I had put German measles, mumps and chickenpox behind me when I was about three years old. I smiled every time I heard that there was an outbreak of an infectious disease in the district for it gave me a glimmer of hope that the prison that adults called Sgoil na h-Àirde would be forced to close for a while!

The shoals of herring were so dense along the coast that the ebb-tide was sometimes leaving fish along the shore. In those days, I didn't know where the Baltic States were. What I did know was that every year, the people there ate hundreds of tons of salt herring packed into barrels on the Mol a Deas in Steòrnabhagh. The fishing-boats at that time used to come to Bàgh Phort Mholair – lots of them – to collect nets that had been given out to be mended by village *bodaich*. My pals and I were on the beach from morning till night, asking questions and volunteering to do chores and looking forward to growing up. We couldn't imagine doing anything more satisfying than drift-netting on board a 'Fifie' or a 'Zulu'. Those were big vessels with sails so big you could wrap a house in one of them. The crew's wellington boots were always covered in silvery scales and, indeed, some of their trousers could also have done with a good wash. During the days that the fishermen were after the shoals, they went about unshaven and unwashed, but as happy as Larry. That's when the fishermen were happiest, when the herring were filling the drift-nets with silver – and their pockets too. And that is how we boys also enjoyed life at its best – ragged, scruffy and unwashed and away from the terrible scrutiny of women.

During the few days that the big-sail vessels were anchored in Bàgh Phort Mholair, the crews on board were hard at work, preparing to set off for the fishing grounds. Some came ashore for nets, some for

Preparing to set off for the fishing-grounds

drinking water or for oatmeal, which was always less expensive in the villages than it was in the town. Some of the younger members were always on the lookout for pretty girls, and there were plenty of pretty girls in our parish, I can tell you.

One day, I was sitting alone at Giollaman, a flat rock well known to the fishermen as it was the half-tide landing stage at Port Mholair. I was watching a fisherman in a ten-foot dinghy about to set off on its return trip to its mother-ship. As I watched him prepare to draw on the oars, I was just bristling with envy. The fellow turned to me and said, 'Aren't you Tarmod Uilleim's son? How would you like to come out to the big Zulu sitting there at anchor, and have dinner with the skipper of the famous *Cuidich an Rìgh*?'

My chest filled out with pride as I accepted the invitation. I was helped on board and I was immediately led to where the cook was busy with his bubbling pots and pans. Before I had got properly used to my surroundings, the cook presented me with a large bowl of soup with a large lump of boiled beef smiling up at me from its middle.

How true the old proverb: *Balach fireann 's e ri fàs, dh'itheadh e mar mhilleadh brà!** You can be sure that I dined very well that day. The crew must have had a good laugh to themselves watching me scoff the lot.

'Go on, cook' said the skipper, when I had finished, 'give him another trencherful and, this time, make sure you give him a proper piece of beef!'

I ate until I could eat no more. I thanked the cook and went up on deck with the skipper and spent an hour or so helping to coil a big thick rope that was covered in clatted tar.

'Have you enjoyed yourself this morning?' asks the skipper.

'The best morning of my whole life,' says I.

'How would you like to come to sea with us, until the school re-opens?'

Join a Zulu and see the big, wide world! What young fellow could refuse an invitation like that?

'I will give you this sgumair then,' says he, 'and you can use it to capture the herring that falls out of the net when we're hauling. You can have that herring to yourself to take home to your mother, or to sell for your profit.'

The *sgumair* was like a spoon-net with a handle about six feet long. I tried working it in the sea, but the skipper saw me and shouted, 'Quit mucking about with that just now! You'll learn how to work it soon enough when we're hauling. Now, go ashore and tell your mother that you're engaged as a coiler on the *Cuidich an Rìgh*.'

* A strong, growing boy can consume as fast as a quern can produce meal.

I couldn't believe my luck. And I will never forget the first day we set sail – two hundred-odd sailing-drifters, two or three sails on each, heading down north past Ceann an t-Siùmpain, with only a breath of wind to stir them along.

The *sgumair* proved to be very profitable, for we ran into an enormous shoal of herring off Tolastadh. It was possible for me to give my mother three or four shillings every week I was working. But it wasn't just the *sgumair* that kept me occupied while I was on the *Cuidich an Rìgh*. There were twelve big bundles of rope, hundreds of yards long and every bundle of it as heavy as lead because it was clatted with tar. That rope was called the 'ground-rope', because it was attached to the foot of the drift-nets so as to drag them down towards the bottom. Rows of corks at the top held the nets upright like a huge curtain. Coiling the 'ground-rope' as it was being hauled wasn't my only duty. When we were berthed at Steòrnabhagh, I also had to run errands. 'Go for the bread! Go for the skipper's Black Twist! Go for the baskets! Go for this! Go for that!' I was having a slave's life, but I was young and very capable of tackling every task to which the skipper challenged me. Oh, he had only to open his mouth and I would up and jump, in spite of the fact that I was only thirteen years of age. It was a great compliment to be given the title of 'Crew member of the *Cuidich an Rìgh*'.

The herring season came to an end in Steòrnabhagh and, at the same time, the German measles went off to attack some other parish. The school reopened and all the children trudged off up the road to Druim Oidealar like prisoners re-captured after a jail-break.

'Iain, you'll be wanting to go back to school now,' says the skipper. 'The *Cuidich an Rìgh* is going off to Fraserburgh on Monday forenoon on the tide. It's such a shame that you haven't left school yet, and us without a cook an' all.' I answered with a big black lie.

'Och, my schooldays are over!' says I. 'I will have reached school-leaving age next Tuesday. My mother asked me to tell you.'

It was just the answer the skipper wanted to hear, and I am pretty sure that he knew I was lying. In the morning, my mother sent me off to school as usual – or so she thought. Little did she know that when all the other children would be coming home from school that afternoon, I would be in Cuan nan Orc,* well away, on my outward voyage to Fraserburgh. We entered Wick the next morning and I sent a telegram home to tell where I was. It said, 'Enjoying a cook's life. Right as rain. Plenty herring. Son Iain.'

I can well believe that if she had got a hold of me that day, my mother would have called in the neighbours to help her tie my legs

* The Whales' Ocean.

with a halter, just as she did on the crabbed cow we had. My mother had quite a sharp tongue on her when she got going. Anyway, by the time we reached Fraserburgh, I was in a totally different world. The uproar and industry of the North-east of Scotland amazed me and every second lingo I listened to was a different brand of English. Folk were there from Yarmouth, Port Rush, Gourdon, Barra – from all over the place – and everybody trying their best to make conversation. It was in Fraserburgh that I saw my first train and, watching it so brightly painted as it moved along the coast, I thought it was a most wonderful sight.

The work I had to do was not at all easy. In fact, at times it was sometimes difficult. When the *Cuidich an Rìgh* was on the fishing-ground, I only got two or three hours' sleep at a time, whether it was during the day or night. As the 'Coiler', I held the lowliest rank on board the *Cuidich an Rìgh*. Because of that, I wasn' t due a wage, just a lump sum the size of which depended on the overall takings of the boat. Mind you, the skipper and the crew treated me very well and they always praised my hard work.

The morning catch at Lowestoft

At midnight, the lads would start hauling the end lines, and me with them helping them as best I could. More often than not, I was responsible for the capstan, the only piece of machinery on board driven by steam. The capstan was used to haul in the nets. Every quarter of an hour or so I was sent below to shovel more coal on to the boilers. I had to have pots and kettles boiling on the stove all the time, so as to give the lads a cup of tea whenever they felt in need of one. Making the tea and dishing it out was no problem to me, but I also had to wash the dishes. Once the nets were on board, the crew would sit down to eat. And, boy, did they eat! At the one sitting, they could devour close on a basket of herring either boiled or roasted. So you see, I didn't have a moment's peace, but I hasten to say that my time on the *Cuidich an Rìgh* was one of the best times of my life. I learned more at the fishing in that one season than I ever learned at Sgoil na h-Àirde!

Life at sea was always eventful and uncertain. You never knew what the weather was going to do to you. It had you *air bhiod* [on tenterhooks] all the time. You never knew if there was going to be much herring in the nets. But from the start, the skipper and the rest of the crew showed that they knew what they were doing, and I felt safe in their company. Like most of the fishermen I've known, they were religious. The skipper said grace before the meals – a very short one, mind – when we were in the thick of the herring shoals. He also prayed long and hard, morning and evening, and the crew took good care never to offend the Almighty if they could help it. In August, we sailed to Shetland, and fished there for six weeks. On a lovely clear day, something happened that caused me to go hide my face so that the skipper would not see how upset I was.

It was a beautiful day. There was only a light 'blabber' of wind so that we were making little progress, though we had every yard of sail aloft. When a smart-looking Lowestoft steam drifter came by us, her skipper came out of the wheelhouse and hailed us, asking if we would like to be towed out to where the herring shoals were. He would have been very surprised if the answer had been 'no'! He arranged for a line to be put aboard the *Cuidich an Rìgh* and soon we were under way, moving forward at a nice brisk pace. Our skipper invited me to the steering-wheel for a turn, to try to keep our vessel steady in the wake of the steam drifter. The job took more muscle than I had in my arms and I soon gave it up. But, by Jingo, didn't I think highly of myself for having stood, all by myself, holding the helm!

'Admiral John MacLeod, RNR, doesn't half steer well!' one of the boys teased. I enjoyed being teased like that, for I was only a young lad.

'What's RNR?' I asks.

'Runaway Rascal,' quips the skipper.

The men laughed and went out on deck to prepare the nets. Suddenly I heard shouting, and the next moment, I spied two men in the sea, having fallen overboard from the Lowestoft drifter dead ahead. After a few moments' hesitation running back and fore, two crewmen on the drifter threw off their clothes and jumped into the sea to try and help those struggling in the water. They were good swimmers, but one of those who had fallen sank just as the rescuers were about to reach him. His body was never recovered. The men of the *Cuidich an Rìgh* severed the tow-rope with an axe and the Lowestoft boat slowly came astern to where the second fellow was lying face-down. The crew hauled him aboard but he was found to have drowned. Our two drifters returned to Lerwick, with herring-baskets attached at half-mast. It was a sad, sad day. The men of our two boats behaved as grieving brothers that day and an awful silence fell over the *Cuidich an Rìgh* as we made our way back to port. Two days later, we all attended the funeral. In those days, there was true friendship between the crews of boats, no matter where they came from.

We returned to Steòrnabhagh at the beginning of September 1903.

At Steòrnabhagh, McBrayne's passenger steam-ship *Claymore* and a Zulu herring-drifter waiting to be unloaded

In Wick, when we were on our way back home, the skipper gave me two pounds and ten shillings. A millionaire could not have felt happier.

I bought presents for my mother – a cashmere shawl, a china teapot and a bottle of whisky. I arrived home late one evening, and when my mother saw me, she was overjoyed. She didn't have the heart to give me a telling-off. That had to wait till morning! I brought out the shawl and teapot I had bought her and she had tears in her eyes as she took them – my first ever purchases. Then I ventured to take the whisky out of my bag and, as I expected, she was not over pleased. I told her that I didn't want her to regard me as a child. 'All the men brought home a bottle of whisky. Why should I be different?'

I managed to persuade her to take a sip before she retired for the night, and when she was gone, I poured myself a handsome noggin. With my head in a swim, I felt really proud of all that I had done. Lying in my bed in the dark, I chuckled with glee, for the whole world was now at my feet. Little did I know then that the School Board was on my tail, determined to pull me down a peg or two before I was very much older.

Discipline and the Provost Sergeant

The 'whipper-in'* of the school was nicknamed the 'Poidhleat', who came from the village of Siadar. On the first morning after my return from Fraserburgh, he arrived at our house before I had properly wakened up, to deliver a summons for my mother and me. That was a very bad day for us. My mother, dear soul, did nothing but shout at me whenever I came by her, for the shame I had brought upon the family. Well I knew, though, that it was not the family she was worried about but what the School Board were going to say to us both and, more so, what they would do to my stern!

There was no patchwork trousers for Soolivan this time! Off we went to Steòrnabhagh, quite neatly dressed. I had on a clean gansey and moleskin trousers and the tackety boots which the skipper had given me as a present in Fraserburgh. My mother wore her new cashmere shawl. It was heavy going on the journey, as the weather was blustery and showery, and I must admit to feeling really downcast as we trudged the ten miles to the court-house. I ignored the provocative birds peering at us from the Sanndabhaig trees, just leaving them chirruping on their roosts.

When we entered the court-house, my jaw tightened and my body

* Compulsory Officer.

began to shake for it could remember better than myself the weals in my *tòin* [backside] after my previous visit.* Five sour-looking fellows were sitting on the bench, formally dressed, with their scented hair and moustaches combed, and their faces so clean and shiny that they must have spent the morning getting ready. They were a handsome bunch all right, and when they started talking with their solemn, high-falutin' words, I couldn't understand half of what they said. In the middle chair was the very fellow who had sentenced me for taking His Majesty's telephone-bell and spoon – a self-important little man who, more than anybody, enjoyed his own sarcasm. Anyone listening to his tirade against my mother would have thought that she was a stupid idiot. Oh, he fairly bombarded her with shells from his six-pounder! He accused her of giving me too much leeway and said that people like her should not have had a family. While I was listening to Mac an Diabhail, I said to myself, 'Another year or two, and I will be out from under your authority and pity you if I ever meet you man-to-man. I'll make you apologise for all the insults you have heaped on my mother today.'

The other men were more moderate. They questioned my mother in Gaelic on the subject of my behaviour and, as usual, she did her best, poor soul, to defend me. Was I a delinquent and a rascal around the house? Did I obey her or was I defiant? She replied in a slow, steady voice, not much above a whisper. 'Taing do Dhia!' she says, 'my son is very kind to me. But he's an adventurous boy who hasn't got the example of a father for him to follow.'

Then they turned to me with their questions.

'Why', asked one, 'did you run away from school?'

'I did not run away from school,' says I. 'The school was closed with the German measles, and because my mother is nothing but a poor widow, I went out on the boats to earn some money.'

That answer winded them a bit. They gathered their heads together in a pow-wow, and, after a few minutes, the chairman turned to me and told me that I had to answer one question truthfully.

'Are you willing to return to school, or are you intent on running back to the fishing?'

Anything to please them, I thought! I can well remember the look of relief on my mother's face when they let me off. What relief I also felt to be told that they weren't going to play 'blind man's buff' with me again.

The joy on my mother's face fairly lifted my spirits but the anger I felt for the School Board still burned within me. And it burned

* Soolivan wrongly assumed that the School Board had authority to sanction the use of the birch. Statistics show that, in fact, even the courts in Scotland rarely resorted to use of the birch against juveniles.

stronger still when we sat on herring-barrels on South Beach Street, and my mother suddenly began to cry. It's a shame that the guilt I felt when I saw her weeping didn't change my ways.

Instead, it came second nature to me to do the opposite of what was expected of me. All the time I was at school, I envied the boys home from the Militia, because of their neat appearance. They were so clean and immaculate, I just couldn't wait to join the ranks. One day, after coming ashore in Steòrnabhagh, did I not meet Murdo MacDonald, son of Dòmhnall Tharmoid – him an army captain, at home on leave. He looked like an ornament newly purchased from Bùth Sheumais (James MacKenzie's shop). There was me in my drab canvas jumper, scaly fishing-trousers and wellies as grubby and

Murdo MacDonald
'. . . like an ornament out of Bùth Sheumais'

unkempt as a bundle of rags on a tinker's cart. That day I said to myself, 'Soolivan, why aren't you as posh as the son of Dòmhnall Tharmoid? Some people might say that you would be just as handsome as him, if you was properly presented!'

Through the post, I received a recruiting-book telling about the Militia, and, at the age of fourteen, I signed on. Wasn't I proud when they sent for me to go to Fort George, having been enrolled in the 3rd Seaforth Highlanders – one of the most famous regiments in the whole of the British Empire. I had not been at Fort George for long before I discovered that there was more to the life of a soldier than looking smart. There were the difficulties of getting up early, learning proper speech, learning how to salute an officer, marching, presentation, spit-and-polish, and heeding the Provost Sergeant. Oh, the Provost Sergeant was a difficulty all right! He was like a hippopotamus – short in the leg, small beady eyes, a large mouth and a voice like thunder.

Since I was so young, the other men took advantage of me. Do this! Do that! I prayed to God, 'Please make me bigger! Please make me older!' It had not been my intention when I entered the Army to be a slave to anyone. No, sir! I told the other boys that, and I even told the Provost Sergeant. Eventually, a couple of regular soldiers whom I had befriended persuaded me to tell the Colonel. Well, being as green as a cabbage-leaf, I took their advice. I asked the Colonel if I could have a word in his ear and you can only imagine a little of what he said to me in return. I got an earful for my insubordination and thirty days confined to barracks. If the truth be told, there was another small matter which helped to earn me my punishment that day. It's more than my life is worth – even at my ripe old age – to say that there were thieves in the Seaforth Highlanders in those days. Somehow I had managed to lose my kit-bag with every item that the King had gifted me – my coat, my sheet and twenty cloths that were provided to keep my gun looking nice and clean.

Those thirty days were torture. The corporal gave me every horrible job there was – shovelling coal, peeling potatoes, scrubbing floors. If they had let me do these chores at my own pace, it would not have been so trying. But the bugler was a lad from Inverness just about two years older than myself. Whenever he sounded the bugle, I had to leave what I was doing, and chase off up to him. You bet that Inverness lad enjoyed his job all right! He thought it hilarious to see me coming pounding along the parade-ground from wherever I had been. I hated him for his smirk.

I was forbidden to drink in the canteen or even to enter through its door. But one sweaty afternoon, after I had finished the day's chores, I asked the bugler if he would report me if I was to have a pint of ale in the canteen. Oh, he wouldn't say a word, he says, so long as

I promised to come out as soon as he sounded the bugle. All right, then, off I went and drank as fast as I could. When I came out, the Provost Sergeant was waiting for me with a black scowl on him. He gave me such a dressing-down in front of all the other boys that it made the pint I had drunk leave through my pores as sweat! The next time I heard the bugle, I ran to the bugler, pushed my nose right up against his, and called him the most unsavoury names I could muster in Gaelic and in English. At Fort George, the Army hadn't taught me much about soldiering but I had picked up some useful English words along the way.

'One fine day,' says I, 'I will repay you for your treachery, you rotten little toe-rag!'

Well, it wasn't a nice thing to call him, right enough, but I can tell you that on more than one occasion, I was called a lot worse than that by the Provost Sergeant. The bugler just stood there smiling, for he quite enjoyed seeing me digging myself deeper in the mire. But he who laughs last laughs longest! I paid the young smirker back a lot sooner than he expected. I knew the route he took back from the canteen at the end of the night. While peeling the vegetables, I chose a nice healthy turnip and went with it into a cubby-hole. When the bugler opened the door to the dormitory, I threw the turnip overhand as you would a grenade. It hit him right on the side of the head. As soon as I saw that I had made a direct hit, I ran to the back of the barracks, climbed in through the window of the toilet, and lay on my bed as if reading a book. In five minutes the Provost Sergeant came into the room, with two military policemen.

'On your feet, MacLeod! Out of here on the double!'

I was taken to the guard-house and the Provost Sergeant started to question me. I wouldn't admit to anything. Another officer came and together the two began to question me, but all they would get out of me was that I was on my bed reading all the while. In the end, they had to let me go. On the following day, I heard that the bugler was in hospital. Evidently, the blow I had struck was heavier than I intended. A week later, when he returned to his bugle, I approached him and asked where he had been.

'You know fine well,' says he, running his fingers over his head. 'But before you leave Fort George, you'll get what you deserve. I promise you that, you Heilan' coward!'

I wasn't really a coward, for I was never afraid of punishment, but there was no point in trying to tell that to the bugler. I was just angry, and maybe also I was disappointed that I was not allowed to dress up immaculate like Murdo MacDonald, the son of Dòmhnall Tharmoid.

That was just an example of the little skirmishes that went on between some of the young lads in the camp. For me, bigger skirmishes were to come. The Provost Sergeant told us the next day that we were being drafted to another camp. Where? I never found out. But we had to leave Fort George as soon as possible, and go to the nearest railway station which was at Campbeltown (or Ardersier, as it is known today). All the preparations were made to transport the 1,250 soldiers at Fort George to some distant destination. About 600 of us were marched to a train that was supposed to depart at eleven o'clock in the morning and another 600 (myself being one of them) on another train due to leave at two o'clock in the afternoon. Anyway, the first train failed to arrive until six o'clock the following morning. Imagine that – well over a thousand troops in that small village, cold and unfed and without sleep for most of the night.

By sunrise, the troops had become very impatient and some of them began to break things. When the train did arrive, they rampaged through it like a plague of locusts. The police from Inverness and, as far as I can remember, from as far away as Perth were summoned to the Campbeltown station to try to quell the mêlée. At one point I didn't think I was going to make it out alive. At last order was restored and officers directed us back to Fort George. For the damage they had done at the station, a fine of twelve shillings and six pence was imposed on every member of the 3rd Seaforth Highlanders.* Nor was that the last stramash I was involved in before leaving the Militia. The Provost Sergeant got a hold of me one day, shortly before I had completed my year. He says, 'There's a law in this regiment that every soldier must pay all his debts, before he leaves Fort George.'

'But I don't have any debts,' I says.

'Maybe not money,' he replies, 'but there's more than one kind of debt in an army camp.'

He took me behind the barracks, where the bugler and two or three other soldiers were waiting for me. Oh, everything was all arranged before I appeared on the scene. Even a referee! There was to be no kicking or biting, we were told. We had to shake hands and come out flailing. My goodness, what a battle we fought. We went at each other, hammer and tongs, until our knuckles were swollen. I hadn't fought anyone by fisticuffs for a couple of years – not since I had left over from scrapping in the disused quarry at Druim Oidealar. The Inverness boy was strong enough, but he was a much better bugler than he was a fighter. Although I was two years younger than him, I gave him as good as I got. The two of us had bleeding noses and faces so swollen that we could hardly see out of our eyes. When the referee declared the peace, the bugler and I shook hands and

* The relevant pages have been torn from the regimental records so that the official account of the events described cannot be traced.

agreed that we had done each other enough damage and we left it at that.

Returned home, I was looking a bit the worse for wear. People were saying, 'Soolivan has been to the wars again!' I told everyone that I intended going back to the Army as a regular, but in my heart I knew that never would I return of my own accord to His Majesty's kilted battalions.

In Them Thar Hills!

There was a time in my life when I took a terrible dose of gold fever. It started after I discovered a vein of gold in a cliff at Ceann an t-Siùmpain. Well, to be truthful, it was Calum Ned who found it, and he would have done me a big favour if he had kept his discovery to himself.

I was born in 1889 in an age when there were five or six boys in every island household. Big families everywhere. It also happened to be the golden age of rock-climbing in Lewis. In the summer and autumn, you'd find boys like us swarming over the cliffs like a plague of mice in the thatch. Me and Calum Ned and 'Cròchan'* were keen rock-climbers. The three of us were fondest of the cliffs at the Siùmpan and over by Seisiadar. Elsewhere in the Rubha, boys from other villages were doing the same thing, and I can tell you that there were some terrible cliffs further up the Rubha, especially in Pabail Iarach and in Suardail, on which you could put your life in danger every day of the week and especially when the adults were in church. Anyway, on that special day, the three of us – Calum Ned, Cròchan and myself – were climbing in Caolas a' Ghrianan, in the north face of the Cnap, when all of a sudden Calum Ned shouts, 'Soolivan! Look at that, right in front of where your foot is!'

I shifted my position to have a dekko and I heard Cròchan say, 'Glièidh mi agus mo chiall! Seall air an òr!' [It's a streak of gold in the rock!]

I can see it now: a yard-long streak of gold, about three inches at the broad end and tapering to nothing. Excitement! I tell you, I nearly let go my hold of the rock to which I was clinging – which would have been an unwise thing to do, for I would have plunged into eternity. So excited was I by that gold streak in the rock that we went scrambling off home and told everybody that we had discovered another Yukon. Before you could say *sgian* [knife], people were arguing about who

* Calum Ned was lost in the HMS *Bulwark* disaster in 1914; 'Cròchan' (Murdo Campbell) spent a total of eight years as a POW in Germany during the two world wars.

could lay claim to the fortune at Cnap Cìleag. Two or three people figured that Calum Ned and Cròchan and I would become millionaires.

Our good fortune caused the wisest *bodaich* on the Sràid to debate the subject into the wee small hours of the next day. In the end, it was decided to refer the matter to the person in the village who was thought to have the most gumption. And that was the Captain of the lighthouse. Stands to reason, you see: a man with a collar-and-tie and with no Gaelic had to know about mining gold and that! Because of Ivor Nèill's land-dispute with Admiral Jack, we all knew that the lighthouse authorities couldn't claim any territory at Ceann an t-Siùmpain outside the perimeter wall of the lighthouse station and that put Cnap Cìleag about 250 yards beyond their reach. So far, so good! Och, in the marrow of our bones, me and my pals began to hear streams of guineas clinking into our pockets. It was a wonderful sensation and I already began to feel a growing craving for cigars. My ambitions began to soar. I would build a huge store that would put Innis Uilleim's in the shade; and I would marry some well-to-do coloured lady from Havana where they make cigars and rum. Oh, *a charaid ort*, there would be no stopping me then.

Once told of our good fortune, the Captain of the lighthouse sent for us. 'Now, lads,' he says, ' I want you to take me to the very place where you found the gold.'

No problem. We met up with him on the shoulder of the Siùmpan and headed off downhill towards Cnap Cìleag. When we started scrambling down the grassy section of the cliff-face, the Captain began to panic and got so scared that he was near losing his dinner! 'Come back up here, you idiots,' he yells. 'I wouldn't go down there for all the gold in China!'

Oh, he wouldn't put a foot near the edge of the cliff. Can you

Pabail Iarach: 'a lot of terrible cliffs . . .'

imagine that: a man who made his living on top of the lighthouse tower, having no head for heights. No, he wouldn't budge and he couldn't even bear to see us on the cliff-face.

'Now, boys,' he says, 'come here and I'll let you in on a wee secret. It's well known that the rocks hereabouts have what they call "fool's gold". It's worthless rubbish. Not only that, but even if it turns out to be the real thing, the gold wouldn't belong to you. It would belong to the Matheson family who own the Island of Lewis, and that includes the mining rights.'

With that, he turns on his heel and disappears off to the lighthouse. Och, well, easy come, easy go – that's what everybody up on the Sràid told everybody else. The long and the short of it was that the disappointment had us all in the dumps for days. Calum Ned and Cròchan began to believe that they had imagined the whole thing. Not me! I knew what I had seen and I couldn't get that streak of gold out of my head. Still can't. Today, nobody believes that the discovery of gold at Cnap Cìleag ever happened, but I know it did. Calum Ned lost his life in the First World War and Cròchan's memory can't stretch back beyond his years as a prisoner of war of the Germans. *Co-dhiù*, I was desperate to find somebody who would believe my story and was honest enough not to try to rook me out of a share of the loot. It took

Innis Uilleim, the merchant, with his wife and family

me until the following summer to come across such a man.

Now, in our end of the Rubha, there was a good number of old soldiers who were after learning the pipes while they were in the Seaforth Highlanders, fighting in the Boer War. In those days, when couples got married, you could hear the loudness of their weddings miles away. That was because of the noise of the pipes and the hooching and pooching of the barn-dances. Having said that, I believe that the best piper I ever heard was a *ceàrd* – a tinker who used to visit us with his pony and spring-cart every summer. His name was Alasdair Dòmhnallach and he lived with his wife and young family in one of the tinker huts at Tong. That was only his winter headquarters, mind you. For the rest of the year, he just wandered all over the Gàidhealtachd, earning a living any way he could.

My mother was always good to the tinkers, even though they looked different from other Lewis folk and spoke a funny kind of Gaelic. Alasdair Dòmhnallach was a gifted man, and whenever he and his wife got a plate of broth in our house, he would repay us with a tune on his tin-whistle or on his chanter. He was first class on both. It always ended up with us children dancing about like dervishes when he played the reels.

But what I liked most about Alasdair Dòmhnallach was that he didn't mind giving us boys a ride on his spring-cart. Of course, this was before the age of buses and tourers, you understand. Getting a ride on a spring-cart was a great treat in those days. In winter, when they weren't on the road, the tinkers used to sit at home making pails and things out of sheets of tin. Then, when the weather improved, they would hitch their horses to their spring-carts and off we go – pails, basins, jugs, mugs, horn spoons and little ornaments made from animal bones. What a wonderful life! I envied Alasdair Dòmhnallach

The promontory of An Grianan (nearest), with the bulbous Cnap Cìleag sandwiched between it and An Siùmpan

so much for his freedom that I figure I was a *ceàrd* at heart. Mind you, I didn't fancy being married to his wife. She was a thin, pale-faced, nervous sort of woman, dressed in grey clothes and with a huge tartan shawl wrapped round herself and her baby. She never said much but became twitchy and bright while her husband was entertaining us. I think she would have liked to get up and dance with us but she didn't have the courage. Aye, they were ordinary folk who never pretended to be anything more than what they were – common or garden *ceàrdan*.

I decided to tell Alasdair Dòmhnallach about the seam of gold in Cnap Cìleag and to invite him to go with me to see the gold for himself. I trusted him, you see. No problem: Alasdair Dòmhnallach said he would like to see the treasure, so off we went on the spring-cart, me and the wife and baby sitting in the stern and Alasdair up front, leading the pony. I can tell you that I got some funny looks from the women who met us coming in from the Sliabh Mhònach with their creels of peats on their backs. I could hear them cackling and saying, 'Where is Soolivan off to with the tinkers? Perhaps he's going to sell them his "fools' gold"!'

As we were approaching Geodha nan Crùbag, I came off the spring-cart and ran ahead of Alasdair over to the Geodha Ruadh. In due course, he arrived with the pony and spring-cart. The Geodha Ruadh is quite a sight, as you know. When you stand on the edge of the chasm, you feel that it is drawing you into its darkness, so you've always got to take a step or two back. When Alasdair got used to the scene and I showed him the challenge of Cnap Cìleag, he drew breath. I explained to him that, to see the streak of gold, we would have to climb down to near the high-water mark. He stood thinking for a while considering the challenge. Well, he stood and he stood. Then, of a sudden, didn't the tinker wifie start sobbing.

'No-no-no!' she was saying. She held her baby up before her husband. 'Look at our Jeannie. Don't go leave us.'

With all her whimpering, I knew that I was in for another disappointment.

'Tell you what I'll do,' says Alasdair. 'I don't think you'll find any real gold in that rotten rock. But as it so happens, I know where there is a real hoard of gold coins hidden. No need to risk your life to get to it! It's a secret, 'ille, but you shared your secret with me, so I'll share mine with you.'

Och, Alasdair Dòmhnallach could see that I had put all my faith in him and that he had let me down. He cleared his throat and he says, 'I'll swear on our baby Jeannie's head, 'ille, that I'm not telling you a lie. I must put you on your word of honour that you won't tell a living soul about my secret.'

I told him I wasn't the kind of fella who was likely to give away a secret like that.

'There's a store of gold coins hidden at the other end of the Rubha,' he says. 'Only my brothers and me know where to look for it. If you join us and keep your mouth shut on it, we'll give you a share.'

I promised that I wouldn't mention his secret to a soul. On the following Friday first thing, I was to meet Alasdair at the peat-stacks at the last house before you come to Gob na Circe in Suardail.

A dhuine bhochd, was I excited that I was going to get a share of the tinkers' hoard of gold coins! Who wouldn't be? And me only about fourteen or fifteen years old an' all. When I got home, I told my mother that I had to go to my seanairs'* house in Pabail Iarach and that I'd be back on Saturday night. I wouldn't tell her the reason why I suddenly decided that I must visit my grandparents. She must have thought that I had begun *caithris na h-oidhche* before I was out of short trousers!

As the crow flies, the distance from my grandparents' house in Pabail Iarach to Suardail is no more than two miles. So bright and early, I got up and was at the end houses of Suardail long before Alasdair Dòmhnallach had started to climb the Cnoc.

Where the cart-track peters out at the headland, I loitered about for ages. Then, at last, I saw Alasdair come plodding his way up to me leading his pony and spring-cart. Even from a distance, I could see that the face on him was wearing a scowl. He soon showed me why. 'Do you not see the three ponies grazing over there by the headland? Those belong to my cousins. The trustairean [villains] have beaten me to it! Come on down here with me.'

He led me to a gully called Grèinigeadh not a quarter mile from the houses. Before we reached the cliff-top, we could hear plenty of activity below us. The beach was heaving with tinkers who were squabbling and arguing as they turned over boulders and searched under them. Alasdair Dòmhnallach turned to me and said, 'Tha mi duilich 'ille! I'm sorry, lad! My brothers must have shared my secret with all our cousins. There's a pirates' hoard of silver dollars hidden in them rocks. There will be trouble tonight if we don't find it.'

I knew that the tinker clan would be on me like hornets if I joined in the fun. Before we parted, Alasdair offered me one of two silver coins that, he claimed, were part of the pirate's hoard.

'But you told me it was a hoard of gold coins! ' says I.

I was so *troimh a chéile* [miffed] that I refused to take his coin. Though I was as upset as upset can be, he made me take one of his tin whistles.

* Iain & Margaret Graham, 26 Pabail Iarach.

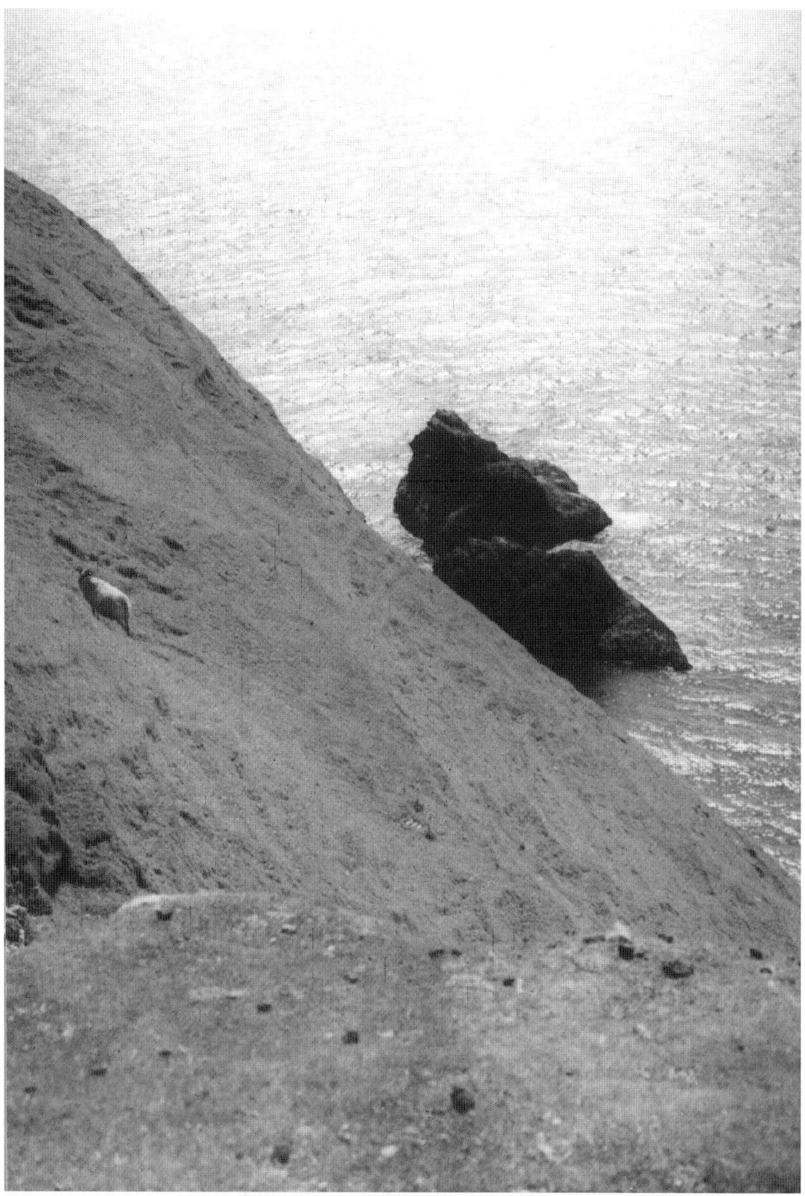

'It's not gold or silver,' he says, 'but after all, a tin whistle is better than nothing at all!'

You know, I discovered early in my life that Admiral Jack of the lighthouse was not the only bull-shitter in town! That morning at the far end of the Rubha, Alasdair Dòmhnallach proved to be another of them. I walked home miserable, trying to get a tune out of the tinker's tin-whistle while every dog between Suardail and Siadar barked at the noise I was making.

To date, my search for gold had failed, but America was there for the taking. When I reached Cnoc Chùsbaig, I threw the tin-whistle as far as I could into the moor. My mind was made up. I would pack my bag and seek my fortune on the far side of the Atlantic Ocean.

The grassy slope of Gréinigeadh (The Green Gully)

Historical Note

The story of the Grèinigeadh hoard of silver coins began in Gibraltar on 19 May 1821. On that day, a schooner called Jane *left Gibraltar bound for Bahia in Brazil. Her cargo was a valuable one, consisting of about 100 barrels of beeswax, numerous bags of aniseed, hundreds of jars of olives, scores of boxes of raisins and six wooden casks so heavy that the crew had difficulty in bringing them on board. It was somehow discovered that the casks contained a large quantity of silver coins. Within three weeks of putting to sea, the mate and the cook murdered the captain and commandeered the ship. At a position west of the Canary Islands, the* Jane *altered course and sailed northwards. The mutineers intended to reach the north of Scotland, where they would share the loot before dispersing to places where they might enjoy their ill-gotten wealth. Meanwhile, the barrels brought up on deck were found to contain large canvas sacks in which were a total of 38,180 silver dollars. The casks were broken up and the staves thrown overboard. The sacks of dollars were hidden in the sides of the ship.*

Eventually, the Jane *was within sight of Barra and anchored off Vatersay. The mutineers went ashore and acquired a sheep, geese, ducks and butter which they bartered for boxes of raisins, jars of olives and a lump of beeswax. They also bought a large boat and a sail for which they paid £20. While at Vatersay, the visitors heard mention of the presence of a revenue cutter, called* Prince of Wales *which was operating in the Minch, under the command of Captain Oliver.* The* Prince of Wales *was charged with the seizure of vessels found to be carrying contraband of any kind, but particularly illicitly distilled whisky, the production of which was commonplace in the Outer Hebrides. The mutineers decided that it would be too risky to sail the Minches. Off Pabail Iarach, they prepared to scuttle the* Jane *and duly provisioned the boat purchased at Vatersay. Off Suardail, three members of the crew were sent below to cut holes in the inner skin of the* Jane*. Meanwhile, the sacks of silver dollars were transferred to the boat. By eleven o'clock, there was total darkness. Holes were knocked in the outer skin of the schooner, which immediately started to fill with sea-water. With the wind in a jib and a spinnaker, she sailed off in a*

* His name is commemorated in 'Oliver's Brae' on the outskirts of Steòrnabhagh.

northerly direction and was soon swallowed up in the night. The crew now set a course for the Scottish mainland, which they hoped to reach by late morning. However, a storm blew up and forced them to run before it. Off Rubha na Circ in Suardail, the boat was driven towards the shore and ended up lying broadside on to the beach at Gréinigeadh. The sacks of silver were hastily carried on to the beach, where the mutineers began to share the money, with the mate and the cook (the ring-leaders) taking more than the others.

Unfortunately for the mutineers, their boat had been sighted from the shore while she was beating off Suardail, and no sooner had she arrived at Gréinigeadh than news of her presence was quickly carried to Steòrnabhagh. Later in the day, Ruairidh MacIomhar, Surveyor of Customs, visited the scene with three companions and interviewed the strangers. The erstwhile mate of the Jane *claimed that they were from the brig* Betsy, *which, they claimed, was wrecked at Barra Head; and that her crew had abandoned ship in two boats, one of which was under the command of the captain. Meantime, he claimed, he and his companions were attempting to sail south to Liverpool. It was a plausible enough story. But as the Customs men were leaving the scene, a young Maltese boy who had been cabin-boy on the* Jane *ran after them and blurted out the truth. Local men were hastily recruited to help guard the prisoners and the loot. Later in the day, the mutineers were handcuffed and taken to Steòrnabhagh, whence they were transported to Edinburgh on board the* Prince of Wales.

The half-submerged Jane *came ashore at Tolastadh. Half a ton of beeswax from her cargo also came ashore and was sold by Customs officials for the sum of £45. At the mutineers' trial in Edinburgh, a jury found the mate and the cook guilty of murder and piracy and, on 9 January 1822, they were hanged at the foot of Leith Walk. The rest of the crew had turned King's Evidence.*

Of the 38,180 silver dollars in the hold of the Jane *when she set sail from Gibraltar, only 31,213 were recovered. In other words, nearly 7,000 silver dollars had 'disappeared'! In his book,* The Gaelic Vikings, *James Shaw Grant claims that, at one time, some of the pirates' silver dollars were common enough in Steòrnabhagh: '. . . it was said that, for many years afterwards, you could not cash a pound note without getting Spanish money in the change.'*

Chapter Two

The Brave New World

Within the past three centuries, countless numbers of Scots have emigrated to North America. During the Clearances of the eighteenth and nineteenth centuries, thousands were forced to leave their homes in the Highlands and Islands and shipped to the New World. But apart from those who crossed the Atlantic against their wishes, there were many others who

Lewis emigrants of the 1920s boarding ship at Steòrnabhagh

emigrated seeking adventure, or escaping from religious persecution or punitive taxes imposed by their landlords.

In the seventeenth century, most people of British descent were concentrated in the thirteen original colonies of the country known to us today as the United States of America. Those colonies were Virginia, established in 1607; Massachusetts, in 1620; Maryland, in 1634; Connecticut, c. 1635; Rhode Island, in 1636; Delaware, in 1638; New Hampshire, in 1638; North Carolina, in 1653; South Carolina, in 1663; New Jersey, in 1664; New York, in 1664; Pennsylvania, in 1682; and Georgia, in 1732.

In 1604, France began to colonise the basin of the St Lawrence River. Its settlements there laid the foundation for New France, a country that was to develop its own culture – 'a blend of French roots, Aboriginal customs, and adaptations to the new land'. For several generations, New France prospered, with its major settlements at Quebec and Montreal.

The French had a monopoly of the Canadian fur trade until two of their traders defected to the English and revealed to them a route to the rich trading grounds to the north and west of Lake Superior. After that, English traders, working from the shores of Hudson Bay, were able to penetrate far into the interior, bypassing New France, which lay to the south. In 1670, the Hudson's Bay Company (HBC) was incorporated by royal charter, granting the company a monopoly over the fur trade in a region consisting of one-third of the area occupied by today's Canada. Over the years, a great many Orcadians and Hebrideans were employed by the HBC. The company's trading expeditions began and ended in London, but the last port of call for its ships was Stromness in Orkney, where they were provisioned before starting their voyage across the Atlantic Ocean.

In 1773, nearly a thousand people emigrated from Lewis to North America. In the following year, two ships, the Friendship *and the* Peace and Plenty, *set sail from Steòrnabhagh, each carrying more than a hundred emigrants bound for Philadelphia and New York respectively. Among the passengers bound for New York was Alexander Mackenzie,* the future Canadian explorer. Then aged twelve, he travelled with his aunts to join his father, who had joined a United Empire Loyalist regiment near New York. With the American*

* The house in which Sir Alexander Mackenzie was born stood on the site of what is now Martin's Memorial Church, Steòrnabhagh.

War of Independence about to erupt, the Mackenzie family migrated north to set up home in Montreal.

The HBC based an agent in Steòrnabhagh to recruit men for the fur trade in Canada. Those men were engaged for a minimum of three years and were given free passage there and back. Many took advantage of those terms, and in 1811, more than a hundred left the island for a new life in northern Canada. A number of them married First Nation (Red Indian) girls. Whereas most of those chose not to return to Lewis, a few did return accompanied by their wives. Searching for a river that would open up a route between central Canada and the Pacific Ocean, Sir Alexander Mackenzie discovered and charted the largest river in Canada, the 2,500-mile long Mackenzie River. Instead of a new route to the Pacific, he found that the waters of the river poured into the Arctic Ocean, which he reached on 14 July 1789.

Disputes over trading rights between Britain and France led to the Seven Years War (1756–63), each country fighting for dominion over the northern half of the North American continent. The British colonials (Americans) were pinned up against the Atlantic seaboard, with only the HBC in the north challenging the French trading monopoly. With thirty-three times the population in less than half the land area, the British found the need to expand into territory claimed by the French. When they entered the Ohio Valley, which was controlled by France, war resulted.

The decisive battle between the two colonial powers was fought at Quebec in 1759. The British General Wolfe, guided by the Fraser Highlanders, scaled the Heights of Abraham overlooking Quebec and defeated the French. Once New France fell, some of the Scots who had had a measure of success in the fur trade, though based in the Thirteen Colonies, moved north to Montreal and founded a rival to the HBC. It was called the North West Company, and so bitter was the rivalry between the two organisations that when their respective traders met, even on neutral territory such as Steòrnabhagh, brawling often broke out. In 1821, the North West Company of Montreal and the HBC merged, with a combined territory that was extended by licence to an area reaching the Arctic Ocean in the north and the Pacific Ocean in the west.

During and after the war, the large numbers of people who had remained loyal to the British crown moved out of the colonies. It is estimated that about 40,000 fled to Canada and formed the basis of the English-speaking society in that country. The newcomers greatly strengthened Canadian society, for they included graduates, lawyers, merchants, craftspeople and farmers. They swelled the populations of Ontario, Quebec, New Brunswick, Prince Edward Island and Nova Scotia (including Cape Breton).

Today, virtually all Scots have blood relations living in Canada, a country which came into existence on 1 July 1867 when four eastern British North American provinces were united as a federation.

John Alexander Macdonald (1815–91), Canada's first prime minister, was born in Glasgow. His first term in office was marked by nation building. Manitoba, centred on the Red River settlement on the Prairies, joined the confederation in 1870. British Columbia, on the west coast, was enticed into confederation in 1871, having been promised that a transcontinental railway would be built within ten years to link it with eastern Canada. Macdonald also added Prince Edward Island and British Columbia as provinces in 1871, and acquired the territory that eventually became Alberta and Saskatchewan.

One of the most far-sighted decisions of the newly fledged government was to promote the building of the Canadian Pacific Railway, which was to unite Canada physically from coast to coast – a distance greater than that between Scotland and Nova Scotia. The Rocky Mountains in the west of Canada formed a natural barrier that was difficult to penetrate. The section of railway along the steep and treacherous walls of the Fraser Valley was especially difficult to build. It took 15,000 men seven years to build 382 miles of this route, which claimed the lives of between 700 and 800 workers.

On the great plains of central Canada, immigrants had not waited for the railway to arrive. The government had encouraged large groups of people to move into the wide-open spaces in the middle of the country. In 1874 it created the first of its 'collective settlements'. About 7,500 German-speaking Mennonites whom Catherine the Great had allowed to settle on the steppes of Russia, but who had abandoned that country owing to religious persecution, were allowed to settle in Saskatchewan. Several hundred Jewish refugees, also fleeing from persecution in Russia, arrived in Winnipeg. Having taken flight after the eruption of Mount Hecla, 1,250 Icelanders arrived in 1875 and founded a settlement on Lake Winnipeg. There, they combined farming with commercial *fishing. At the same time, Swedish farmers began to move northward from the Dakotas, and, by the early 1880s, English gentlemen farmers were trying to establish themselves in southern Saskatchewan. As the railway moved across the Prairies, on the flatter stretches at the rate of three miles per day, it spawned villages and small towns. By 1891, there were still only quarter of a million people living on the Prairies. Well over half of them were newcomers to Canada. On 7 November 1885, east met west when Donald A. Smith* ceremonially joined the two sections of the Canadian Pacific railway. He drove the symbolic 'last spike' at Craigellachie, in British Columbia.*

*This task of building the railway from the Atlantic coast to the Pacific was a huge undertaking which, as it transpired, was constantly fraught with financial problems. Even when the work was complete, the railway company appeared to be in jeopardy. It took a minor uprising of a mixed race called the Métis to impress on the Canadian government the value of the CPR. In 1869, Louis Riel, the political leader of the Métis, had led an uprising against government-backed agencies which were riding roughshod through territories which, by treaty, belonged to native people. Riel came out of exile in the United States after the first Northwest Rebellion to lead the second insurrection in 1885. Inadvertently his actions demonstrated the national security benefit of the CPR. Troops and militia from the east were mobilised, travelled west over the nearly completed CPR main line and managed to quell the 1885 rebellion in a matter of weeks. To quell the rebellion of sixteen years earlier had taken months and a circuitous trip through the USA. The federal government then agreed to secure CPR's outstanding loans. With the CPR completed in 1885, regular passenger services across Canada were initiated by the following summer. The Canadian Northern Railway, incorporated in 1899, opened up territory to the north of the CPR. It ran through Edmonton and over the Yellowhead Pass to Vancouver, opening up the northern Ontario wilderness on the way. By 1914,** Canada had more than 30,000 miles of railroad, the highest ratio of track to population in the world. By 1921, two million people lived on the Prairies, almost a*

* (1820–85). Born at Forres.

** In the First World War, seventy-three men from the Rubha served with the Canadian Army and Navy, of whom eleven were killed in action, and as many wounded; see pp. 107–19. A handful also served with the armed forces of the USA, Australia, New Zealand and Rhodesia.

quarter of the country's population. Of those, 800,000 had been born abroad. Between 1910 and 1913, almost 1,400,000 people settled in Canada. At that time, there was a huge surge of immigrants from the British Isles, the largest since the 1840s. One of the Rubhaich who, in his late teens, began to feel the urge to cross the Atlantic Ocean, was the elder son of Tarmod Uilleim of No. 11 Port Mholair.

In 1907 when he was about eighteen years of age Soolivan took the plunge. He travelled to Glasgow with his three sisters who, it is believed, had found employment in factories or as servants to well-to-do families in the city. With his emigration papers in order, he kissed his sisters goodbye and took the train to Greenock.

Worlds Apart

In those days, news was conveyed by word of mouth. Very often what was being reported as news wasn't news at all – just idle gossip. Apart from local scandals, news of important events in distant places took months to reach as far as our end of the Rubha. People often added colour to each titbit as it travelled along the villages. They weren't just telling lies. Not at all! They just wanted to make dull news sound more interesting. A triviality could be converted into a real whopper within a couple of hours. You could start a non-existent war between Egypt and Patagonia at the drop of a hat and commit terrible slaughter on battlefields without anyone getting hurt. The *bodaich*, smoking their clay pipes, sat round the fire considering the carnage and recalling their own experiences of Crimean battles, hurricanes in the China Sea, fisher-fights in Wick, and other forms of mayhem. The *cailleachan,* on the other hand, preferred standing together in the open air, some knitting socks and some with their arms folded, discussing recent reports of disgraceful acts of fornication or, failing that, whispering re-worked scandals of long ago. My friends and I enjoyed eavesdropping on the *bodaich* and looked forward to a time when we too could leave the island so as to get a proper slice of life. Although I had been given a good drubbing while I was in the 'Malishy' at Fort George, it didn't discourage me from pushing off the island once more. I finished with the winter fishing of 1907 and stayed at home all through the spring of 1908, helping to plant potatoes and to cut peats but, all the while, dreaming about the huge, exciting world beyond the distant horizon.

Innis Mòr Campbell down by the Cladach was the only person in our part of the parish receiving newspapers regularly. I suppose his policeman son sent them home to him from Glasgow. It so happened at that time that one of Innis Mòr's newspapers found its way into our house, and it was through it that I learnt of the big job opportunities in the New World. As soon as I got hold of a writing-pad and pen and ink, I wrote away to say that I was ready, able and willing to emigrate to Canada. It was autumn before I received word that my application had been accepted and that I would shortly be invited to accompany other Lewis folk on the voyage out. What excitement the day I got that news! Next thing, I was at the road-end surrounded by well-wishers and my mother giving me a tearful farewell kiss.

'Now, remember,' she says, 'to lead your life as I have taught you from the Bible and the catechisms! Remember to say your prayers at night and never take the Lord's name in vain!'

Of course, she said all that to me in Gaelic. It was the last time I saw my mother. Looking back to those times, I am truly ashamed that I caused her to shed so many tears on my behalf. I'm ashamed that I ignored her advice while she was living and even more after she was gone. You ask me why did I not take my mother's advice. A fair question! Well, it didn't help that she appealed to one or two of the

Washing blankets – a communal activity

churchmen in our community to advise me on how I should behave myself in the New World. How could anyone take some of those guys seriously – fellas who had spoken ill of me a few years earlier because I had gathered herring for our family on a Sunday. No doubt their advice was well meant, but I rejected it as so much hot air.

At Greenock, three hundred people from Lewis went aboard the *New Media* – an almighty vessel, the biggest ship I had ever laid eyes upon. It wasn't only Highlanders who travelled on the voyage. There were Greeks and Russians amongst them – all with the same dream. We sailed out through the beautiful scenery of the Firth of Clyde in good weather. But as soon as we lost sight of the Mull of Kintyre, the sea turned nasty, coming at us from the west with big, ugly waves – and it stayed on like that for three long days. Of course, the Lewis folk were as used to rough seas as cormorants. We weren't like island men of today! There are men in our villages today who have never even had a pint of sea-water flow under their buttocks! Very different from the hardy souls of my young days.

Some crew-members of the *New Media* were severely seasick, and a lot of the passengers became fearful that the vessel was going to sink. Buckets of weeping and praying! As best they could, the Gaelic women comforted those who were afraid.

At last, when the sea calmed, everyone settled down and made friends and told each other that it was all going to be worth it, once we arrived in the New World. A day or two later, we noticed a group of Russians standing at a porthole and nervously watching the ocean. They never seemed to move from the same spot. The white-caps had given way to long gentle ridges, and so, like many of the passengers, I decided to go for forty winks even though it wasn't yet bedtime. In those days I could sleep anywhere at the drop of a hat. I lay down on the deck with my head on my jacket and prepared to doze off. There was nothing to be heard but the distant throb-throb of the engines, the roar of the sea on the bows and the occasional cry of a young child.

I was wakened by the cold and saw that a lot of passengers were already moving about. In the morning light, I saw that the same group of Russians were still standing by the porthole. A lad from Tolastadh and I went to another porthole on the starboard side and saw, just a few miles away, something that astonished us – a square, white mountain larger than Mùirneag, sitting on the horizon. The iceberg was in view for about an hour, and by midday another one came into view, and then another. For the whole day, the mountains of floating ice were within a few miles to starboard. The sight of them was enough to make us all shiver.

On the last leg of our journey, we were allowed on deck, and late one evening, land was seen rising out of the mist. What excitement!

Everyone crowded to the rail to get our first glimpse of the New World. The ship ploughed on towards Halifax in Nova Scotia and, in the morning, we got up to find Canadian Customs men and a couple of doctors climbing on board.

Apart from what I was wearing, everything I owned was in my suitcase – two shirts, two shifts of underwear and four pairs of socks. I haven't the faintest idea why I carried a suitcase, when all I owned could have fitted into my pockets! Anyway, that was how I went ashore in Canada – the Promised Land. My stomach was wailing with hunger and my suitcase was wailing with emptiness, and, boy, did I feel ready and able to fill them both!

From Halifax trains took us far into the heart of Canada until, after days of weary travel, we reached a station about a hundred miles from Kenora. That was in the far west of Ontario, a place I got to know quite well in due time. There were sleighs to meet us, with plenty of blankets to keep us warm. They were strange-looking buggies, the sleighs – contraptions we had never seen the like of before. The Gaels felt a wee bit foolish sitting in them, as they were brightly coloured, and adorned with bells that jingled like an English Morris dancer. What laughing and joking went on! The horses were also decorated in the same hilarious manner, and when they went prancing through the dark in all that ting-a-ling, we felt ridiculous – though I cannot explain why!

When the journey ended, we were told that we had to complete on foot. We walked for mile after mile through countryside littered with rocks and broken forests, and many's the time I wished that we were back on our sleighs again, ting-a-ling or not. At last we reached the camp – a bunch of wooden buildings and canvas tents. That was the end of the line.

It was a place buzzing with hundreds of men. Not a female of any description in sight. It reminded me of the army camp at Fort George, but without spit-and-polish, Provost Sergeant or bugler. Thank the Lord for that!

There were forty people in each cabin, all from differing backgrounds. Plenty of food. Good food! Chinese came to the camp every day with frozen fish. Our clothes were kept nice and warm in a specially heated room. And, by George, warm clothes were needed, because you couldn't help being in and out of the freezing weather. In our cabin, two Frenchmen had the job of keeping two big log-fires alive. That's all they were paid to do. A very responsible job it was, forever sawing logs, swinging axes and stoking.

At first, we were given four days off work, to allow us to get used to the climate and our new surroundings. Then, it was time to work! Reveille was at six in the morning, and the work started at seven.

What excitement seeing these fellows swarming out with all manner of tools, tearing our way through the land, to make a path for the great Trans-Continental Railway – steam-hammers, axes, picks, shovels, drills. The deer and the other wild animals must have been wondering what hellish monster was coming their way. You could hear the din from a mile away, and that din went on from sunrise to midday. An hour for lunch – that was our only break, until the work finished at four in the afternoon. You can be sure that Soolivan earned his bread on that job, as did every man-jack who was there!

Now, there were lots of Gaelic-speaking navvies working on the Trans-Continental Railway, and I could still name quite a few who were in the same squad as myself. There was one lad who, by his personality and happy-go-lucky nature, became friendly with everybody. He was champion! Lovely fella! His name was Innis Smith, from Borgh on the west coast of Lewis. He was a real handsome, fair-haired young lad, six foot tall. Mind, he was only young – just about my own age, I'd say, but very mature for his years. He was full of the joys of life, and he had a smile and a bright comment whenever you met him. Everyone took to him at once. Innis Bàn made a lasting impression on me. Somehow, he made me proud that he was of the same people as me. I was present when he met his terrible sudden death, and, to this day, it makes me sad to think on it.

Our gang was tearing our way through the side of a tall hill. We could see another gang up ahead of us doing the first rough clearing of obstructions. It was all very well organised with engineers and surveyors in charge of the scheme. By noon, we came up against a shoulder of rock, hard over a fast-flowing river. The gaffer said that the obstruction would have to be removed with 'dinnimite'. There was nothing unusual in that, for the gangs were blowing 'dinnimite' every second day. But I'll never forget that shoulder of rock. And that's because of what happened when the shots went off.

Six holes were drilled about ten feet apart. The sticks of 'dinnimite' were placed in the holes, and the gaffer blew a whistle warning everyone to take shelter.

The fuses were lit, and after three minutes, off went the blasts, one–two–three–four–five with only three seconds between. We stayed put, waiting for the sixth blast. Nothing!

Innis Bàn was crouched ten yards from where I was taking shelter, his hands over his ears. Still, nothing happened. After a few minutes the gaffer rose, shouting to everyone else to stay put. He was away for ten minutes and returned with the news that the whole shoulder of rock was reduced but that the remaining stick of 'dinnimite' was lost in the rubble. Everyone was only too willing to go back to work, for crouching down behind icy boulders in temperatures well under freezing was mighty uncomfortable. Our gaffer was a wee Frenchman – in his middle forties, I'd say – but because his beard was whiteish-grey, he looked as old as Ned, down in the Port there. He shouts, 'Allez, allez, allez!' He was always shouting that, so that he became known to us navvies as 'The Alley Man'. *Co-dhiù*, he shouts, 'Allez, allez, allez! If you see the goddam "dinnimite", don't touch him! Leave him alone and call the sapper!'

Innis Bàn was one of the first on the scene. He carried with him a crowbar which he used for turning the heaviest of stones and rolling them into the gorge below. The gaffer again called for us to be careful. I clearly remember everything that happened on that terrible morning. The usual din started – some men working sledge-hammers and steel wedges; and others shovelling chippings, earth and gravel. An hour went by and we had nearly forgotten the missing explosive. The lunch-time whistle was about to go. I heard Innis Bàn from Borgh shouting something to the gaffer. He would be about a hundred yards from where I was working, but quite a bit higher up.

'There's a drill-hole here in the rock; but I can't see the "dinnimite"!'

He was crouched down as if trying to discover if the drill-hole was empty. The gaffer shouted to him to come down at once, but instead of doing as he was told, he poked his crowbar into the hole. There was an almighty roar and an avalanche of boulders and loose stones rained down on the work-gang. By a sheer fluke, no one was hit by the flying rocks, though the smaller stuff caused some cuts and bruises. The work was stopped at once. Everyone was in a state of shock and in no condition to work. Innis was blown well away from where he had last been. Lying on his back with his eyes still open, he was placed on a makeshift stretcher and carried to the first-aid cabin. When the doctor examined him, he found that part of the crowbar had penetrated his brain. He died that same night. The camp went into mourning. The French gaffer was grief-stricken and looked as if he had aged ten years in as many hours.

The funeral was held on the following day and it was very sad for the Gaels to see the remains of a fellow countryman laid to rest in the frozen wilderness of Canada. After a very brief service, the burial took place and a small wooden cross was placed in the earth to mark the grave.

The gaffer came to me and asked if I would come to his tent for a glass of brandy. In the evening, I did as he asked. To my surprise, he broke down in tears. Because Innis Bàn and I were from the same island, he had assumed that that we were related.

He said, 'How terrible for his parents to hear that their fine young boy is buried in this dreary place!'

I promised the Frenchman that if I ever returned to the Isle of Lewis, I would travel to Borgh to tell Innis Bàn's folks of the deep sorrow of the gaffer and all who worked with him. The years passed and, by the time I returned to Lewis, I had a lot more on my mind than the death of Innis Bàn. I never did go to Borgh. Now, in my old age, that omission weighs heavily on my conscience.

Note

While on holiday in Lewis in the 1970s, I visited Borgh and searched for relations of the Innis Bàn who had been killed in Canada. To my surprise, I discovered that Innis Bàn of Borgh, who had been working alongside Soolivan on the railway, had returned to Lewis hale and hearty! The young man who was killed was, in fact, Calum MacIver, also tall, fair and personable. I had the pleasure of being introduced to Anna, Calum's sister (elderly but sprightly), living at No. 5 Borgh.

'I am pleased that you have come to our home with the story that Soolivan himself should have delivered those many years ago. Unfortunately, apart from me, all those who were dear to my brother have long since passed on.

'But let me tell you a strange story. Calum and I were close in age and, from the very earliest, the best of friends. We did not hold any secrets from each other. I was not happy that he was going off to Canada with the other young men of the district, for I knew that his going would leave a void in my life and in that of our entire family. Anyway, on the day before he left us, he travelled to Steòrnabhagh and bought a new suit and shoes. He wanted to be well-dressed for his great adventure! The shoes were black, I remember. He wore them for a time inside the house to "break them in". All was well. But the first time he wore them outside, he returned in a panic. He said, "Chan eil e 'n dàn dhomh a bhith fada beò an Canada." [My time in Canada is destined to be short! Look at what has happened to my shoes!]

'I looked at the shoes and saw that the heels had come off them both. I told Calum not to be silly, that the damage to his shoes proved nothing but that it was an example of bad workmanship. I helped him to pin the heels back on to the shoes from the inside. My brother left us feeling depressed and sure that misfortune awaited him in Canada. We received only one letter from him. In it, he said that he was enjoying life. A day later, we were informed of his death.' CF

I caught a chill and was ill with a high fever, sweating like a pig. They placed me in the very bed in which Innis Bàn had died. Luckily, I was there for only two or three days, but I continued weak for some days after that. A number of men, including myself, had become unhappy with our working conditions. Though I was not back to my full strength, I decided that I had had enough. Four of us decided to abscond, and on a very cold night, we sneaked out of the camp.

I had snowshoes on, dungarees on top of moleskin trousers I had preserved from my fisherman days, a big heavy jumper, two pairs of gloves and a beaver hat. We plodded west through the snow and rested at a rail camp about twenty miles further on. After we had eaten, we continued on to the next camp. We probably covered a hundred miles, walking most of the way. Somewhere along the way, we did manage to 'borrow' a sleigh which made the last half of our trek easier, three pulling and one resting. We finally threw in the towel at a rail camp where we recognised some lads from home. We were given work there by two Scots brothers surnamed Gordon, and spent the month of May 1908 with those friends. Hard manual labour all the way, working all the hours you cared to work. At the end of the month we received a handsome wage – nigh on $50 each. For four months we did odd jobs, working hard during the months and, within a few days of being paid, blowing our pay-packets on booze and gambling. I'm sorry to say that, even at that young age, I was learning some very bad habits.

With the first clouds of autumn beginning to peep over the horizon, we set off for the next village, Kenora. We got rooms in the King Edward Hotel and, while there, were told about the wages paid to the wheat-workers of Manitoba. Four days later, we caught a train from Kenora to Winnipeg, less than two hours' ride to the west. Being ignorant Lewis bums, we didn't know what was the time of year when farmers came into town to hire hands. But in Winnipeg we discovered, as it was well into the fall, that there was little chance of getting work on the wheat farms until the spring. Now, I cannot recall the name of the hotel we stayed in, only that it was owned by an Edinburgh man – a real gentleman who was very good to us. He advised us to go on to Selkirk, as there was a likelihood of our getting work there. Off we go to Selkirk, a quiet village, plumb in the middle of the wheat-lands.

We managed to get lodgings in a house on Clive Street, and to this day I still remember the woman of the house – Mrs Dennis, who again was very hospitable. Soon after we arrived at Selkirk, I was walking down the street and saw an old boy coming towards me. He looked just like a Lewis elder on his way to kirk: a smart coat, a sparkling

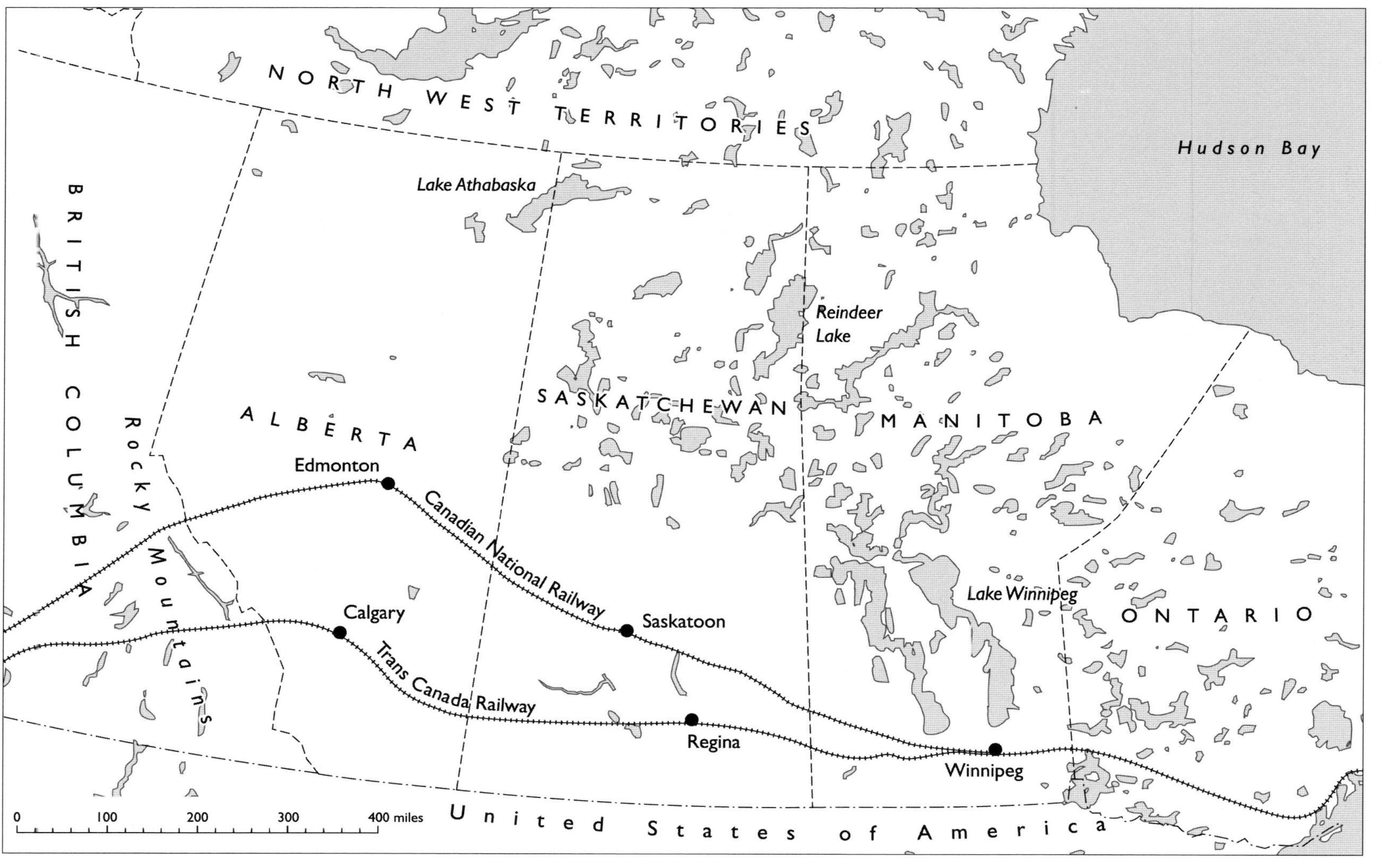

NORTH WEST TERRITORIES
Hudson Bay
Lake Athabaska
Reindeer Lake
BRITISH COLUMBIA
Rocky Mountains
ALBERTA
SASKATCHEWAN
MANITOBA
ONTARIO
Edmonton
Canadian National Railway
Saskatoon
Lake Winnipeg
Calgary
Trans Canada Railway
Regina
Winnipeg
0
100
200
300
400 miles
United States of America

clean face, his hair neatly combed, and his beard reaching down to his belly-button. He wished me a good day in English, and asked where I was from.

'I am from the Old Country,' says I, 'and I have come into this one-horse town to find work!'

'Sin thu fhèin, a bhalaich!' says he. 'If I was a gambling man, I'd bet you are from Lewis like myself. And I'd also bet that the places where we were born weren't far apart!'

It turned out that the man came from Ness, thirty miles from my home village. Although I knew that I had relations in Ness, I couldn't tell him who they were – something that disappointed him. However, the stranger (whose surname was MacLeod) was convinced that we were somehow distantly related – that I looked like his mother's folk.

'Come with me,' says he, 'and I shall take you to a family who will certainly give you a job.'

'Beggars can't be choosers!' says I to myself, but I did not wish to turn my back on the three boys who had come to Selkirk with me without telling them where I was going. Anyway, the fellow persisted, and so I went with him to the livery stable to pick up his horse and buggy. After that, off we went.

We travelled for about twelve miles to Clandiboy, near the banks of the Red River. We arrived at his farm – a big affair with a large timber dwelling-house and steading, and with lots of trees all around. *Ach, a dhuine bhochd*, when I met the woman of the house I was bowled over! A Red Native woman she was – a large, stout, timid woman who said not a word for the whole time I was in her home. What a difference from the cackling *cailleachan* back home in Lewis! I learned during my time in Clandiboy that a Red Native woman makes the perfect wife – a good housewife, never moaning or bitching, but with a well-filled, round figure that would keep any man warm at night!

We had a good meal of venison, cabbage and corn-on-the-cob, washed down with whisky heavily diluted with water. I followed the example of my host, re-filling my glass several times from a large pewter jug, that must have held a half gallon of whisky!

After the meal, Mr MacLeod sang '*Hóró mo Nighean Donn Bhòidheach*' and I sang '*Hóro Bharabal Phàdraig*'. Then off we went to visit neighbours, the pewter jug safely stowed in the back of the buggy. What a laugh we had!

Firstly we went to the house of one of the MacLeod sons called Norman, the same name as my father had when translated into English. I wish that I had a picture of that Norman to show you. A half-caste he was – a tall, good-looking fellow with a strong, healthy, muscular body on him and shiny brown skin. Facially, he resembled

This map shows places in the Prairie provinces well known to Soolivan his father, but his dusky skin and his long black hair plaited down his back were definitely not inherited from the Gaels. He said very little to us. Like his mother, he believed that silence is golden.

Next we went to visit a Leódhasach [Lewisman] living about ten miles from Clandiboy – a man from the village of Pabail. MacAulay by surname, he had been in Canada for many years and was married to an English woman. When he heard I was from the Rubha, he made a great fuss. What a welcome! The man threw question after question at me, for he was as homesick as a pigeon. Like Mr MacLeod, he wished that he could one more time smell peat-smoke, *spealtragan* [filleted herrings] on the 'pry-pan' and the sea-air of Lewis. When I told Mr MacAulay that my mother had been born and brought up in Pabail Iarach, he realised that he had been in school with her.

'Have you ever been to Eilean Phabail?' says he.

'Been to Eilean Phabail? Two summers ago, I swam from Eilean a Chàis to Eilean Phabail. It was a very calm day, of course.'

What a liar I was. Because it doesn't matter to anybody, I can tell you now that I was not much of a swimmer but I thought my claim would impress him – which it did. It was becoming clear to me that our island people had penetrated to the most remote corners of the British Empire and that I was likely to meet strays like myself wherever in the world I went.

Mr MacAulay himself had an unusual history. He had run away from home as a youngster and ended up in the Yukon at the time of the Gold Rush. Two years there and he had earned what he considered to be a small fortune. He came back over into Manitoba to the Red River, got married and headed off to find a community where other Highlanders were settled. His wife was as curious about my background as he was. She says, 'Did you come as far as Manitoba on your own?'

Her question brought to mind the three boys I had left in Selkirk and who must have become concerned about my sudden disappearance. I told them of our desertion from the Trans-Continental Railway.

'As a matter of fact,' says I, 'the four of us were together in a lodging-house in Selkirk until three days ago. One of the lads is called Alasdair MacAulay from the village of Pabail in the Isle of Lewis and he is known as Alasdair "Knox".'

A few minutes later, I saw Mr MacAulay drive away from the house in his buggy, a very quick getaway! Within a few hours he had my three friends and me reunited. Alasdair 'Knox' turned out to be his nephew, whom he had not seen since Alasdair was a small child. I'll never forget the night we spent together, talking and singing in Gaelic into the wee small hours. Though Mistress MacAulay understood very little of what was being said, she seemed to enjoy the company.

At last, it was time to part company. I returned with old Mr MacLeod to his home and spent two days there without hearing any mention of work. Sitting at breakfast on the third day, Mr MacLeod says to me, 'Iain, my boy, I have raised a family of boys and not one of them has stayed in the family home to help us here on the farm. How do you feel about coming to work for us for a year, living with us in the house as if you were family? If we get on well together, you can stay on and take over the farm when the wife and I kick the bucket! After all, we are of the same blood!'

What an offer! And what a fool I was in those days! I wouldn't listen to a word the man said. I told him that I was by nature a rolling stone and that I just couldn't stop in the one place.

'Och!' says I, 'I haven't explored even half the world yet!'

In the end, my host accepted my decision and not another word was said about the matter. For the first time, the lady of the house smiled at me when we finally said goodbye. I am sure that, from her point of view, my decision to leave was a welcome relief – though, to be truthful, I can't imagine why.

Crashing Billows on the Prairies

Many's the sight I've seen, and many's the thing I've done in my time. Many's the person I've known and long since forgotten. But there are some things that happened long ago that have burned themselves into the memory and will stay there until my dying day. What I am about to tell you I have shared only with a very few friends, for I hold the memory of it close to my heart. It is to do with young love, which is the sweetest and the most painful love of all.

As you already know, I started working when I was no more than a young lad and, since then, was pretty well employed continuously in one kind of manual labour or another. For sweat and exhaustion, nothing I did during all that time, compared with that of work on the wheat-farms of Canada. *Gu sealladh Dia ort!* There was a brute of a machine there vomiting sheaves out at an almighty rate! It was pulled by a great big horse with the eldest of the Henrich sons in charge of it. The job given to Alasdair and me was to keep up with the rig, putting the sheaves standing as stooks of eight. Of course, we were both used to stooking oats or barley from our own young days on the crofts. But in Canada, you had to work ten times faster. I tell you truthfully that there was no time to take breath or stand listening to womenfolk chattering on about this or that! No, sir, not a woman in sight – just me, Alasdair, the Henrich boy and Crazy Horse! Mind you, for over four silver dollars a day, we felt it was worth getting knackered.

The family was very good to us. Five meals a day: breakfast when we got up; another breakfast at eight in the morning; a packed lunch for having between twelve and one; a proper dinner at four in the afternoon; and a big supper after we washed up in the evening. That's if you had the energy to make it to the table! Whenever the day was done, I would collapse into bed, dreaming of the sight and sound of all those lovely silver dollars jingling in my pooch, at the end of our contract. For a boy from a poor background like me, there was no sight nor sound more pleasing.

Anyway, after several days of the same routine, something very strange happened. It was between the hours of twelve and one and Mrs Henrich came to where we were working to deliver our packed lunches. The son went off to feed and water the horse at the farmhouse. Alasdair and I sat on the stubble to eat lunch. After the farmwife had gone, I said to Alasdair that I fancied taking a walk. Not that there was much to see on the Prairie owing to the wheat growing up to your elbows, and the scenery being as flat as a pancake. Mile after mile of golden grain. The two of us wandered through the uncut wheat – away from where we had been harvesting but, all the time, within sight of the top of a huge silo that was part of the Henrich steading. After a while we came to a fence marking the edge of the section, one strand of wire on wooden stakes.

'This must be the boundary of the Henrich's lot,' says Alasdair. 'In this sea of grain, they need something to show where one man's lot ends and another's begins.'

We sat in the wheat having a smoke, one thing that old Henrich told us never to do! Och, well, we said to ourselves, we are safe enough here – the two of us, half a mile from the steading and not a living soul to know where we were. We made sure that our matches were extinguished, and everything was fair and dandy. All that could be seen to give away our presence was the fragrant blue smoke of our cigarettes curling up among the ears of wheat. Not a sound to be heard but the sigh of the Prairie wind travelling over the thousands of acres of grain.

Ach seo ort, not five minutes had gone by before I had the strangest experience of my life! As if a cold spirit had brushed across my hair, the sound of a human voice came to me – a girl's voice singing a song that I had known since my childhood. Fear of the voice made me spring to my feet and peer about. I found Alasdair standing wide-eyed beside me.

'Did you hear a girl's voice?' he asked.

'Quiet!' says I. 'There it goes again – a girl's voice! And it's coming from over there! Listen!'

As we stood, the sound came to us more distinctly, and the words were unmistakable.

'. . . bha'n crodh a' geumnaich a ceann a chéile . . .'

As quietly as we could, we slipped under the perimeter wire and moved forward through the wheat, in the direction of the voice. As we moved forward, as quietly as we could, the voice gradually became more distinct.

'. . . Bha'n tobht aig Anndra, 's i làn de dh'fheanntaig . . .'

The thought suddenly struck Alasdair that our lunchbreak was over and that the Henrich boy would be standing waiting for us with his ever-eager horse.

'Taigh na galla to the horse!' I whispers. 'I'm going to find out where that Gaelic singing is coming from, if it's the last thing I do!'

The voice suddenly stopped, so we began to move more quickly. Fifty yards or so further on, we broke through into a clearing of about half an acre where the wheat had been harvested. At the far edge of the clearing sat a young girl. She had been knitting until she heard the *rusbadaich* of us approaching her through the wheat. I don't tell a lie – she was petrified. And no wonder, seeing us two half-clad ruffians approaching her out of nowhere.

Alasdair spoke to her in Gaelic. He said, 'Na gabh eagal, a ghràidh. Cionnas a thàine tu an seo?' Don't be afraid, he told her. We are Gaels from the Old Country.

She was standing clutching her knitting.

'I'm sorry, I don't speak Gaelic. It's my grandparents who have it.'

The poor girl was almost speechless, and it took us a while to convince her that we were honest lads employed by the Henrichs as farmhands. In the end, she relaxed and seemed as pleased as we were that fate had brought us together in that lonely place in the middle of nowhere.

'I was never so frightened in my whole life!' says she. 'When I saw the disturbance in the wheat, I thought you were a bear coming to attack me!'

After she recovered from her fright, the girl invited Alasdair and myself to tea at her grandfather's house on the following Saturday.

Saturday was the only day that we stopped at six in the evening. Sabbath on the Prairies was as churchy and lazy as it is back home! Alasdair and I returned to our work and didn't speak more than a word or two to each other for the rest of the afternoon. Each of us had his own thoughts. The girl was very attractive. We hadn't asked her name, nor had she asked us ours. Before we slept, we both wondered whether our encounter in the clearing had been a trick of the imagination. We could hardly wait for Saturday to arrive!

On Saturday evening, Alasdair and I washed and shaved and put on our cleanest clothes. There she was at the gate of their back yard waiting for us, dressed in a pretty green dress with white frills and a dark blue velvet ribbon in her hair. Funny that I should remember how she looked all those years ago! As you will have gathered, she made quite an impression on me! We shook hands with her and then she took us into the living-room. Sitting by the fire was an elderly couple – him with a kind, rosy face on him and bright, light-blue eyes; and her looking frail with a white apron on, and with her white hair tightly combed back and tied in a bun.

I will never forget how kindly we were received in that house. The MacLeods were true Gaels, very friendly and hospitable, with scarcely a word of English spoken in the home. They told us that, owing to some epidemic, they had lost their three sons in the previous three years. What a tragedy!

The eldest – the father of the girl – had died on New Year's Day. With Sheena, their grand-daughter and some help from neighbours, the old couple had spent nine very long months fighting a battle to keep the farm going. Now, when the wheat was being harvested all over the district, there was nobody to help them but one young lad who had come with a neighbour's reaper and cut a small fraction of the crop. The three of themselves were left to stook the sheaves. It was obvious that they would lose the rest of the wheat if they didn't get help.

Well, Alasdair told them, much as he would like to help them, that Mr Henrich had been a fair employer and that he could not break his contract with him. The old man said that he understood the position and that it was typical of Alasdair, as a Gael, that he should have a conscience about such matters. Unlike Alasdair, I felt that my own Highland people came first. If I were to turn my back on that family in distress, my conscience would always bother me. And I said so! And when I did, our old host didn't try to persuade me to stay with the Henrichs!

Now, I would be telling lies if I said that the prospect of living close to young Sheena did not help me make my mind up! I offered to come back on the following Wednesday to work for the same wage as I was getting from the Henrichs. That would be fine, they said.

So that is how it was. On the following Wednesday, I took my suitcase over to the house of Norman MacLeod who said he was from near Dunvegan in Skye. And there we lived together, four MacLeods – all of us together as content as four peas in a pod!

As soon as I could, I set to work on the harvest. The two of the young Henrichs came over to give us a hand, and after a hard slog, working fifteen-hour days, we managed to save most of the harvest. Even though I was exhausted, I was buoyed up by the presence of the girl. Wherever she was, near or far, my eye always wandered to where Sheena was. There was only a couple of years between us and she became prettier with every passing day. I stayed on for seven or eight months without any thought of leaving and, during that time, a strong bond developed between me and her. The spring sped away and, looking back, I was happier then than at any time in my life. How true were the words composed by William Mackenzie, the great bard of Siadar – himself for years in Canada, thinking of his homeland:

Fàsaidh smal air òr, is fàsaidh còinneach air an aol;
Is thèid a' ghrian a chòmhdachadh le ceòthan is droch shìd.
Na lusan 's bòidhch' 'san t-samhradh bheir an geamhradh gu
neo-bhrìgh,
Ach gaol far 'n téid a dhaighneachadh, cha téid air chall an tìm.

[Gold will tarnish and lime become moss-grown;
And the sun shall be overcast with mists and storms.
The most beautiful blooms of summer will yield to winter
and wither;
But true love where it is rooted will forever remain.]

How sad that, at that time, I was so young and foolish that I didn't ponder on these words. One evening, Norman told Sheena and her grandmother to hurry off to bed as he had important business to discuss with me. When we were alone, he poured me a stiff whisky. Himself swallowed a good mouthful before he stood up and quietly made a speech at me.

'Iain,' says he, 'hard though it may be for you to believe it, I was once as young and virile as you. My sight is now going a bit, but not so much that I cannot see that you and Sheena are becoming very attached to each other. I am becoming dull of hearing, so I am not going to say definitely that I have heard the squeak of her window being opened in the dead of night. Now, what I want to say is this! Sheena is only sixteen years old but my wife and I would allow her to marry you if that is what she wishes. If you marry her, this farm and all our property will become yours – everything along with our blessing. You'd be like our son, since we have none of our own left now. On the other hand, if you have no intention of staying with us, you must decide at once to follow a road elsewhere.'

Since I came to the Prairies, it was the second time that an old man had offered me property on condition that I settled down. This time I was sorely tempted. I didn't have an answer for Norman MacLeod on the tip of my tongue. I took a long *deoch* from my cup and shook him by the hand, saying that I would give him a definite answer before

The headland of An Ceanach, at the foot of No. 11

breakfast on the following morning.

Lying on my bed, I wondered what I should do. Sheena would be expecting me as usual at her window but I did not visit her that night. I felt strangely far away from my homeland. Would I be happy spending the rest of my days marooned in the heart of Canada? As I pondered what to do, I began to hear the great flow-tide billows of the Minch crashing against the Ceanach at the foot of my mother's croft. How could I choose to be like those old Gaels I had met, who had put their roots down on the Prairies, but forever craved for the homeland of their childhood which they would never see again?

'Mar a thèid cuilean an ròin an comhair a chùil chon na mara, sin mar a rinn mise!' [Just as the seal-pup backs to the sanctuary of the sea, so also did I!]

I got up and gathered all my clothes together and folded them into my suitcase. Like a thief in the night, I stole away from Norman MacLeod's farm, and before day broke I was many miles away.

Often, as I sit here in Port Mholair having a quiet cup of tea at this table with 'Marilyn Monroe'*, my mind wanders to things I have done and might have done better. I think of that lovely girl and the pain I must have caused herself and her folk out there on the Prairies. In the long run, I probably did the right thing in turning my back on what her grandfather was offering.

* Soolivan's affectionate nickname for his wife.

Looking back, though, I often wish that I had stayed long enough to explain to Sheena why I had to desert her. Deep down in my heart, I know that that was the decent thing to do. On the other hand, I know that if I had stayed to tell her, I would not be here right now!

RIGHT CROSS TO THE CHIN

Work on the wheat over, all the hired hands went off to roost elsewhere. I returned to Selkirk to be with my mates from back home. For a few months I took odd jobs. That was the great thing about the New World. You were given the chance to try your hand at almost anything you fancied and I ended up doing a whole assortment of work.

One morning, I woke up shivering with the cold, and when I went to the window, I saw that it was snowing heavily. My landlady said that a giant plague of locusts was eating up the greenery and turning everything to a white, lifeless desert! Lake Manitoba froze solid.

I had made a load of money on the farms, but after lodgings and buying clothes for the winter, my nest-egg soon dwindled. Roderick Smith of Borgh sent me a message reminding me of his invitation to get in touch with him as soon as I came back from the wheat. He knew very well that I badly needed help. By that time, I had a taste for 'John Barleycorn'. My thirst was such that I approached Roderick and

With Seònaid of No. 7, Soolivan and Shonag returning from a day's peat-cutting

asked him if he would allow me to work in his Wholesale Liquor Store. I figured that there would be perks of booze going there! No flies on him, though!

'That's the last place I would give you a job, son!' he says. 'Only teetotallers are allowed to work in the Liquor Store.'

He gave me a fistful of dollars to tide me over, and told me to wait a few days until he could find me work paying a decent wage. It was during that time of bumming around that I discovered that the Old Man's son was a boxer – a very successful boxer: Lightweight Champion of the Prairies. At that time, brute strength and skill at fist-fighting were far more important to people than they are today. To the working classes, there was no-one more highly regarded than boxers or even street-fighters. Successful politicians, businessmen, doctors – they all had their place, but, in the pecking-order, they came behind World Boxing Champions like John L. Sullivan, Gentleman Jim Corbet and hard men like that.

Roderick Smith's boy was called Jock. He was about my age but not as sturdily built. I was told that his mother was Sioux but, looking at him, you could never tell that he wasn't from the west side of Lewis. He was as open and friendly as his mother was quiet and shy. Anyway, since finding out about Jock's prowess, I began to haunt the gym – a converted Dutch barn with a ring and punchbags of various weights suspended from the rafters. Jock was preparing for a big fight and I watched him closely as he got his body and mind into tip-top trim by skipping, shadow-boxing and pounding the punchbags. Against sparring-partners, he looked lethal – almost impossible to hit. His footwork was superb, and when he trapped a fellow in a corner, his arms and fists went to work on him so fast and accurately that you just felt sorry for the fellow on the receiving end. Of course, the sparring-partners were professionals in their own right – mean, tough guys who had some boxing ability but whose careers in the ring were over.

You just had to admire the way Jock handled those fellows. They just could not lay a hand on him. One morning, at the ringside, Roderick whispered in my ear that the three sparring partners had decided to find an easier way of making a buck and had given notice to quit. And who could blame them! Anyway, Jock was appealing to his friends to help him prepare for his big fight by sparring with him now and then for a few rounds. As you can imagine, I was flattered that I was asked, but not very keen to go into the ring and receive a mauling.

'Don't tell me you're afraid of Jock's punches!' says Roderick. 'I thought that you'd be the first to volunteer, Soolivan! Och well, I might as well be taking off my togs myself and giving the boy a few minutes of my own time.'

Though he was a religious a man, you could see that he was very proud of his son. Of course, he was well up in years – not able to last one minute in the ring.

'Very well then,' says I, 'I can't defend myself for toffee, but I'm

Soolivan in his prime

willing to go in for a round or two if that will help.'

As you know, I had enjoyed a bit of a reputation as a fighter when I was a young brave and the last thing that Soolivan needed at that time was to be humiliated. Secretly, I was dead keen to 'put my dooks up' against Jock. On the other hand, I knew that I couldn't cope against anyone as fleet-footed as the Lightweight Champion of the Prairies!

Old Man Smith explained that I was not being engaged as a replacement sparring-partner. Yet, if I was willing to help out, I would be handsomely rewarded for each two-minute round. Who happened to come sauntering into the gym at that time but Alasdair MacLeod, one of my pals, the kind of guy who liked watching a scrap but was useless in a fistfight. Now, I'm not just saying that against my friend! He was a big, hard-working lad but you could make his nose bleed if you looked at it too hard.

'Soolivan can give Jockie a run for his money if he tries,' Alasdair announces, like a fellow who knows a lot about fighting form! 'Come on now, Soolivan: don't pretend that you don't fancy your chances against the Champ!'

Jock winked at me and signalled that he was waiting. The trainer gave me the necessary togs and helped put on my gloves – the first boxing-gloves that I ever put on my mitts! You wouldn't believe how clumsy they are if you are not used to wearing them. I would have been far happier squaring up with my naked fists but I didn't get a chance to argue. The side of my head was soon warmed up by a sharp left hook. That was only the start of the bombardment! Knock after knock on my head, hitting me hard whenever I prepared to throw a punch. No sooner had he scored a hit than he flitted away like a bluebottle to some far corner of the ring. The son-of-a-gun! Ding-ding! End of round one. Alasdair was beside himself with excitement, enjoying the spectacle of me being taught a very painful lesson.

Roderick was in the opposite corner telling Jock to go easy on me. Obviously, they had expected me to do better. I was very embarrassed that I hadn't once landed a decent punch. Round two, the same – me exhausting myself, trying to block Jock off into the corner so that I could pulverise him! But he was agile as a cat and avoided all my attempts to land a *tàrnach*. Ding-ding! End of round two. One more round to go, thank God!

In the third round, Jock hit me with a left and right to the solar plexus. That was one of his knock-out specialties. The punches hurt me right enough, but I pretended to be worse hurt than I was. I back-pedaled into a corner and he followed, intending to deliver a volley that would finish me off. He whipped in a left uppercut to straighten me up and held his right glove low, ready to deliver. In that split second, I saw that his head was unguarded so I threw a full-bodied right which landed flush on his chin. Down he went, flat on his back with all his lights out!

In an instant, Roderick and the trainer leapt into the ring. Before Jock even began to stir, I was out of there, desperately trying to get my gloves off, pulling on the laces with my teeth. Instinct told me that if Jock were to come after me for what I had done, I should be able to defend myself bare-fisted. When Jock got to his feet and looked about him, he was surprised to see me standing outside the gym door peering in, looking like the cat that had stolen the cream! Everybody laughed and I felt very foolish. Training was stopped for the day. Later, Jock looked me up.

'Soolivan,' he says, 'I fell for the oldest trick in the book. You caught me a beauty but don't think anything of it. If you can be bothered to learn how to box, you have the punch to make you a very useful middle-weight pro.'

In the Smiths' gymnasium, I began to understand the difference between boxing and bare-knuckle fighting – as different from each other as night is from day. Having said that, when you are in a bare-knuckle fight, you are far more likely to win if you can box. And the reason for that is that a boxer has learned the art of self-defence. Pity the fellow who goes into a fight with his temper fired up, but without the skill to defend himself.

Never again did I manage to crack a hard punch on Jock's chin. But as the days went by, I began to learn how to carry my arms to shield my head and chin and how to use my feet to carry my body away from the worst of Jock' s hurricanes! That was the most useful thing I learned – how footwork helped you avoid taking heavy punishment.

By the end of a month, Jock and his trainer were convinced that I could do well in the professional ring. Unfortunately, there was one thing I lacked – something which is essential for anyone considering any career, whether it be as a boxer or even a church minister: will-power. Whenever I passed the pub and saw my mates carousing together, I regretted the commitment I had made to the Smiths. I am not proud of the fact that my dedication did not last long. One evening, I went on a wild spree and, on the following morning, went bleary-eyed to the gym. The Old Man smelled the drink right away and, there and then, put an end to my plans to become a professional boxer. Jock and I continued to be friends and I believe that if he is still alive today, he will remember me. He used to say that my right hand could flatten any of the best middle-weights at that time fighting out of Winnipeg. Unfortunately, I never found out, one way or the other. I guess I just didn't have the discipline to see me through.

Wolves

Cap in hand, I again went to Roderick Smith to ask if I could have a job in the Wholesale Liquor Store. He laughed at me and said that I definitely could not. However, he suggested that I might be interested in going back on to the Lake with him – not to fish, but to catch wild animals. I jumped at the chance.

Before the end of the week, seven of us set off for a remote island somewhere out in Lake Manitoba. The island was known as the Lake Camp. Roderick himself was there along with two of his sons and three Red Natives. We holed up in small cabins no bigger than moor shielings.* What a clever way they had of catching the animals! We would travel some distance from the cabins and bury fish bait laced with strychnine, several inches under the snow. Using big brushes, we would then sweep the snow to get rid of our tracks. No wolverine or skunk would go near the bait if it suspected that it had been planted there by humans. The bait was laid in the evening. In the morning, we went back to see if any animals had taken it. The method was similar to the way we worked small-lines back home in Lewis – putting down the baited lines in the evening, then going out first thing in the morning to take up your catch. It was impossible to foretell the results of your evening's labours. Some mornings, we would return to the cabins with our sleighs laden with carcasses. Other mornings, nothing.

We played cards late into the night, but everyone spent at least half an hour sharpening the flensing-knives. When the frozen carcasses were brought in, they were flayed and the skins stretched on wooden frames. I cannot pretend that I enjoyed the work but the pay was good.

One of the Indians and I had been out laying bait one day, and returned to the camp in the twilight. Not a soul about – just Roderick sitting by himself in the mess cabin.

'Where are all the fellas?' says I, settling myself down by the fire.

'The Red Natives haven't yet returned from baiting but Iain and Kenneth have gone off to Winnipeg.'

Why had they gone off to Winnipeg? Och, I knew that they had been keeping something from me.

'Jock is fighting in Winnipeg on Saturday night and his brothers felt they had to be there to support him.'

'A chiall, gléidh mi!' says I, 'why didn't anyone tell me that Jock

* Bothies of traditional design, occupied by members of crofting families to tend their cattle while on the open moor. For 'shieling', the OED gives: 'A piece of pasture to which cattle may be driven for grazing'. Co a chreideadh nach e 'àirigh' *shieling*?

was having a fight? I would have gone with them and shouted Gaelic war-cries that they would have heard in New York!'

'The boys know that you would like to be there, but we need to have at least five men here to keep the camp running as it should.'

Roderick knew full well that I was disappointed, and tried his best to buck me up. Next morning, when my mate and I returned with half a dozen animals on our sleigh, the Old Man called me over and told me that our stock of bait and groceries was running low. Would I be game to travel to the nearest store for supplies?

'No problem!' says I, though I didn't have the faintest idea what he meant by 'the nearest store'.

The Natives saddled the mare and hitched the sleigh on to it. Roderick gave me a list of things to get but no money. The custom was that you didn't settle up with the store until the end of the trapping season.

That was all right, but where was the store?

'Now, Iain,' says he, 'this journey is going to be a test of your strength of character and stamina. Listen very carefully to what I have to say! The store is on the lake shore a few miles from here, across the ice. The time is now after ten and daylight will begin to fade before three in the afternoon. It will be pitch black by half past three. You'll arrive at the store long before midday. The mare is a wise old cratur and already knows the way. But here's a compass for you just in case you feel you need it!'

Oh, I remember it as if it was yesterday! It was freezing cold, so Roderick insisted that I put half a dozen skins round me. I pocketed the compass, which was a little bigger than a pocket-watch.

'Don't dawdle in the village now,' he shouts. 'Just give my list to Ross MacDonald and he'll help you load the sleigh. Then come straight home!'

As I moved off, I heard him shout, 'Remember, north-east going and south-west coming back!'

The mare set off at a canter. She knew the way all right. Though the air was extremely cold, the weather was fine – clear-blue sky and not a sign of any kind of trouble. For ages, there was nothing to be seen but the buttocks of the mare trotting on before me and a spray of powdery snow thrown up by her hooves. From time to time, I checked my compass to make sure that the mare was on course. She was. At last, I saw a hint of house-tops appearing distant on the horizon. The village was a small settlement of no more than a dozen houses. The General Store was just above the pier. Without a word from me, the mare pulled the sleigh right up to the front door. Ross MacDonald came out and patted the mare. He told me that they knew each other from way back. I gave Ross the Old Man's line, and within twenty minutes the work of loading the sleigh was complete.

'A real one-horse town!' says I, looking about me.

'Sure is that,' he replies. He was a canny sort of fellow. Nothing much to say. Just wanted to go inside to read his book.

'Isn't there a hotel hereabouts?'

'Nope!'

'Nowhere where I could get a pint of beer?'

That seemed to wake him up!

'Hey, fella,' says he, 'nobody travelling across the ice in the depths of winter takes alcohol. Come on in and I'll give you a coffee if you wish.'

Ross MacDonald wasn't Scottish, you see. He was a Canadian. You could see that by his accent and the way he was so respectful of the lake. Mind you, the fella was only trying to be helpful, I'm sure. But as he was laying off, what did I see over his shoulder but a sign saying 'Saloon' stuck on a building not much bigger than a good-sized shed. Without further ado, I told Ross that I was going for a pint and that I would be back in ten minutes.

Ross shook his head. 'It's your skin, boy!'

I left him tying the mare to a post. He shouts after me, 'Old Man Smith would not be pleased if he knew that his messenger was drinking in the saloon!'

Now you might say that Soolivan hadn't learned a damn thing up to that point. My problem was that I was strong-willed and ignorant and thought that I knew best. I was soon to learn otherwise!

The inside of the saloon was as dark as the inside of a black-house but I could sense that there were two or three loafers lounging on seats, enjoying the heat from a big log stove. By the light of candles flickering on a shelf, I could make out where the barman was. I made for him and ordered a double scotch and a pint of ale. I downed the dram and then heard a voice raised at me from the far corner of the room.

'A Thighearna, what is the son of Tarmod Uilleim doing in a saloon at the back of beyond?'

In that remote, god-forsaken place, who had identified me by my father's name? Who was it but a fellow whom we called 'Ruagan' at school. A hard case! He was already drammed up but he ordered two double scotches from the barman at once. After we had drunk these, he wouldn't allow me to go until I had stood my hand one more time, so I went and ordered another two doubles. When our glasses were again empty, he staggered to his feet and ordered more. By that time, I was feeling quite merry and burst into song – '*Hóro Bharabal Phàdraig*' – my favourite song in those days! What a lovely ceilidh we were having, chatting about our school-days together at Druim Oidealar and all the characters we knew.

When I saw the barman lighting lamps at the windows, I suddenly remembered the mare tied in front of the General Store. All at once, Roderick Smith's warnings began to ring in my head.

'A mhic an t-Sàtain, you have lost me the daylight!' says I in a panic. 'Night will be on me before I'm halfway back to the island.'

Ruagan thought the situation I was in very funny.

'Here, Soolivan!' he shouts as I stagger to the door, 'you've left a nickel on the table! You'll be all right, my son! Just keep on singing '*Hóro Bharabal Phàdraig*' to the mare and she will dance across the lake!'

O, mac an t-Sàtain! The mare was still standing in front of the General Store, her head drooping sadly and her reddish coat made grey by the hoar-frost. I untied her at once and didn't even pause to say goodbye to Ross MacDonald. Though fuddled with the drink, I managed to mount the sleigh and shouted, 'Gee-haw!'

The mare knew what she had to do. She wheeled round and set off with me steaming drunk on the sleigh. It was dark before we were half way across the lake – so dark that I couldn't read my compass. I had no idea whether the animal could find her way back to the lake camp in the dark. The thought crossed my mind that if I were to fall off the sleigh, I would be unable to run after it and would freeze to death very quickly. I clung on to the reins for dear life.

Above the sound of the hooves pounding on the ice and the swish of the runners of the sleigh, I heard another sound coming at me from somewhere over in the dark. It reminded me of the baying of my old dog Diamond whenever we imprisoned him in the barn. I strained my ears to listen, but it was no longer there. After a while, I heard a yowl closer by and realised that we were being stalked by wolves. Well, I tell you the truth – the thought of being torn apart by a pack of wolves sobered me up in an instant and my mind became as alert as it is now!

Wolves on the ice

I began to shout, 'Gee-haw! Gee-haw!' to the mare. Not that I needed to. She was in a panic and galloped as best she could, with her breathing becoming as loud as a blacksmith's bellows. The howl of the wolves gave way to short barks as they came closer until, in the end, I fancied that I could make out the dark shape of the pack closing in from left and right, like Atlantic rollers after a storm gathering speed before crashing against the shore. Both the mare and I were terror-stricken.

Thank God, help came before it was too late. I heard a kind of short rumble on the ice ahead of me. When a second rumble reached my ears, I realised that it was a shot from a gun. Then came another and another – each time coming nearer. Within a minute or two, a Native on horseback reached us. He blasted off a couple more shots before throwing me a lantern. He never uttered a word, just took the reins of the mare and rode on into the night. What a relief to see the lights of the lake camp and then to reach safe haven. Roderick was there waiting.

'Thank the good Lord, you made it!' he says. 'Don't say a word now! Just go in to the fire and thaw out!'

It took Roderick and the Natives the best part of an hour to calm down the mare. When they came in from the stable, the Old Man looked very dour and said, 'Soolivan, you and I will have to have a serious talk as soon as you've eaten first thing in the morning.'

I scarcely slept, partly because of exhaustion and partly because of shame. At breakfast, Roderick was waiting for me at the table. He spoke so kindly to me that I felt like weeping.

'Now, Iain', he says, 'life is cheap in this corner of the world. Because you failed to take good advice, you very nearly lost your life last night. You would not listen because your life has become ruled by alcohol. I'm sorry, a Ghàidheil, that we have to part like this, but as soon as the boys return from Winnipeg, you will pack your bags and go to Selkirk and there terminate your employment with me. I refuse to have your death on my conscience!'

I missed Roderick Smith and I missed his son Jock even more. I never managed to see Jock box in any of the towns I was in. However, I did read about him from time to time and, although I lost touch with him, I never forgot what Jock taught me. Indeed, I'd go so far as to say that what he taught me saved my life on more than one occasion.

Two Bulls a-Fighting!

I was handsome in those days. There was not a *peic* of fat on my body. Pure muscle and it was as hard as the sole of your shoe. It's not in my nature to boast but you can take my word for it that there weren't many men in the Highlands who would take me on. Not that I was looking for a fight, you understand. But, after a few years in different kinds of employment, I felt that you have to stand up to be counted when trouble brews. Trouble seemed to follow me around. No doubt about it, in those days I was living in a hard, cruel, dog-eat-dog world where your best friends were your fists. While I was in Canada, I kept myself fit, always hammering or chopping wood and walking many miles each week.

Let me tell you about a fight I had with an Irish workmate. It was a fight that I should not have fought – but one caused through my pride and folly. I am not proud of the way I was. But I have come to accept that the way I was wrong and shameful, so I feel that I can tell you my story without being seen as bragging about my escapades.

The Irishman, a strapping fellow in his mid-forties, with a crooked nose and looking pretty rugged, had been working at the sawmill since he was a teenager. He liked to tell stories and to sing Irish songs, especially when he had a drink in him. He was popular enough, though, to be honest, I did not care for the habit he had of telling us lads how much stronger and hard-working he was than the rest of us. Och, I'm sure that the man didn't really mean anything by it, but when you're a young fellow and somebody is making a habit of putting you down, look out. Something will have to give.

After work one evening, he says, 'Now what a pity it is that it isn't morning all over again. You all look so weary and done in, poor bastards. As for me, I feel as fresh as I was at sun-up. Full of energy I am, just as when I got out of bed!'

'Listen to the old fellow,' says I. 'I'll bet you that I can run faster and farther, and lift heavier weights than any Irishman this side of the North Atlantic.'

A bhalaich ort, the fat was in the fire! A foolish mouth is one of the burdens that's carried by the young – especially if you are as cocky and full of yourself as I was. The rest of the lads were sitting on the logs we had cut, listening to the argy-bargy and hoping that our difference of opinion might lead to something more physical. The Irishman began to get worked up, big-time. Oh, what a big fellow he was, much more broad-chested than big Lawdy Campbell living down the brae there.

'Listen!' says he, turning up his shirt-sleeves. 'My name is Eugene Sullivan, cousin of John L. Sullivan, World Heavyweight Boxing Champion. I have been Bull of the Woods here since Lord knows when! And let me tell you, you loudmouth, puny little critter, nobody comes into this territory and tells me that he can do anything better than me – anything from farting to fighting – and that includes you!'

'Champion farter!' says I. 'A real big noise, right enough!'

The boys roared with laughter. Eugene was furious to be put down by a raw youngster. I wasn't really spoiling for a fight, though everybody else thought I was. Even though he was much bigger than me, I had nothing to prove by fighting a man twice my age. In fact, I tried to calm the fellow down but he would not have any of it. His temper smouldered on so that, in the end, he called me some very unpleasant names and challenged me to fight him. Well, in the circumstances, I'm sure you'll understand there was nothing for me to do but to take up the challenge.

We walked together round to a sort of meadow behind the sawmill, the lads following hard on our heels. Eugene was three-stone heavier than me but I had youth on my side. He fought in the style of the bare-knuckle fighters of the old days, standing upright and square-on, his feet anchored on the same spot, and his clenched fists held forward at waist level. My stance was very different. I had learned the crouching, swaying, probing style of boxers like Jock Smith and I kept my fists well up to protect my head from the ponderous swings of my opponent.

Jinking this way and that, I managed to land a couple of lefts high up on his head and then with my all my might, hit him with a right on the chest, just below his heart. And what a chest! Punching Eugene Sullivan was like punching the trunk of a giant sequoia. What a strong bugger he was. He didn't even flinch. As my efforts to catch him off

Soolivan and the 'Bull of the Woods'

balance continued, he tipped me over a couple of times with glancing punches but I wasn't really hurt – although the boys put up a mighty shout every time Eugene appeared to get the upper hand. If the Irishman and I had been the same age – well, I'm old enough now to admit it – I would have been scuppered. But in the end, Eugene's age began to tell on him, and as he became more and more breathless, I managed to land more and more telling punches about his broken nose. Now, you would find it difficult to guess how the fight ended! That son-of-a-gun managed to get hold of me by the shoulders and threw me as far as he could. I stumbled back on my heels and fell over in a heap. Looking up, I saw him standing over me with his hands on his hips and a big grin on his face.

'Now there you are, you young devil,' says he. 'Let that be a lesson to you.'

'Fair enough,' says I. 'You proved that you're still Bull of the Wood!'

He and I both knew that, if the fight had continued, Eugene would have ended up on his back, sooner rather than later. But my heart was not in fighting a man old enough to be my father. We parted with a handshake and the boys' appreciation of the fair fight. The weeks went by and Eugene and I became good friends. Many's the time he said to me that if I had been a few stones heavier I could have become as good a fighter as the great John L. Of course, he didn't really mean what he was saying, but to be hearing it did me an awful lot of good at the time!

'You have the Gaelic and the glib tongue,' he would say. 'And you have the Sullivan fighting spirit but you don't have any money. You are nothing but a homeless bum – just like myself!'

ABOVE NIAGARA FALLS

I had been working with an Irishman called 'Munster' O'Boyle on the Canadian Northern Railway and met him again in Niagara when I was looking for work. He was only one of a handful of Irishmen I met throughout my life who was not called either Pat or Paddy! Now, that is no exaggeration. Not a Murdo nor an Alasdair in the whole of the Irish population. If my friend Munster had been called Pat or Paddy, I would probably have forgotten him years ago. As it was, he was fortunate enough to come from a place in Ireland called Munster and that made him easy to remember.

But I have another reason for remembering Munster O'Boyle. It was he who brought together myself and a lad who had been a fellow-sufferer with me at my old school here at Druim Oidealar.

I had not seen Dòmhnall Bàn since our schooldays when the tyrant Caoidheach ruled the roost. Because he was six or seven years older than myself, I looked on him as one of the 'big boys' of the school and, of course, at that time he really was much bigger than me. When Munster O'Boyle brought us together, Dòmhnall Bàn turned out to be not at all as I expected. He was a couple of inches shorter than me and was as bald as an American bald eagle. So far as I can remember, he had no teeth. Not that that mattered, you understand. He was a nice fellow, *càirdeil* and easy-going and, like me, never one to say 'no' to a good dram. As soon as we met, we headed for a pub and drank our fill. That's the way our lives were in those days. One evening after work, Dòmhnall Bàn and I made our way to Scottie's Bar, a pub at the outskirts of the town that sold genuine Scotch whisky. It was a bit up-river, as I remember it, but the thought of getting a gulp of good whisky rather than rye kept us going. As we

Niagara Falls

walked, the lights of the village dwindled and, above the roar of the river, we could hardly hear our own conversation.

Scottie's Bar was jam-packed with Scots. It was just like the Star Inn in Steòrnabhagh on a Saturday night. Someone over there singing, another crying, everybody with a glass in his hand and enjoying himself. Dòmhnall Bàn was an awful fella for laughing. When he was in school, he was forever in trouble with the teachers because they couldn't bear to hear his cackling. His condition didn't improve with the years. All he needed to get inside him was a double whisky, and he began to cackle like a two-stroke engine. The more alcohol he drank, the louder his cackling became. When he got really drunk, his laughter made him roll about on his chair, bringing him to the attention of everyone in the bar.

In those days in Canada and the United States, they served tasty snacks in public bars. At Scottie's Bar, we ordered a bowl of hard-boiled eggs. Now, I cannot remember what caused Dòmhnall to behave the way he did, whether he had taken a bet, or whether he was just fooling around. In any case, he put a whole egg into his mouth and when he tried to chew it, he began to choke. What a commotion there was, with two or three locals trying to unstop the fellow's mouth so that he could breathe. A bouncer who didn't understand what all the fuss was about came over and told us to make less noise or else to continue our shenanigans outside. Suddenly, Dòmhnall managed to swallow the egg, turned to the bouncer and said in a loud voice, 'What's the matter with you, man? Surely you should have the good sense not to interfere when a Scotsman is rebuking his son for trying to choke his father?'

Not able to make any sense of what he heard, the bouncer shrugged his shoulders and retreated. Dòmhnall Bàn took up his cackling where he had left off and rocked on his chair so that everybody around him was in fits of laughter. Soon, the bouncer returned to our table and said, 'You two guys had better clear off home and sleep it off!'

Dòmhnall Bàn and I weren't in a fit state to argue. We left Scottie's Bar holding on to each other and staggered along the path, following the bank of the river. I remember groping for the rail between me and the river, then suddenly finding myself under water with the torrents roaring about me.

'Soolivan,' says I to myself, 'as sure as death, you'll drown if you don't grab hold of some dry land before you go over the Niagara Falls!'

Drunk though I was, I was scared. The Falls is only about twelve to fifteen miles from where I fell. The river current is so strong that it wouldn't have taken me long to reach there and, although I was drunk, I was well aware that less than half an hour was all that separated me from eternity.

Dòmhnall Bàn is dead – died many years ago – but what he did for me that night certainly saved my life. He ran along the path above me shouting like crazy, 'Man overboard! Man overboard!'

I saw a bridge approaching and made a lurch towards one of its supports, but the current was too strong for me. Shortly after that, I saw another bridge approaching and the current carried me directly to one of its supports. I managed to wrap my limbs round it. The pressure of the current was crushing me against the pillar. The ice-cold river water was numbing my body and driving the life out of me. I have no idea how long I was there. Though my strength was ebbing, I knew there were people above me, shouting encouragement.

After what felt like an eternity, ropes were thrown down to me, but none of them came anywhere near me. Big blinding lights were trained on me from somewhere on the far bank. At last, a fellow came down on the end of a rope and plunged into the river behind me. He kept talking to me while he was fastening a second rope round my oxters. I wasn't understanding much of what he was saying, for by that time I was almost unconscious. As soon as the rope was securely fastened, he called for his helpers above to heave away. I can remember lying on my back and, through my chattering teeth, trying to thank the people around me for saving my life. In fact, I believe that I was crying.

The man who had saved me was an off-duty policeman. No sooner was he safely back on the bridge than he collapsed unconscious and was rushed away to hospital. As for myself, I was so drunk, cold and confused that I didn't know where I was being taken. I remember Dòmhnall Bàn's cackling and his telling the crowd, 'I am the wet man's father. He's as *fliuch* [wet] as a fish!'

That kind of nonsense. Dòmhnall Bàn was drunk and didn't realise how close I had come to death. I cannot remember anything of how I was transported from the bridge to safety. I do recall lying on a couch in the home of a kind Canadian lady, with Dòmhnall Bàn trying to get me to drink endless cups of coffee.

Sober by morning, my old pal and I awoke with my body and limbs swollen. When I got up to walk, my thighs, legs and feet were nearly twice their normal size. Later in the day, I managed to hobble about, and when I felt well enough two or three days later, I went straight to the hospital to visit the policeman who had saved my life. We found him in a side-ward recovering from exposure.

'By all the laws of nature,' he says, 'you should have died in that icy water. Beats me how your heart kept beating considering the time you were in the river.'

'My blood,' says I, 'was so full of Scotch that it's a wonder the Niagara River didn't start to boil around me!'

He didn't laugh at my joke. Not even Dòmhnall Bàn raised a smile. In the cold light of day, I began to realise that, for some strange reason, Fate had decided to give me one last chance. Probably for the first time in my life, I became depressed and made for the East Coast. Deep down, I just wanted to go home.

END OF THE GREAT ADVENTURE

I had not managed to make my fortune on the *Criothnachd* – that's what we used to called the Prairies of Canada in those days. Having left the *Criothnachd*, a thousand miles behind me, I found myself on the Atlantic coast where I had started – in Nova Scotia. On a raw winter's day a couple of years before the outbreak of the Great War, I arrived by train at Halifax, a busy port with a harbour built round the Bedford Basin. As soon as I left the railway station, I got a whiff of the cold, salty wind of the open Atlantic. It was a wonderful sensation and I was refreshed at once. What a brave sight the Bedford Basin was, with at least twenty ocean-going ships, mostly flying the flags of their European ports of origin, tied at the wharves while others, newly arrived after their voyages, were lying off, waiting to be berthed.

It used to be said that there were as many Gaels in Canada as there were in Scotland. I cannot say whether that's true or not, but I noticed in Halifax as soon as I arrived that when you'd go into a shop, you would very often hear English spoken with a Highland accent. Though I couldn't read a word of my own language, I used to buy a newspaper printed in Gaelic. The long and the short of it was that I was as homesick as a parrot and spent a lot of time down by the wharves, looking for lads from home. *Is ionmhainn leis gach neach a choltas*! Or as they say in English: 'to each his own'!

A Donaldson boat had just arrived from the Clyde and I was down by the docks, outside the gates of the Customs shed, waiting for some of the crew to start coming off her. A red-faced fellow in a Customs uniform walked past me. Then back he comes and says in a Canadian accent, 'Who are you waiting for, fella?'

'No-one in particular,' says I. 'I'm just a homesick Highlander hoping to meet someone off that boat who can speak to me in my own language!'

'Có ás a tha thu?' says he. And as if there was a possibility that I couldn't speak Gaelic, he says it in English, 'Where do you come from?'

The fellow had been born in Halifax of Harris parents and was as

Hearach as the An Cliseam*– a real friendly fella. But what would you expect of a man whose name was a twin of my own – another John MacLeod! After he knocked off work, he and I repaired to a pub on Brunswick Street. We sat there for an hour or so discussing seamen whom we both knew, working on ships out of Glasgow. At that time, Scottish shipping-lines had vessels in and out of Canadian ports all the time. John invited me to his home for supper. A good-looking young wife he had, and a string of children. His father was sitting by the hearth, and by his side a dog, which obeyed its master's Gaelic commands. The children pretended to be learning Gaelic from the dog, which they called Spate. Apparently the dog was descended from a bitch that the old man MacLeod had smuggled in when he emigrated, all the way from Harris.

The MacLeods' supper was just the kind they might have been having if they had been in Harris – one of my own favourites – *feòil-réisgte agus buntata* [peat-smoked mutton and jacket potatoes]. It brought back to me the memory of joints of salt beef and mutton that crofters back home had hanging for weeks in the smoke above the peat fire and kept there until they were so black with soot that it was difficult to believe that they were fit for human consumption. But what beautiful food when the meat was washed and prepared for the pot. The meal caused me to feel more homesick than ever, and I knew then that my Canadian adventure was at an end. I decided to return home to Lewis and to the simple life. My share of the fortunes being made in the New World had somehow passed me by. In fact, by that stage, I did not have much more money than I had when I stepped ashore in Canada from the *New Media.*

I had to wait in Halifax for about a fortnight before I got a berth on a ship as a deck-hand. The ship, a 'Baron boat',** was to my liking, but before I managed to get enough money behind me to take me home to Lewis, the Kaiser had built a fleet of battleships and an army, and was ready to go to war. As it was throughout my life, trouble seemed to be following me wherever I went.

After a couple of years at the deep-sea sailing, I paid off ship at Greenock. That was in June 1914. War was declared a month later. But I was very happy indeed to be on the train taking me north from Glasgow, my mind full of plans for enjoying myself with the pals I had known in my youth. Unfortunately, those plans were never realised.

* Hearach, a native of Harris which together with Lewis form the largest island of the Outer Hebrides. An Cliseam, in the north of Harris is over 2,600 feet high and is the highest hill in the archipelago.

** The so-called 'Baron' boats, most of which were built at Port Glasgow, belonged to the H. Hogarth & Sons Shipping Co. of Glasgow. They were steam-driven cargo ships: *Baron Belhaven*, *Baron Inchcape*, *Baron Dalmeny*, etc.

From the beginning, all the able-bodied men were called to arms, so that there wasn't any opportunity for relaxation or celebration.

The men of Lewis were mostly in the merchant fleet or in the infantry. Once hostilities got under way in earnest, reports of casualties came flooding into the Àird post office every second day.

Now, I hear you say, 'Why wasn't Soolivan in the merchant fleet or else in the infantry?'

Well, my 'Malishy' papers somehow got lost. Perhaps the old Provost Sergeant, hearing that Soolivan had emigrated to Canada, had heaved a sigh of relief and tossed them on the fire! Whatever happened to them, I was not conscripted. Coward that I was, I wasn't too keen to go to the Front in France to get massacred along with the rest of the boys! You will remember Murdo MacDonald of the Royal Bucks Hussars? He was the dashing regular army officer who had impressed me so much with his immaculate uniform and smart looks, before I went into the 'Malishy'. Well, then, Murdo arrived home from a military hospital, having been so badly mangled at the Front that he never walked again. Instead of going to the recruitment office, I took a job on a Steòrnabhagh drifter and contributed to the war effort by helping to feed the multitude! Quite a lot of the neighbours turned against me, for they thought I should have been killing Germans instead of catching herring.

Those were depressing days. The *bodaich* sat in the ceilidh house, puffing smoke and scarcely uttering a word. Many of the *cailleachan*, on the other hand, stood about as usual, but no longer talking tittle-tattle! Now they had serious news to discuss – news that caused them to spend a lot of time weeping.

All the families living down by the Port were surnamed Mac-Kenzie or, in Gaelic, Clann 'c Anndra. That was because they were all descended from Anndra MacKenzie who was one of the original settlers in Port Mholair. My old flame, known as Shonag, daughter of

Three great liners of the early 1900s: *Mauretania, Columbus* and *Empress of Canada*

Iain MacKenzie, shone brightly once more. At the weekends, I spent much of my time in her company down by the Port – particularly after her folks had gone to bed. Her mother, known as Bantrach Iain [Iain's Widow], wasn't one for joining the rest of the *cailleachan* in their worry-sessions. She was a strong-minded, big-busted woman, always ready to fire off a salvo in this direction or that. She never had much time for me. A little bird told me that she usually referred to me as 'Diabhal Mòr na Sràide' – The Big Devil from up the Street!

One evening after supper, I walked down by the Port and was hanging about waiting for the folk's bedtime when I heard loud wailing. As I passed by Shonag's door, I heard Bantrach Iain crying out, 'If only women like us could get hold of that black-hearted devil, we would tear him apart!'

The thought entered my head that she was talking about me. I became so curious that I slowly eased the door ajar and ventured in. The widow was wiping her streaming tears away with her white apron.

'Oh, Iain, a ghràidh [dear], have you heard the terrible news?' she cried. 'Ned next door has just received word that his son Calum was lost in a disaster at sea. It happened a week ago, on the twenty-sixth of November. If I could, I would choke the German Ceusar* myself for all the murders he's done!'

Just as I was preparing to set off for Greenock to join my old ship, I got a telegram from the Army giving me a telling-off for not reporting for duty months before. They gave me twenty-four hours to report at Fort George.

I travelled to Kyle on the steamer, the *Sheila*, not very sure whether I was heading for Greenock or Fort George. In the end, I chose Greenock and found that there was a hell of a war waiting for me.

Calum Ned, who was lost on HMS *Bulwark*

* Ironically, the Gaelic word for 'Kaiser' also means 'the one who crucifies'

Chapter Three

The Mad, Bad Old World

Extract from the Preface to the second edition of *The Roll of Honour for Lewis and Harris, 1914–1918.*

The Royal Naval Reserve was started in Stornoway in 1874 and. for a long time, was drilled annually at the Battery Station there – in its day, the largest single station in the United Kingdom. According to official reports, the physique and efficiency of the Reservemen were surpassed by none. In later years, actual service on board a man-of-war has been insisted on and the local Training Station has been discontinued. This splendid RNR contingent, numbering about 2000, promptly answered the mobilization summons of the Admiralty on the memorable 2 August of last year. It must, however, be kept in mind that the connection of Lewis with the Navy has been very close for fully a century, though the recruitment was not large, and that in this war, up to date, several Lewismen of the regular Navy (apart from RNR seamen), have conspicuously distinguished themselves.

The old Artillery Volunteers (1st Ross-shire) Stornoway, was supplanted some years ago by the new organization, the Ross Mountain Battery (T.F.), and the Stornoway Company thereof is now valorously fighting in the dreary and blood-soaked slopes of the Dardanelles. With the Company are 41 of the secondary pupils of the Nicolson Institute. Nothing redounds more to the high credit of the Island's endeavour in this world conflict than the voluntary enlistment of young men of Lewis birth or extraction, both at home (though furth of the Island) and in the colonies, the States, the Argentine and elsewhere in foreign parts. From Canada alone, 250 Lewis lads are now in the trenches in Flanders . . . Alas, that with all the military enterprise and pageantry the toll of life and limb by land and sea has been distressingly severe. Already the death casualties alone are well into the third hundred and every week now, little groups of men, maimed and hopelessly war-worn, are finding their way to the family hearths in all parts of the island.

The story of the achievement of the Island of Lewis by land and sea is a glorious one. The recital of its losses in the finest of its manhood is, alas, harrowing and in no phase of the war was the cry of lamentation nor the agony of anxious hearts absent in any village in the land. The fact that out of a population of less than 30,000, over 1,000 gave up their lives, not to reckon the distressingly large proportion of wounded and permanently disabled who have been straggling back to their mourning homes, has stirred the hearts and won the admiration of our kinsmen everywhere, and of the nation at large.

Port Mholair

2. MACLEOD – DONALD, Canadians: killed in France, 1917, aged 18.
4. MACDONALD – MALCOLM, RNR: torpedoed. NORMAN, Gordons: killed in France, 1917, aged 19.
5. MACDONALD – ALICK JOHN, RNR: drowned, 1917, aged 22.

MACDONALD – DONALD, Sergt. Seaforths: killed at Hill 60, 1915, aged 27.

5. MACLEOD – JOHN, Seaforths: twice wounded.

MACKENZIE – MALCOLM, RNR: lost in *Bulwark* disaster, 1914, aged 29.

MACKENZIE – MURDO, RNR: died Mesopotamia, 1915, aged 41.

7. CAMPBELL – NORMAN, Seaforths: gas poisoned; prisoner in Bulgaria.
13. MARTIN – MALCOLM, RNR: torpedoed; saved from the *Iolaire* disaster.

MARTIN – ALICK, Seaforths: killed in France, 1916, aged 22; brother JOHN, Ross Mountain Battery; severely wounded at Gallipoli.

14. MACDONALD – MURDO DAN, Lieut. Camerons: killed at the Somme, 1916, aged 29.
15. MACIVER – KENNETH, Seaforths: severely wounded; brother ALICK, Seaforths: wounded thrice.
18. MACLEOD – NORMAN, Canadians: wounded; brother ANGUS, 2nd Lieut. Seaforths; killed in France, 1917, aged 28.

CAMPBELL – MURDO, Gordons: six times wounded; POW.

MARTIN – WILLIAM, RNR: drowned in the *Clan MacNaughton* tragedy, 1915, aged 22.

Port Nan Giùran

1. MACLEOD – ALICK, RNR: lost in the *Iolaire* disaster, aged 42.*
5. GRAHAM – JOHN, Lieut, Canadians: wounded.
6. MACLEOD – DONALD, Gordons: killed at La Bassée, 1914, aged 20.
8. MACKAY – Donald, RNR: drowned when his ship was mined, 1917, aged 40.

MACIVER – MURDO, New Zealanders: asphyxiated 1917, aged 30.

9. CAMPBELL – KENNETH, RNR: died of pneumonia, 1918, aged 23.
10. MACLEOD – WILLIAM, RNR: drowned on HMT *Lydian*, 1915, aged 28.

MACLEOD – ALEXANDER, Gordons: killed France, 1914, aged 20; brother ANGUS, RNR: interned in Holland; released on medical grounds, died 1916; brother ALEXANDER, Gordons: killed in France, 1914, aged 20; brother NORMAN, RNR: lost in the *Iolaire* disaster.

11. MACDONALD – MURDO, Royal Bucks Hussars: severely wounded at Gallipoli; brother DONALD, W. O, RN: lost when his destroyer was mined, 1917, aged 41.
12. MACDONALD – MURDO, Seaforths: killed France in 1916, aged 20.
15. MACDONALD – KENNETH, Seaforths: wounded.
17. MACLEOD – MURDO, RNR: asphyxiated, 1918, aged 48.

* The Armistice bringing the First World War to an end was signed on 11 November 1918. In the early hours of New Year's Day 1919, the armed yacht *Iolaire* transporting 260 Royal Naval Reservists home to Lewis and Harris foundered on a reef at the entrance to Steòrnabhagh harbour. More than 200 drowned.

The yacht *Amalthoea* was based at Steòrnabhagh and re-named *Iolaire*

Brocair

3. MACLEOD – DONALD, RNR: severely wounded; brother ALICK JOHN, RNR: lost in the *Iolaire* disaster.
4. MACLEOD – DONALD, Gordons: killed in France, 1916, aged 20.
5. MACLEOD – JOHN, Black Watch: killed in France, 1918, aged 21.
6. CAMPBELL – DUNCAN, Seaforths: mortally wounded at Aisne, 1914, aged 22.

Na Fleisearan

1. GRAHAM – ANGUS, RNR: lost in the *Bayano* disaster, 1915, aged 30.

GRAHAM – CHARLES, Gordons: twice wounded.

2. GRAHAM – ANDREW, Seaforths: wounded in the firing line, aged 17.
4. MACASKILL – JOHN, RNR: lost when his ship was mined, 1917, aged 37.
6. MACKAY – JOHN, RNR: wounded and disabled.

MACDONALD – ANGUS, Seaforths: killed Mesopotamia, 1916, aged 20.

MACLEAN – RODERICK, Seaforths: wounded.

MACDONALD – DUNCAN, Canadians: killed at Vimy Ridge, 1917, aged 31.

GRAHAM – NORMAN, RNR: lost in HMT *Robert Smith,* 1917, aged 19; brother MURDON C. RNR: died in hospital, 1918, aged 18.

MACLEOD – ANGUS, RAMC: died 1918, aged 24.

Àird

1. MACKENZIE – ALEXANDER, RNR: lost in the *Iolaire* disaster, aged 42.
3. MACIVER – ANGUS, RNR: killed in action, 1917, aged 42.
4. MACLEOD – DONALD, Sergt. Gordons: twice wounded; brother FINLAY, RNR: died of pneumonia contracted while in service, 1919; brother KENNETH, RNR: drowned, 1918, aged 33.
5. MACKENZIE – JOHN, RNR: killed when ship was torpedoed, 1918, aged 28.
6. MACDONALD – DONALD, RNR: died April, 1917, aged 27.
7. SMITH – ALEX, Capt., Canadians: twice wounded; brother MALCOLM, Canadians: killed in France.

10. MACLEOD – MURDO, RNR: lost in the *Iolaire* disaster, aged 43; brother NORMAN, Canadians: severely wounded; brother DUNCAN, Sergt. Gordons: thrice wounded.
11. CAMPBELL – NORMAN, Seaforths: wounded; brother THOMAS, Gordons: wounded five times.
12. CAMPBELL – NORMAN, RMB: wounded Gallipoli, died in hospital, 1915, aged 20.
13. CAMPBELL – JOHN, RNR: lost on HMS *Bayano*, March 1915, aged 20; brother WILLIAM, RNR: died June 1918, aged 32.
14. MACKENZIE – THOMAS, Sergt. Seaforths: twice wounded.
15. MACDONALD – JOHN, Seaforths: killed in Mesopotamia, April, 1916, aged 22.

Taobh Loch An Dùin

MACKENZIE – ALICK: lost in *Iolaire* disaster, aged 42.

MACIVER – ALICK, RNR: severely wounded in mine explosion.

SEISIADAR

3. MACAULAY – JOHN, RNR: drowned at sea during a storm; 1914; aged 61.
4. MACLEOD – DONALD, Canadians: gassed.
5. MACDONALD – DONALD: lost in the *Iolaire* disaster, aged 40.

MONTGOMERY – NORMAN, RNR: lost in the *Iolaire* disaster, aged 39; Cousin ALEXANDER, Sergt. Seaforths: killed at Hill 60, 1915, aged 28.

7. MACAULAY – MURDO, RNR: lost in the *Iolaire* disaster, aged 34.
9. MACAULAY – JOHN, Canadians: killed in France, 1916, aged 24.
11. MURRAY – WILLIAM, RNR: lost in the *Iolaire* disaster, aged 23; brother JOHN M., Transport Service: twice torpedoed.

MACDONALD – NORMAN, Seaforths: killed in France, 1916, aged 21; brother WILLIAM, Sergt. Canadians: gassed.

12. MACLEOD – ANGUS, Sergt. Argyll & Suth. Highlanders: wounded; brother KENNETH, Canadians: twice wounded.
13. MACAULAY – PETER, Seaforths: killed in France, 1917, aged 24; brother MURDO, Seaforths: gassed; brother DONALD, RNR: lost in the *Iolaire* disaster.

14. MACLEOD – WILLIAM, RNR: lost in HMS *Sanda*, 1915, aged 23.

MACLEOD – KENNETH, Seaforths: killed at Hill 60, 1915, aged 21.

15. MACKENZIE – MURDO, RNR: lost in the *Iolaire* disaster, aged 45.

20. MACDONALD – JOHN (Sen.), RNR: lost in the *Iolaire* disaster, aged 33; brother JOHN (Jun.) RNR: lost in the *Iolaire* disaster, aged 26.

21. MACRAE – DONALD, RNR: died 1919; aged 26; brother John lost when his ship was torpedoed, 1918, aged 28.

22. MACKAY – DONALD, RNR: lost in the *Iolaire* disaster, aged 22; brother COLIN, Sergt, Seaforths: died of his wounds in Mesopotamia, aged 27.

23. MACLEOD – NORMAN, RNR: lost in the *Iolaire* disaster, aged 29.

24. MACLEOD – JOHN, Canadians: wounded.

Siadar

3. MACLEAN – DONALD, Canadians: twice wounded; brother ANGUS, Canadians: killed in France, 1917, aged 31.

7. MURRAY – KENNETH, RNR: lost when his ship was mined, 1918, aged 27; brother Alasdair, Canadians: wounded.

9. MACKENZIE – DONALD W, Canadians; wounded; brother JOHN W., Canadians: wounded.

14. MACASKILL – DONALD, RNR: lost in the *Iolaire* disaster.

15. MACDONALD – ANGUS, RNR: POW in Austria; died on his way home after the Armistice was signed, aged 29.

16. MACAULAY – DONALD, RNR: lost in the *Iolaire* disaster, aged 38; brother MURDO, Canadians: killed in France, 1918, aged 29.

19. MACIVER – ALEXANDER, RNR: fired the distress rockets from the ill-fated *Iolaire* in which disaster he lost his life, aged 42.

22. MACDONALD – ALLAN, RNR: wounded; POW in Germany.

MACKAY – ANGUS, RNR: lost in the *Iolaire* disaster.

1. Newlands MACAULAY – MURDO C., North'land Fusiliers; brother KENNETH, North'land Fusiliers: wounded.

4. Newlands MACKENZIE – KENNETH, RNR: lost in the *Iolaire* disaster, aged 27.

Garrabost Iarach

4. GRAHAM – ANGUS, RNR: lost with HMS *Invincible* at Jutland, 1916.
5. MURRAY – MALCOLM, RNR: lost with HMS *Invincible* at Jutland, 1916

MACKAY – NEIL, Canadians: wounded & discharged.

6. GRAHAM – MALCOLM, Seaforths: wounded; brother ALLAN, Seaforths: killed in Mesopotamia, 1916, aged 18.
8. MACSWEEN – MURDO, Seaforths: killed in action, 1916, aged 19.
21. MACMILLAN – DONALD, Canadians: wounded.
23. MACLEOD – DONALD, RNR: died in hospital, 1917, aged 22.
25. MONTGOMERY – GEORGE, RMB: wounded.
28. MACKAY – JOHN, Seaforths: twice wounded, once gassed.
29. MONTGOMERY – DONALD, Camerons: killed in action, 1917, aged 19.
30. MACLEOD – JOHN, RNR: drowned in the *Iolaire* disaster; brother ALEX, Seaforths: killed in action in France, 1916, aged 23.
39. MACKAY – JOHN. RMB: wounded.
43. MACDONALD – MALCOLM, Sergt. Gordons: killed in action, 1915, aged 21.
44. SMITH – JOHN, RNR: died in Holland; brother ALEXANDER, Gordons: wounded.
48. SMITH – JOHN, RNR: lost with ship in the White Sea, 1916, aged 47.
50. MACKAY – MALCOLM, Canadians: wounded; brother MURDO, RNR: drowned when HM Yacht *Sanda* was mined, 1915, aged 24.
51. MACKAY – JOHN, Canadians; seriously wounded, POW in Germany; leg amputated.

MACKENZIE – KENNETH, Canadians: killed in action in France, 1918, aged 28; brother MURDO, RMB: died from his wounds, 1915, aged 19.

52. GRAHAM – MURDO, Seaforths: gassed in France, 1915.

MACKAY – ALEX, RNR: drowned when HMS *Merse* was mined, 1917, aged 31.

Church Street

CAMPBELL – DONALD, RNR: died in hospital in Chatham, 1917, aged 51.

MACKENZIE – NORMAN, RNRT: drowned in the *Iolaire* disaster, aged 19.

Garrabost Uarach

1. MACSWEEN – GEORGE, Gordons: killed in Flanders, 1915, aged 24.
2. MACDONALD – JOHN, RNR: lost at sea, 1918, aged 19.
5. MACDONALD – DONALD, Sergt., Seaforths: killed in France, 1918, aged 25.

MACKENZIE – JOHN, Gordons: killed in action, 1916, aged 19; brother EVENDER, Seaforths: killed in action, 1916, aged 19.

MURRAY – KENNETH, Gordons: severely wounded.

8a. CAMPBELL – DONALD, Gordons: died of pneumonia, 1916, aged 23.

9. MACLEOD – MALCOLM, Canadians: severely wounded; right arm amputated.
10. CAMPBELL – DUNCAN, Gordons: killed in France, 1915, aged 21; brother JOHN, Camerons: killed in France, 1915, aged 19.
11. MACLEOD – DONALD, Camerons: killed in action, 1916, aged 20.
14. MACKAY – ANGUS, Camerons: wounded.

Garrabost Ur

12. LEE – JOHN, Gordons: wounded.
13. MACLEOD – JOHN, Canadians: gassed, discharged, 1916; brother NORMAN, Canadians: killed in France, 1916.

Pabail Uarach

1. MACKAY – NORMAN, Gordons: killed in action, 1916, aged 25.

MACLEOD – DONALD, RNR: killed during a collision, 1916, aged 36.

MACDONALD – EVANDER, Scottish Horse: killed in France, 1918, aged 25.

GRAHAM – ANGUS, RNR: discharged and died at home, aged 19.

3. MACKENZIE – MURDO, Scots Guards: killed in action, 1914, aged 31.

MACKENZIE – ALEXANDER, Seaforths: killed in France, 1915, aged 31.

7. MATHESON – JOHN, Canadians: killed in action, 1915, aged 33.

14. MURRAY – NORMAN, Scots Guards: killed in action, 1916, aged 19.

MURRAY – MURDO, Seaforths: twice wounded; brother NORMAN, RNR: drowned 1918, aged 18.

17. SMITH – JOHN, RNR: lost in the *Iolaire* disaster, aged 46.

MACLEOD – RODERICK: torpedoed, discharged ill owing to exposure.

19. MACDONALD – DONALD, Seaforths: wounded in France, 1915.

20. NICOLSON – COLIN, Canadians: killed in France, 1917, aged 21; brother EVANDER, Canadians: wounded in action.

22. MACKENZIE – DONALD, RNR: lost in the *Iolaire* disaster.

23. MACKENZIE – RODERICK, Seaforths: severely wounded in Mesopotamia; brother JOHN, Gordons: killed in action; brother DONALD, Canadians: died of wounds, 1917, aged 25.

23. MACRAE – NORMAN, Canadians: killed in France, 1917, aged 27; brother ALEXANDER, Mercantile Marine: drowned on SS *Buffalo*, 1918, aged 20.

25. MACLEAN – MALCOLM, Seaforths: killed in action, 1916, aged 23.

26. STEWART – JOHN, RNR: drowned 1917, aged 28.

27. MACLEOD – JOHN, RNR: drowned at Calais, 1916, aged 27; brother KENNETH, RN, drowned off Italy, 1918, aged 24; brother NORMAN, Canadians: wounded in action and discharged.

Geilir

32. SMITH – DONALD, Lieut. Seaforths: twice wounded and died of pneumonia while returning from Mesopotamia, 1919, aged 26.

33. MACLEOD – JOHN, Gordons: killed in France, 1914, aged 19.

34. MACAULAY – MURDO, Seaforths: killed in action, 1915, aged 20; brother ALEXANDER, Canadians: killed in France, 1917, aged 36.

34. CAMPBELL – DONALD, R.G.A.: wounded in the Balkan advance, 1914.

37. CAMPBELL – NORMAN, Sergt., Seaforths: killed in France, 1914, aged 35.

39. MACLEOD – DONALD, Seaforths: wounded in France, 1915.

42. MACLEOD – DONALD, RNR: died of pneumonia in Ireland, 1919, aged 22.
43. MACLEOD – JOHN, RNR: lost in the *Iolaire* disaster, aged 41.
47. MACKENZIE – RODERICK, Canadians: severely wounded in France; brother EVANDER, Arg. & Suth. High: wounded, 1918.
51. MACMILLAN – MALCOLM, RNR: lost in the *Iolaire* disaster, aged 46.
MACLEOD – DONALD, Seaforths; killed in Mesopotamia, 1916, aged 20.
52. SMITH – DONALD, Sergt. Seaforths: wounded in France.

Greenpark

MACIVER – KENNETH M., Capt. South African Rifles: killed accidentally in Nyasaland, 1918, aged 38; brother JAMES, Maj., South African Rifles, wounded; brother WILLIAM M. Sergt. Rhodes. Infantry: killed in France, 1918, aged 36.

Pabail Iarach

2. GRAHAM – ANGUS, Seaforths: wounded.
3. STEWART – PETER, RNR: lost on HMS *Otway* 1917, aged 34.
4. MACLEOD – DONALD, Seaforths: killed in action, 1917, aged 20; brother RODERICK, Gordons: twice wounded.
6. SMITH – JOHN, RNR: died in hospital in Gronigen, 1917, aged 39.
8. MACLEOD – NORMAN, RNR: died of pneumonia, 1918, aged 39.
15. MACLEOD – JOHN, Seaforths: killed in action in France, 1915, aged 27.
19. MACIVER – JOHN, RNR: lost in the *Iolaire* disaster, aged 46.
21. CAMPBELL – KENNETH, RN: died in Chatham Naval Hospital. 1917, aged 42; brother JOHN, RNR: died in Chatham Naval Hospital, 1915, aged 34.
27. MACLEOD – JOHN, RNR; drowned on the East Coast, 1917, aged 45.
29. MACLEOD – JOHN, RNR: died at Mudros, 1917, aged 46.
MACDONALD – ALEXANDER, RNR: lost in the *Iolaire* disaster, aged 42.

33. MACLEOD – MALCOLM, RNR: drowned 1916.
34. MACIVER – MALCOLM, RNR: killed in Mesopotamia, 1916, aged 22.
36. MACIVER – MURDO, RNR: drowned in the *Iolaire* disaster.
37. MACDONALD – WILLIAM, RNR: drowned 1918, aged 36.
MACLEOD – DONALD, Seaforths: killed in action, 1915, aged 20.

Pairc
41. MACIVER – KENNETH, Gordons: killed in action in France, 1914, aged 19.
42. MACRAE – MALCOLM, RNR: died at Grimsby, 1916.
MACRAE – NORMAN, Canadians: died of wounds, 1917, aged 29.
43. MACDONALD – MURDO Gordons: severely wounded, 1914.
44. MACDONALD – WILLIAM, RNR: lost in the *Iolaire* disaster, aged 21; brother DONALD, drowned, 1917, aged 24; brother ALEXANDER, Gordons: wounded.
45. MACIVER – ANGUS, RNR: killed near Arras, 1917, aged 27.

An Cnoc

2. MUNRO – JOHN, Canadians: wounded; brother JOHN M., Gordons: killed in action at La Bassee, 1914, aged 19.
4. MACLEOD – MURDO, Sergt. Canadians: wounded at Passchendale.
5. MACLEOD – ALEXANDER, Gordons: thrice wounded and discharged, 1917; brother MALCOLM, RNR; lost with the SS *Mereddio*, 1917, aged 20; brother ALEX JOHN, Sergt. Canadians: killed in France, 1918, aged 25.
8. MACLEOD – MURDO, Seaforths: wounded.
11. NICOLSON – ANGUS, Gordons: killed in France, 1915, aged 18.
12. CRICHTON – ANGUS, RNR: drowned in *Iolaire* disaster, 1919, aged 41.
13. MACKENZIE – JOHN, Gordons: killed 1915, aged 18.
15. CRICHTON – MALCOLM, Canadians: twice wounded; brother DONALD, RNR: drowned in the *Iolaire* disaster, aged 23.
17. MACIVER – MURDO, Gordons: wounded. DONALD, Canadians: severely wounded.

17. MACLEOD – MALCOLM, Canadians: wounded; died of pneumonia, 1919, aged 28.
18. MACLEOD – ANGUS, RNR: drowned in the *Iolaire* disaster, aged 23.
18. MACLEOD – GEORGE, Canadians: severely wounded; brother DONALD, Canadians: died of his wounds in England, 1918, aged 31.
19. MACLEOD – JOHN, RNR: died of pneumonia, 1919, aged 28.
20. MACDONALD – DONALD, RNR: died 1918, aged 30; brother DONALD, RNR: died 1917, aged 23.
21. MUNRO – KENNETH, RNR: served at the Battle of Jutland; died 1918, aged 25.
23. MACLEOD – KENNETH, RNR: accidentally killed on board ship.
24. MACKENZIE – JOHN, RNR: enlisted aged 17; died 1917, aged 21.

MACKENZIE – KENNETH, Seaforths: twice wounded; lost right hand and fingers from the left.

28. MARTIN – NORMAN, RNR: transferred to French warship; lost at sea, aged 24.

Suardail

1a. MACKENZIE – KENNETH, Seaforths: died in Turkey, 1917, aged 24.
2. MACDONALD – JOHN RNR: drowned at the Dardanelles, 1915, aged 17.
5. MACKENZIE – RODERICK, RNR: lost in the *Iolaire* disaster, aged 32.
11. CRICHTON – COLIN, RNR; joined 1916; died at Portsmouth, 1918, aged 18. DONALD, HLI: wounded.
13. MACDONALD – MURDO, RNR: lost with HMS *Hollington,* 1917, aged 27.
15. MACLEOD – MURDO, RNR: lost when his ship was torpedoed, 1918.
16. MACKAY – MURDO, RNR: lost in the *Iolaire* disaster, aged 32.
19. MACLEOD – JOHN. Lieut. Seaforths: killed Mesopotamia, 1916, aged 42. FINLAY, Sergt. Canadians: wounded.
22. MACLEOD – DONALD, RNR: died at home, 1917, aged 38; brother TORQUIL, Sergt., Seaforths; killed in action, 1917, aged 30

24. MACMILLAN – RODERICK, RMB: wounded in action.
26. CAMPBELL – ALEXANDER, RNR: lost in the *Iolaire* disaster, aged 18.
28. MACLEOD – ALEXANDER, Sergt., Seaforths: wounded in action.

AIGINIS

5. MACLEOD – MALCOLM, RNR: lost in the *Iolaire* disaster, aged 19.
7. MACLEOD – RODERICK, Lieut. West African Frontier Force: severely wounded.
8. MACKENZIE – DONALD, RGA: wounded in action and discharged; brother RODERICK, RNR: lost when the SS *Borg* was torpedoed, 1918, aged 20; brother MURDO, Cameron Highlanders of Canada: killed in France, 1918, aged 23; brother MALCOLM, Gordons: died of his wounds in France, 1915, aged 19.
10. MACRAE – ALEXANDER, RNR: lost in collision off the Butt, 1916, aged 25.
13. MACKAY – MURDO, RNR: died in Plymouth, 1917, aged 26.
16. MACASKILL – ALEXANDER, Gordons: frostbitten; brother MALCOLM, RNR: died of pneumonia in Kirkwall, 1918, aged 31.
18. MACLEOD – JOHN, RMB: wounded at Suvla Bay, 1915, died aged 22; brother ALEXANDER, RNR, wounded.
19. CAMPBELL – KENNETH, Seaforths: died of his wounds and pneumonia in France.
20. MACDONALD – FINLAY, Gordons: twice wounded.
21. MACSWEEN – KENNETH, Seaforths: killed in action in France, 1915, aged 21.
24. MACLEOD – RODERICK ROSS, Gordons: killed in action, 1914, aged 17.

MACKAY – ANGUS, Seaforths: wounded; brother DONALD, Lieut. Seaforths: died of wounds in France, 1918, aged 31.

25. MACDONALD – HECTOR, Seaforths, promoted King's Sergt. for bravery: died 1918, aged 23.
26. MACDONALD – DONALD Gordons: wounded in France, 1915; brother NORMAN, Gordons: thrice wounded.

27. MUNRO – TORQUIL, RNR: died of pneumonia in Glasgow, 1919, aged 24; brother JOHN, Lieut. Seaforths: killed in action, 1918, aged 28.
28. MACIVER – MALCOLM, RNR: lost in the *Iolaire* disaster, aged 37.
31. MACLEOD – MURDO, RASC: thrice wounded.

A tribute by Lord Leverhulme

Lewis is proud of the fact that it supplied 6,172 men wearing His Majesty's uniform on sea and land and we all mourn that of these, 1,151 were called to make the supreme sacrifice. Blood was poured out like water, money was counted as dross until our one-time most powerful military foe was defeated and crushed. Not until liberty and civilisation were made secure and safe, not until our homes, mothers, wives and children were freed from the menace of the invader, did the efforts of our unconquerable Lewismen cease. They and their comrades were the saviours of the British nation, the saviours of the Empire; they were the liberators of mankind. Not until victory was assured did our valiant Lewismen return home to their beloved Island, to their anxious mothers, their loving, waiting wives, their bonnie children and the crofts they knew and cultivated. They have not been demoralized – they have been ennobled by their sacrifices.

When peace was restored in November 1918, many of the men who survived the Great War returned to their homes traumatised and disillusioned. They felt that the capitalist classes had used them as pawns in a struggle that had claimed the lives of millions. Soolivan was dismissive of those in authority whose many voices praised 'our glorious dead'. His experience at the Dardanelles had made him a republican who wished to see the British aristocracy stripped of its wealth and power. A few months before he died in 1956, Queen Elizabeth and Prince Philip drove past his house on the way to the official opening of a new installation at Tiumpanhead Lighthouse.

'Help me to the window,' he said, 'so that I can see the granddaughter of the fellow for whom I sacrificed half a kneecap and half a calf! Go tell her the fellows who lost their lives have not been 'ennobled by their sacrifice'. They did not give up their lives willingly. Their lives were sacrificed in defence of the ruling classes and their way of life!'

My hair began to go grey. I had the feeling that the Germans were determined to take my life. In the end, I discovered that it wasn't the Germans who were hell-bent on killing me but the goddam Turks. They didn't try to kill me just once. They spent a whole fortnight at it!

In 1915, I was on a minesweeper, a converted Grimsby trawler sent to clear mines in the Dardanelles. For some reason that I have not yet been able to understand, the forces of the British Empire and the French were fighting the Turks. It was stupid not to have the Turks on our side. Excellent fighters they were. They stood up against everything that our fleet and armies threw at them.

Our battle formations steamed over to the far corner of the Mediterranean and tried to force their way through the Dardanelles – a narrow strip of sea like the kyle between Skye and the mainland. The Turks had laid mines all over the place – everywhere, except in a narrow channel that they had kept secret from everybody but themselves. Before British and French fleets could pass through the straits, a flotilla of minesweepers was sent in to clear the mines. Most of those minesweepers were converted trawlers, sturdy enough against gales at sea but not very sturdy against heavy-duty shells.

As soon as our fleet arrived off the Turkish coast, all hell broke loose. While they were still several miles offshore, big powerful battleships like the *Agamemnon* and *Queen Elizabeth* opened up against the shore batteries, their huge screaming shells passing over our trawler. We thought that nobody on the receiving end of a bombardment like that could live through it. But that bloody Turk would not budge. For every shell that our ships sent ashore, he replied with two of his own. The biggest ships in the Royal Navy had to stay out of range of the shore batteries during the day. At night, of course, the gunners could not see targets or calculate their range.

The minesweepers trying to clear the mines had to venture in close during the night and were well within the Turk's range. Whenever we heard the shriek of an approaching shell, we ducked and prayed that we would not receive a direct hit. One of the French battleships called the *Boovy* exploded on the horizon, about twelve miles from where we were working. One moment she was with the other grey giants, roaring away with her guns. Next moment, there was a terrific flash and a noise like a thunderclap. A huge column of smoke rose from where the *Boovy* had been, and when that cleared, nothing of the ship could be seen. That disaster showed what a direct hit in a magazine could do to a ship built as a steel fortress. Thinking of what a shell might do to a flimsy trawler like ours scared us to the jitters.

Our trawler became crowded with men rescued from ships sent to the bottom by enemy action. We must have had at least a dozen survivors on board, sitting about on the wooden deck smoking our crew's cigarettes. Some of them were badly hurt but none of them was complaining. How I wished that I could have treated those lads to a pint of cold ale! Unfortunately, there wasn't even enough water on board to quench everyone's thirst. A destroyer speeding by us signalled a message with its Morse-lamp as it went. Our trawler immediately altered course and began to steam towards the coast. *A Dhia,* where is he taking us now?

The enemy seemed to have got the gist of the order even before our skipper did. Shells began to come in our direction more regularly, one every three minutes or so. At first, the Turk was straddling us with shells sometimes a quarter mile astern, and then a furlong or so ahead. His gunners were working a system by which, sooner or later, they would find our range. Sure enough, the swish of the shells came closer and closer. The sun was so hot that you couldn't bear to touch metal. Everyone was stripped to the waist, with the sweat pouring off us.

The skipper steered a zigzag course but that did not save us. We took a direct hit. I cannot remember much about it. A loud blast, black smoke, hissing steam, a lot of shouting! A couple of fellows by my side were shrieking blue murder. With all the hullabaloo going on around me, I had not realised that I too had cause for shrieking!

The War Memorial overlooking Steòrnabhagh

Shrapnel had cut open my right leg to the bone, just below the knee. Pieces of metal were also bedded in my right arm and thigh. I lost so much blood that I nearly died. While I was on the trawler, it was touch and go. Once they hit us, the Turk stopped paying attention to us. With reduced speed, the trawler was forced away from land. On the following day, we came alongside a hospital-ship to which our casualties were transferred. By that time my leg was numb all over.

Hundred of casualties were on the hospital-ship and a lot of them died before we reached an island called Lemnos, which is about a hundred miles west of the Dardanelles. Unfortunately, many of our wounds stank to high heaven. They looked awful. Mine were no different, and even I found the stench revolting. At a big field-hospital surgeons worked day and night attending to the wounded. But for many, the surgeons' work came too late. Because my knee wound was so deep and angry, the two French surgeons examined it and then told me that I must lose my leg from just above the knee. Bad medicine, my friend! I told them that I would rather die than lose my leg.

'No-one goes off with my right leg while I am in a fit state to consider the matter!'

'Then consider it soon,' says one of the surgeons, 'for you will never be fit until you have had that leg amputated!'

For another whole day I refused to take their advice. I just could not bear the thought of going back to Lewis a one-legged Soolivan. I developed a terrible fever but still would not let them remove my leg. A young American surgeon came to my bedside and asked if he could see the wound. After examining it, he offered to have a go at saving my leg. And save it he did.

Today, I cannot remember the American surgeon's name, though I knew it very well at the time. No matter. I shall always be grateful to him. My leg is not a pretty sight even now, but at least I am a two-legged son-of-a-gun! Losing part of my knee-cap wasn't all that bad, considering what many of my pals lost. They lost their lives.

THE 'BLOODY' AND 'GAYIS'

Following my adventure at the Dardanelles, I spent months in hospitals in the south of England before coming home in the spring of 1916. My constitution was robust and I made a good recovery. But with part of my right calf and knee-cap still over on an island in the Aegean Sea, I was no use to the Allied fighting machine. As a result, I had no alternative but to stay at home until the war ended, which was in November 1918.

I used to go about with a walking-stick so that I would look like a war-wounded. To be honest, the stick was more for show than for support. Every neighbour wanted to be my friend and to discuss with me what it was like to be in the middle of the madness of a modern war. There were lots of war-wounded in the district, all of them suffering much worse than me. The majority of them had fought with the Highland regiments in France and had come back as broken men. There were fellas with only one arm or with one leg; others who were blind or whose minds had been shot through by shell-shock. There were a few whose innards had been so torn that they were being pushed about in wheel-chairs. Those were the *truaghain* in the community who were regarded as real heroes. Take for example, Murdo MacDonald of the Royal Bucks Hussars – the spick-and span soldier whom I used to admire in my young days. Poor guy, he was no hero! He was just unlucky enough to be on the spot when a German shell exploded in the middle of his platoon.

After a few months, it became clear to me that my wounds were not considered severe enough for me to be regarded as a hero. Not a problem – I didn't give a toss. As everybody knows, the war was only a ploy caused by capitalists and politicians who made damn sure that they were at home sipping brandy and discussing the state of the stock market. Wise fellas. I wish to God that I had been a capitalist!

Until the war ended, the stream of telegrams giving news of men killed or missing in action dominated the life of the community. It was impossible to escape from the effects of so much mutilation and death. There was nothing for me to do during the day but slouch by the fire. In the evenings, you could always attend the wakes held in memory of friends killed in action. Wakes were a depressing business. One evening, at a wake in Port nan Giùran, 'Kit' Martin (the son of Calum 'Ain Mhàrtainn from the Clitig) told me that my cousin, the Bloody, had salvaged a barrel of navy rum from the sea in Geodha Mhór Sheisiadar. My spirit was suddenly uplifted! The thought of a year's supply of rum sitting unattended in Seisiadar distracted me from all the droning prayers and sighing going on around me. I leaned over to Kit.

'I am closely related to the Bloody, and I know that he would give a cripple like me a share of his rum.'

Kit shook his head. 'Then he's not the Bloody that I know!'

After the service, Kit and I walked together up the road, discussing a plan of action. Kit was trying hard to be realistic. He was that kind of fellow, always asking questions in an effort to find foolproof answers. *Bu dìomhain dhà!* His was a futile exercise.

'Apparently the barrel is a hogshead,' says he, 'a big, heavy affair that no-one could shift without a crane.'

The amount of alcohol I had drunk since the Dardanelles wouldn't fill a chamber-pot! At the very thought of the Bloody's hogshead, my tongue became as dry as a cork. Of course, Geodha Mhór Sheisiadair was a place I knew well from my school truancy days! *Thighearna*, hadn't I spent much of my schooldays sitting there eating *mircean* and dulse! You bet! I was confident that I could negotiate any of the three paths we used for scaling the cliffs of the Geodha Mhór, even in the dead of night. Aye, I could that – even with my crippled leg.

I became so excited about the prospect of getting a share of the Bloody's booze that I began to think aloud.

'A hogshead holds enough to keep the two of us in a stupor for months!'

'But there a snag!' says Kit who was becoming equally excited. 'The Bloody and his brother Gayis have organised two or three of the boys from the Àird to help them carry the rum in pails to a safe haven. They have probably put as many sentries on the hogshead as the French have on the Maginot Line!'

'Aye, sentries without guts or guns!' says I. 'Don't tell me you're afraid of tackling the Bloody and Gayis!'

Now I should tell you that neither the Bloody nor his brother Gayis was a pushover. In fact, they were both hard men – scrappers whom many a lad of our generation had fought and had lived to rue the day. I was never afraid of either of them, though I knew that, with my game leg an' all, my taking on the two of them could prove to be a big mistake. Back home at No. 11, Kit and I sat by the fire drinking *stiùireag** and debating how best to tackle the problem. As usual, the Sàtan was putting all sorts of wild ideas into my head! He even suggested that Kit and I take the Còta's boat and try to tow the hogshead from Seisiadar to Bàgh Phort Mholair.

After a couple of jugs of *stiùireag*, Kit came round to the opinion that we should leave the cask to the wild men of the Àird.

'No way!' says I. 'Just imagine if that mug you're holding was full of Royal Navy rum. You take a mouthful and let it go trickling down the back of your throat. After three or four slugain of it, you begin to feel a wee bit light-headed. Then, as the liquid gold reaches down into your boiler, your lips would be forced to crack open into a smile. Without your even knowing it, songs would begin to flow from your throat, gun fhiosd! [involuntarily!]'

Well, after that wee pep-talk, Kit gets off the chair.

'I'm off home to fetch a hammer and chisel,' he says. 'I'll get at some of that rum even if I have to knock the brains out of the Bloody and Gayis!'

'Don't forget to fetch a clean bucket as well!'

* Hot or cold water mixed with oatmeal, with sometimes a pinch of salt.

And that's how Kit and I set off in the night like two burglars carrying our tools of the trade. There was a bright yellow moon over the Àird. We walked on the road as far as Druim Oidealar without meeting a soul. We crossed the moor to the left and skulked off down to the Geodha Mhór – at one time, my home from home!

As it happened, it was the full ebb-tide. Peering over the edge of the cliff, we saw what we had come for – the hogshead of rum sitting on the sand like Queen Victoria on her throne! A quick look round to see if there were sentries. Not even one. Kit and I scurried down the familiar cliff-path as fast as we could.

'Where's your terrible Maginot line?' says I.

'They must be afraid of cold steel,' says Kit as he got his hammer and chisel ready to attack the bung. Three or four heavy blows and the bung was out. The rum, thick as syrup, went glug-glug-glug on to the sand. In its raw state, Navy rum is as thick and slow-flowing as Archangel tar. I dipped my thumb in the liquid and put it in my mouth. What a glorious sensation!

'Come on, Soolivan!' says Kit. 'Pass me that flipping bucket!'

We hurriedly put a pail under the outflow, and took off into the shadows just in case one of the Àird boys came along to check from the cliff-top that all was well. It took ages before the first pail was three-quarters full. The glorious smell of rum filled the Geodha Mhór. All the kittiwakes sitting on their roosts above us in the cliffs must have felt quite groggy. For about half an hour, Kit and I sat there like two midwives waiting for the goods to be delivered.

The moonlit hogshead

'Dear me,' says Kit, 'here come the Germans!'

I looked up and saw half a dozen silhouettes appearing over the rim of the cliff. Together we dashed out into the moonlight. Grabbing our share of the rum, Kit and I scaled the opposite side of the Geodha – a mighty feat even in daylight! The Àird boys had arrived down by the cask before they realised that someone else had beaten them to the bung. Surprisingly, Kit and I reached nearly to the top of the cliff, before they noticed us. When they did see us, they started an almighty shouting and cursing. They came after us like Diamond after my boyhood rabbits! On reasonably level ground above the Geodha Mhór, we began to run with our two half-full buckets. After less than a hundred yards, Kit conked out, completely out of breath. And, as he dived into a peat-bank, his pail went flying. I glanced back and saw that he just lay there, playing possum. Even though my game leg was giving me laldy, I managed to hirple across the *pollagan* [peat-hags] trying not to spill any of my liquid gold! I glanced round, once more, to see if I was being followed and saw that indeed I was – stride for stride. I was almost at the Seisiadar houses before I was forced to a standstill. In a few seconds, the Bloody was by my side, blowing hard and bent over with exhaustion.

'You thieving trustar!' he groans. 'Give me that bucket of rum or I'll put you flat on your back.'

'Take another step closer,' says I, 'and I'll wreck the flipping bucket across the side of your head!'

'Come on, a dhuine! Give me the bucket and I'll not tell Gayis on you!'

'Before midnight, you and Gayis will be out cold with the drink. Even at this moment, I'll bet your brother has his mouth under the bung-hole taking his fill!'

The Bloody didn't wait for a second longer. He wheeled round and off he went at the gallop.

Unfortunately, when I looked in my bucket, I discovered that it was no more than quarter full. Still, the amount of rum that I managed to salvage that night proved to be powerful stuff. On board a Royal Navy ship, the rum is always diluted with water. But, being in a kind of hurry to begin to enjoy my hard-won treasure, I didn't waste time looking for drinking water from a well. Instead, I spent three days and three nights in a dark corner of Iain Mac Anndra's barn where I was sure no-one would find me. Even my sweetheart Shonag didn't know I was hove-to in the sanctuary of her father's barn. When the pail was finally empty, I dragged myself home to get something to eat. I was so queasy and haggard that my sisters didn't recognise me.

Even next day, I wasn't feeling very sprightly but, fragile as I was,

I decided to make an effort to be more sociable than I had been of late. The men of the Sràid were short of crew, so I rallied to the call to go out fishing in the Còta's boat. At the appointed hour, I found four of my neighbours down on the shingle, with their small-lines already baited and the boat already afloat in Cladhan a' Phuirt.

As soon as I appeared, Donald MacLeod [Dòmhnall 'Ain Chaluim], a solemn, good-living fella, started to cross-question me.

'All day yesterday,' he says, 'we tried to scratch a crew together so as to get a bite of fish for the people and you were nowhere to be found. Where on earth were you?'

'Not on earth, sir! I was in Heaven with a bucket of rum! Every time I woke up in a dark corner of Iain Mac Anndra's barn, I just took another slurp of rum and was transported straight back to Paradise!'

Mr MacLeod wasn't amused. He was a senior church elder, you see, and wasn't allowed to have a sense of humour. He grabbed me by the shoulders and shoved me off the boat at Giollaman. Och, he gave poor Soolivan a generous dressing-down that day! Looking back, I can see his point in a way.

'Do you think', says he, 'that anyone here would put to sea with a blasphemer such as yourself on board? And you with the breath of the demon drink still stinking on you! Go thee home, sinner, and repent!'

A Chruthaighear, he made my head sore and I was glad to

Dòmhnall 'Ain Chaluim (seated right of centre) with his brother Uilleam and members of their families

withdraw out of range of his salvos! It was a couple of months before I saw any of the Àird boys. When at last they met me on the road by the post office, they said that they had long since forgiven me for my thieving. I wish that I could say the same of my friend Kit! Until the day he died, he couldn't resist reminding me that I had not put aside as much as one gulp of rum from my bucket. It wasn't just the fact that he didn't get any of the Royal Navy rum that bothered him, but that during our assault on the 'Maginot line', he had lost his father's hammer and chisel. Worst still, he had lost his mother's enamel milking-pail.

SUNDAY IN OBAN

When the boys returned from the Great War, they took up the fishing again. I joined the crew of a 'bauldie'* out of Steòrnabhagh. Five of us were on her and one of them was Calum Campbell – a neighbour of mine who had won the Military Medal for killing a lot of the Germans in the trenches in France. Calum, the son of Dòmhnall Bàn Campbell of Brocair, was a big, strapping fellow. His nickname was 'Lawdy' but not everybody dared call him by that name. Nobody knew where the name 'Lawdy' came from or what it meant – not even himself! But Calum was a proud man who sometimes regarded being addressed by your nickname as a kind of insult. It all depended on who you were, you see! Shony MacLeod the merchant could address him as 'Lawdy', but not me. Soolivan was not allowed to call him 'Lawdy', but 'Lawdy' was allowed to call me 'Soolivan'. No matter. That is the way things were between us. Having been decorated in the war, Lawdy was respected by everybody – even though his surname was Campbell. And being tall and well-built, he had an authority that made younger men stand and listen, and refrain from calling him by his nickname to his face. How he came to kill all those Germans nobody seemed to know, for according to himself, he spent the war years in charge of a field-kitchen, always a mile or two behind the Front Line. Anyway, we were all pleased that Lawdy Campbell was with us on the 'bauldie', for he was a strong, hard-working fella, even though he was sometimes very irritable with the cook. Och, the cook had to watch his step with him, right enough! Indeed, we all had to. Nobody wanted to tamper with a man who had already got a reputation for despatching a bunch of the Ceusar's soldiers!

As often happened, there were better prices on offer at mainland

* A small motor herring-drifter named after Garibaldi, the Italian liberator and hero-figure of the nineteenth century. Still popular between the two world wars, it was fitted with a paraffin-burning Kelvin engine.

ports than at Steòrnabhagh. We followed the herring down through the kyles from Mallaig to Oban and earned quite a fair bit of money. One Friday, we had a very good haul which we landed at Oban, and, we got thirty bob a cran for it. We cleaned and repaired the nets all day Saturday, had a lie-down and then headed into town for a pint. It started to rain when we were walking back and poured buckets all night and into the following morning. I can't remember a more depressing Sunday, stuck on the 'bauldie' with nothing to do and nowhere to go. No-one on board cared to listen to any of my stories because they didn't believe a word I said. Lawdy wouldn't tell us any gruesome stories about the Battle of the Somme because he wanted to forget about the war. There was no-one else on board worth tuppence at telling yarns. In that sense, they were a hopeless crew.

It so happened that the cook had forgotten to buy enough milk and sugar for the weekend. Not the first time, he had let us down. Lawdy was furious, for he had been in charge of feeding squads of fighting men in the mud of Flanders, and here we were in peace time in Oban without so much as would give us a decent fly-cup. Och, a useless lump was the cook! As we were strangers in Oban, we didn't feel like going cadging groceries from the boats alongside. Anyway, there we were with no milk or sugar, no stories and everywhere awash

Racing home to market

with the rain. The skipper lay on a bunk trying to ignore the growing air of mutiny. We told each other that it was a pity that we hadn't brought our good clothes with us, so that we could all go to church. We only had our moleskin trousers, jumpers and wellies with us, and we agreed among us that we would feel embarrassed going among people who were in their Sunday best. No – not everybody agreed. I'm wrong in saying that.

'I survived German shells and bullets,' says Lawdy, 'and I don't think a disapproving glance from the occasional church mouse is going to do me any harm!'

Lawdy was like that – always doing the unexpected. Off he went in the rain, dressed in his black gansey and moleskin trousers, sou'wester and wellies. Two hours later, he returned with the news that nobody had given him a second glance. Although he was shivering, and looked as if he was soaked to the skin, he seemed, for some unknown reason, to be in better humour than when he left us. The skipper was still snoozing on a bunk, pretending not to be listening to our grumbles.

'Go on, Skipper!' I says. 'Are you awake, Skipper? Why don't you give Calum there a sip of brandy from your first-aid box!'

The skipper immediately sits up, gives the key to the first-aid box

A good shot of herring

to the cook, saying, 'Why don't you do as Soolivan says! Since everyone is feeling under the weather, pour everyone a tot of brandy!'

When the cook fetched out the brandy-bottle, we saw that it was empty.

'Never mind, cook,' says Lawdy, 'you're doing your best! Make a cup of strong black tea for me while I get changed.'

As I said, Lawdy had returned to us from church, brimful of the milk of human kindness.

'Was it a good sermon, then?' says the Skipper, wondering if Lawdy had caught a dose of religion. Pulling on his dry clothes at the door of the galley, Lawdy says, 'It was all about peace and peacemakers.'

He came and sat at the table and hurriedly downed his cup of black tea. Then, with a grin on his face, he says, 'The sky is clearing up, boys, and we should all go for a stroll through the town. I think I know where we might get something a bit tastier than a cup of bitter black tea!'

And that's what we did. The five of us trooped off the 'bauldie', heartened by Lawdy's bright new spirit. As we walked into the town, he filled us in with the details of a discovery he had made while on his way back from church. While standing for a few minutes in a doorway, sheltering from the rain, what did he see but two young men leaving a pub by the back door. One of them was tucking a bottle inside his jacket.

Lawdy took us to the very place where he had made the sighting. Without a word passing between us, the five of us stood watching the pub door. Before long, a wee man popped his head out, looked this way and that and then stepped out smartly, stuffing a half-bottle in his hip pocket. He came in our direction, so we suddenly pounced on him. After he got over his fright, the fella told us that he appreciated the seriousness of our thirst all right. But he told us not to expect any favours from the pub owners, as we were strangers in the town. 'You can have a drink out of my half bottle,' says the fellow.

The milk of human kindness must have been all over Oban that Sunday!

We all refused the fellow's kind offer, explaining that what we needed was a frothy pint of cold beer.

'You can help us get our beer,' says Lawdy, 'by telling us what we have to do to get the door to open!'

The wee man told us that we had to give two loud thumps on the door followed by two light taps. Fair enough: we approached the door with Lawdy in the lead. He thumps and taps as instructed and, sure enough, the door opens. Within, we saw the man in charge – a mean-tempered fellow looking like an overweight bare-knuckle

fighter, a big beer-belly on him and thick muscular arms. I had seen his kind often enough – a boxer who had won a handful of fights, then lost a hundred; had become a wrestler in middle-age and, because of his cauliflower ears and ugliness, was in demand as a bouncer in back-street dives. Through the tobacco smoke, we could see behind him twelve happy punters drinking at the bar. Our thirst became almost unbearable.

'What do youse want?' says the pug, pumping out his chest.

'Sorry to disturb!' says Lawdy, all apologetic-like. 'We're from the Islands and a friend of ours . . .'

'Guests of the landlord only!' says the pug and, without saying another word, he closes the door.

We all agreed that we were unhappy with the situation. You could hear the door being bolted, a sure sign that the landlord did not want our custom. Lawdy thumps and taps the door once more but much more gently this time. Nothing happens. Then he thumps the door so hard that the noise is heard three closes away. Instantly, the bolt is withdrawn and the door flies open. Looking uglier than before, the doorman's face says it all.

Lawdy speaks as a gentleman should. 'I'm sorry to bother you again but I don't think you were listening the last time!'

'I've friggin' listened to too much already,' says the fellow, flexing his muscles. 'You're not wanted here and if you knock this friggin' door once more I'll flatten youse intruding friggen teuchters into the bay!'

The door closed and was bolted as before.

'What bad language the fellow has on the Sabbath day!' says Lawdy. 'There's not going to be any room for us at this particular inn! Come on then, boys, we might as well go back to the bauldie!'

Military Medal or no, Lawdy was a peaceable sort of fellow. You've got to give him that. And if it had been left to him, the foul-mouthed fellow within the inn would have been left to think that the

Calum Dhòmhnaill Bhàin, alias 'Lawdy'

teuchters at the door had left in fear of his wrath. Lawdy turns away from the door and so do the other boys. Not me! No, siree!

'Wait a minute now, Calum,' says I, preparing to enquire further. 'I'm about to teach that gorilla a quotation from the Old Testament that has just come to me'

'What's that?'

'"Beware Soolivan when he is parched on the Sabbath!"'

I thump the door, which is immediately and loudly unbolted. Suddenly, the door flies open and the doorman steps forward with a screw-top in his fist, ready to crown the offender. He hesitates when he sees that he is no longer dealing with a six-footer but with a fellow at least four inches shorter. I don't wait to explain my mission. Putting my weight on my right foot, I punch him with my best straight right, bang on the button of his chin. The screw-top flies out of his hand. The strength drained out of the pug at the knees and he crumples on to the floor like a sack of potatoes. Stepping over his chest, I look back at the lads.

'What are you waiting for? This way to the drinks counter!'

The barman didn't say a word – just served us with the drinks we ordered. The drinkers round the place pretended that they hadn't seen a thing. Lawdy drank his dram in a single gulp. You could see that he was scared that when the doorman recovered there would be an almighty shindig. For myself, I was not in the least bothered, for I had often enough seen how big, loud-mouthed fellows react when the stuffing has been knocked out of them. As I expected, when the doorman came round, he wouldn't even look in our direction.

'How on earth,' says I to Lawdy, 'how did we ever manage to beat the Ceusar's army if you are a typical British hero?'

Lawdy only smiled.

'If you had been at church this morning, you would have heard a sermon about peace and goodwill. Even you would have accepted that it's always better to turn the other cheek.'

'You mean to say that if the fellow had managed to hit me with the bottle, I should have invited him to have a second go?'

Lawdy didn't have an answer to that. How could he? How could a man who had been decorated for killing Germans in France say anything about turning the other cheek? Of course, you have to remember that Lawdy is one of the Campbells of Brocair who have always had a twisted way of thinking. Lawdy's brother Kenny was made in the same mould, and so is their cousin John Murdo. Upstanding fellows they are in a way, but always hell-bent on causing arguments when they come in here for a ceilidh. They refuse to believe that the cold in Canada can split rocks or that, in the Dardanelles, the heat of the sun was so powerful that you could fry eggs on the 'prypan' without having it over a fire. Kenny even maintains that there is no such thing as Eskimos in North America and John Murdo believes that the world is flat. What can you do with blockheads like that? I hope to goodness that they won't come in here tonight!

MURDER AT SEA

We must have been about two hundred miles south-west of Ireland and heading out. It was a beautiful, calm summer's day. The grey mists of June were suspended somewhere between the sea and the sky. On deck, the crew were busy as usual, some painting, some chipping and so on – everyone absorbed in his work.

From where we were on the fo'c'sle, my mates and I spotted three officers on the bridge, acting as if they were arguing. One of them came on to the wing of the bridge and looked through his binoculars at something up ahead of us. We stood up to have a dekko but couldn't see anything but an area of turbulence on the surface of the sea ahead. As we watched, a huge shape rose out of the turbulence, less than a mile from where we were. It was as big as a Lewis black-house, big and dark grey. All around it, the sea looked as if it was boiling.

It was a whale, of course, a monster of a creature. What a spectacle! It sank for a while. When it surfaced, it leapt clean out of the sea, and when it smacked back down, the noise it made was like the crack from a rifle.

As the ship approached, we realised that what we had seen was not one creature but three. There was one giant right enough, but every so often two smaller creatures also broke surface. These two were killer whales, black animals with white under-bellies that we frequently see in the summertime in the Minch. *Mucan breac*, or piebald whales, we call them. But until that day, I hadn't realised that the *mucan breac* were so fast and agile, and so vicious. *A sheòid,* my heart nearly stopped when I saw what they were doing to a huge whale, many times bigger than themselves.

With us on deck was Gerry Cooney, one of our deck-hands – a young educated Irishman who, I believe, ended up as captain of a Cunarder. He was a mine of information.

'Killer whales stalking a blue,' says Gerry. 'They'll get her in the end. The blue whale is the biggest creature in creation, but not the best able to defend herself, for she has no teeth.'

The killers were like stray dogs tearing at a sheep which was trying hard to escape to safety. The blue threshed and plunged but could not throw off her hunters. The Captain slowed the ship down for fear that we might collide with the animals. A collision with them might have sent us to the bottom, for although she was a happy enough ship, she was just an old, Clyde-built tramp with plates and rivets that sometimes groaned with old age. When we were directly abreast of the struggle, the blue whale surfaced about two hundred yards to port of us. Her movement was slow and she was obviously losing her struggle. The two killers rose as well, tearing at her head. The sea was churning white but a red underwater fountain suddenly sprang from the victim and it was like oil spreading on the sea. The pool of red was flat calm. What a horrible sight it was. Everyone on deck was yelling and making a terrific din with hammers and any tools they could get hold of, trying our hardest to distract the killers. An officer, carrying a rifle, appeared on the port wing of the bridge and we heard him shout, 'Leave her alone, you murdering bastards!'

He raised the rifle to his shoulder, but before he could fire, the Captain arrived on the scene and took the gun off him.

'Our hero arrived too late with his artillery!' says Gerry. ''The killers have ripped most of her tongue out by now.'

As a boy in Galway in Ireland, Gerry had seen a pack of killer whales attacking pilot whales which were following a herring shoal. According to him, the tongue of a mature blue whale can be as heavy as a full-grown bull. Anyway, that was the way of it! The scene of slaughter slipped by the ship. But for quite a long time, you could see astern of us where the poor blue whale had given up the struggle. It was a sad sight, a widening pool of stillness on the surface of the Atlantic with the body of the whale like an upturned barge in the middle of it. I have sailed the Seven Seas from the Tropics to the icy edges of the Arctic, from Shanghai all the way to Buenos Aires, and have never once come across creatures as determined and vicious as those murderous killers. And to tell you the truth, the sight of them sickened me so much that I never again went for a swim in the sea, no matter how hot the weather or how calm. Not a toe would I venture into the briny, in case one of those ruddy brutes mistook it for bait!

My Lucky Moon

In my young days, it was normal for many of the old folk in our village to bow to the sickle moon and to say a wee rhyme, thanking her for coming back out of the darkness. So far as our family was concerned, the sickle moon was not important. But the full moon was quite another matter. For as far back as I can remember, *gealach bhuidhe abaich an eòrna** was a kind of mascot for me. The reason

* The yellow ripening moon of the barley.

for that was that there happened to be a full moon and a spring tide on the night I was born, and apparently MacIver's widow at No. 15 told my mother that the full moon would bring me good fortune as long as I lived. A lot of my friends thought it very strange since I grew up, that I had a habit of looking up at the moon to see whether my luck was in or out.

We left Liverpool heading for Buenos Aires on a clear moonlit night. I bowed to the moon when I saw that she was full. There were other Gaels with me on the ship – boys from Uist and Barra, all of them Catholic. It wasn't long until I discovered that I was the only Protestant in the crew. Not that the other lads gave a tinker's cuss about that. As you know, when young Gaels are together deep-sea, religion is far from their minds. With playing cards and drinks in our hands, we were as happy a crew as ever sailed from a British port. Unfortunately, there was one rotten apple on board – a lean, scowling hard-man called Paddy Manson who kept himself to himself for most of the time. He came from Liverpool. No-one liked being in his company, for he was discontented and crabbed, always complaining about this or that. You knew at once when he was in a foul mood, for the mouth on him puckered up into a kind of snarl. I'm not exaggerating. But I want you to understand that, from the first, I didn't take to that fella Manson.

Because I was not of the same religion as himself, Manson had the knife in me from the start. Every time I happened to be in his company, he put me down with sarcastic comment about my 'stupid way of speaking'. Mocking me to my face he was, and though I pretended that his mockery didn't bother me, it used to get me churned up inside. Manson was the kind of fella who couldn't live without having a whipping-boy – somebody on whom he could pick whenever he felt like it. As you can imagine, it didn't sit at all comfortably with me to find that, out of all the seamen on board, he had chosen me as the one to suffer. Many's the time my temper boiled but, looking back, I suppose that I didn't feel fluent enough in English in them days to give as good as I got. He definitely had a way with words, and cruel though his words were, the rest of the crew couldn't help but smile at things he said. You get the picture.

The temperatures shot up as we pushed into the Tropics. In the meantime, things between Manson and me became cooler and cooler. I knew in my bones that there would be a collision between us before the voyage was over. One night when I was on watch, Donnie Mabach, one of the Uist boys, came to me and put a word in my ear.

'No matter what abuse Manson throws at you, don't raise a hand to him. He is the worst kind of Scouser – the sort who was born with a knife in his hand.'

'Tonight is a dark moonless night,' I says, 'and I wouldn't take him on. But in a fortnight's time there will be a full moon and that will be a different matter.'

Donnie Mabach says, 'Remember that the moon you see when you're in the South Atlantic is a different one from the one we see back home!'

He was very concerned for me, for he knew that I was in a jam. When we docked in Buenos Aires, the crew prepared to go ashore. A couple of the Island boys had invited me to go with them but I told them that, because of Manson, it would be best if I went my own way.

I was first off the ship. Dressed in my Sunday best I was. I thought it likely that the crew would frequent the pubs down by the waterfront, so I walked about half a mile from the docks and went into the first hotel I came to. Oh, you can understand that I was not happy being away from my pals, for I knew that they would have a good *Hóro-Gheallaidh*!*

What an exciting place Buenos Aires is! The air is good and the people are good-looking, especially the girls and young men. As soon as I sat in the hotel lounge and ordered a drink, a senorita came across to greet me. A beautiful girl she was, about my own age, with fine skin and raven-black hair down her back. She didn't have a word of Gaelic – and not much English either! Nor did I know a word of her language. But it is amazing how easy it is for a young couple to communicate when they have romance on their minds. An hour passed, myself and the senorita drinking tequila and learning words from each other. We had reached the stage of holding hands when I heard loud laughter and conversation approaching the lounge door. In the twinkling of an eye, a mob of our crew, Manson included, came bursting through the door. All of them had had drink taken. They made for me and my friend. Manson brought up a chair and sat at the table directly opposite the senorita.

'Your shipmates aren't good enough for you, MacLeod!' says Manson, his lip curled into the usual snarl. 'Is that it, MacLeod?'

The senorita stood up but Manson bellowed to her to sit down. Terrified, the girl did as she was told. Even though she couldn't understand his language, she understood his meaning. Since that night I have often been annoyed with myself for allowing the girl to be treated like that. And I cannot now explain why I didn't deal with the Scouser there and then. Manson again turned on me and continued to taunt me and to molest the girl. Now, I can honestly say that I wasn't afraid of him. Indeed, I was not! I'm telling you the truth. I wasn't afraid of him, though I had come to realise that he was a very

* A lively celebration.

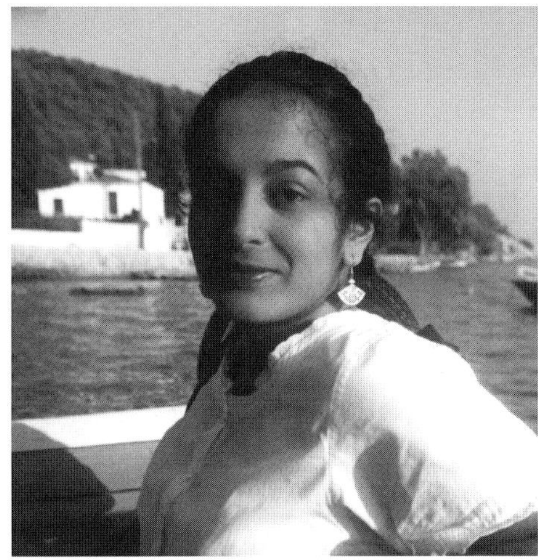

dangerous fella! Perhaps the fact that we were in a foreign country caused me to hold back, but I was struggling hard to control the rage that was building up inside me.

My old friend Donnie Mabach was once more beside me. He says to me in Gaelic, 'Now's your chance, a sheòid, to get your own back! Your friends are around you to make sure that he fights fair!'

Hearing the sound of a language that he couldn't understand, Manson flew into a bellowing rage. It was as if you had thrown a glass of whisky on the fire. He thumped me right between the eyes and I fell backwards on the floor with the table and broken glass all over the place. As I said, I had come in my best suit and did not fancy fighting dressed like that. I sat on the floor dazed, my clothes soaked with tequila. Still sitting on the floor, I put my hand to my forehead and found a lump the size of half an egg. The Gaels were yelling at me to get on my feet and pay Manson for what he had done. But if they were shouting loudly, then Manson's voice was even louder, shouting abuse at me and prancing around jabbing and swinging, in anticipation of what was to come. I got up slowly, and although I felt like belting him, I left my hands hanging by my side.

Donnie Mabach was shouting at me in Gaelic, 'Go on, Soolivan – hit him now, or none of us will ever again consider you a true Leódhasach!'

I headed for the hotel door with the whole mob shouting after me that I was a spineless coward. It was painful for me to listen to their insults, but I didn't look back, just kept going until I boarded the ship. I took off my suit, hung it up, sponged it as clean as I could. The inside of me was on fire with rage.

Within ten minutes, I was in my working togs – simmit, dungarees and sand-shoes. When I went for a wash and saw the state of my face, I was so angry that I cried. An hour passed and then I heard the sound I had been waiting for. From the port-hole, I could see a bunch of our

A pretty senorita

lads laughing and singing as they approached the gangway and began to climb on board. It wasn't long until they started to come down into the saloon. As usual Manson was in the lead. He made straight for me.

'Ah, here's the yellow-belly who refuses to fight for his woman!' he shouts, bending over me so the spittle from his snarling lips was spraying into my face. 'You're a spineless coward, MacLeod. Now I'm going to give you one more chance to prove yourself, and if you decide to run away this time, I swear to God that I shall dump you overboard.'

I got up smartly and, as I did so, I began to wrap a handkerchief round my fist

'Manson,' says I, 'if you're a religious man, now's a good time for you to say your prayers. You've just arrived at the end of the line!'

Manson threw off his jacket and showed me his right, threw a left hook, then tried to connect with a right pile-driver. He needn't have bothered! With my sand-shoes on, I was like a stormy petrel in flight. The saloon was small but not so small that it prevented me from dodging and jinking. When he found that he couldn't corner me, he stopped flailing about with his arms.

'Come on then, nancy-boy,' he says. 'Let's see if you can hit me!'

Well, he didn't have long to wait. With all the pent-up tension and hatred of weeks built into it, my right fist connected with his jaw. He reeled back and I knew at once that the fight was over. His head hit against the stanchion in the bulkhead and he crumpled to the bottom of it – out cold!

Gléidh mi, I thought I had killed him. As the floor on which he sat turned red, Manson's face turned grey. I would not have believed that so much blood could have been inside the one man. What a mess! One of the boys went shooting up the stairs looking for help. Everybody was quiet, thinking that Manson was a goner. The First Officer duly arrived with a first-aid box and immediately departed to call for an ambulance to take Manson to hospital. When he returned, the officer began to question the crew as to how Manson had got hurt. The boys were unanimous. Manson, they said, had come on board reckless with alcohol, had reeled at the foot of the stair and had fallen against the stanchion. In a sense, all of the evidence they gave was true!

I was at the gangway leading off the ship when Manson was being carried ashore on a stretcher. He opened his eyes and tried to speak.

'You'll be all right, old son,' says I, taking him by the hand. 'In a way, tonight was a lucky night for us both. The full moon over Buenos Aires Bay saved your life!'

A voice at my elbow says, 'What pagan rubbish are you talking now?'

It was my friend Donnie Mabach, who had evidently forgiven me for not tackling the Scouser in the hotel lounge, earlier in the evening.

'A charaid,' says I, 'if it had not been a full moon tonight, the *tàrnach* that I landed on Manson would have knocked the fellow to eternity and might well have earned me the Argentinian gallows!'

I spent the next hour ironing my Sunday suit but feeling quite depressed. There was only one way to rescue the evening! I got dressed, and as I was passing the saloon, I looked in and saw the boys playing cards and sharing a bottle of tequila. They hailed me as they would hail a hero. They offered me a glass but I refused it, telling them that I had urgent business ashore.

'Off to visit Manson in the hospital?'

'Manson's path and mine will never cross again,' says I. 'I'm off to the hotel to see what luck I have with the senorita under the light of the full moon!'

Fairies in Philadelphia

When I was a little boy in short breeks, Mòr MacIver, who was Tarmod Iomhair's widow at No. 15, made an important discovery. Mòr was a crafty, intelligent brand of *cailleach*! She was also gifted with having the Second Sight. And because she had the Second Sight, everybody was a little bit afraid of her. In those days, if you had 'the Eye' as it was called, you also had a certain amount of clout in the community. But only with some folk, mind you! Not everybody was afraid of her, and that included me.

One day, when Mòr was down in the croft weeding the potatoes, she discovered that 'pin-kellans' had inhabited her fields of oats and barley overnight. She reported her discovery to this person and that, and being who she was, nobody was willing to question what she said – and least of all, the children. My wee brother Kellan was afraid of the old lady and would never look her in the eye. Unlike Kellan, I liked Mòr! Maybe, that was because she and I had a lot in common, in the sense that we both had a lot of natural cunning.

When Mòr came up with the news of the 'pin-kellans', she gave the neighbours plenty to talk about. What kind of creature were those little 'pin-kellans' that were in the barley and oats at No. 15? Mòr let out that the creatures have human form but, unlike English fairies, they don't have any wings and unlike Gaelic little-folk, they migrate about the countryside so that you're never sure whose barley-field they have occupied. Children wanted to hear more.

'Och, no!' she says, ' they don't have wings! The "pin-kellans" are like humans and from what I have seen of their behaviour, like some of my human neighbours, they are mischievous little buggers!'

Now that I have grown to be a man, I don't think it's any coincidence that the name given to the creatures inhabiting the *arbhar* at No. 15 is very like the nickname of my younger brother Kellan, who, while he was growing up, was the bane of Widow Mòr's life!

One day, when Kellan and I were bare-legged *brogaich* skipping free-range about the crofts, along with my sister' Lydie, Mòr called to us to come over at once and she would show us the wonderful creatures she had discovered living on her croft.

'First of all, children, see the mess those creatures have made in the arbhar* last night!' she says.

What a mess! The field of barley looked as if a herd of cattle had stampeded through a quarter acre of it.

'Now, come on down here, children,' she says, 'and see the tiny, little "pin-kellans" who must have held their annual ball in our field. They must have had a lot of fun, right enough!'

The thing about those tiny creatures was that they were perfectly camouflaged among the gold and green of her oats and barley. So much so, that narry a one of them could I see – however hard I tried. Although Mòr took us to the very edge of the barley field and had them pointed them out to us, only my sister Lydie actually saw them. In the end, Kellan's eyes and mine were watering with eye-strain. My sister Lydie saw them at once and Mòr said that we should be proud of our little sister, for she was the only one of us who had 'the Eye'.

Mòr warned us that if we ever had to go near the cornfields – for example when going to Tobair a' Bhúidseir [Butcher's Well] for a couple of pails of water – we should beware of what the 'pin-kellans' might do to us. Apparently, some of them were aggressive little warriors, always carrying a bunch of tiny darts in their mouths. You were safe enough passing them, so long as their eyes were closed. But if their eyes were open, they were inclined to blow one of their tiny darts at you whenever you turned to go away. One dart could give you arthritis and your joints would seize up. Mòr claimed that a number of folk in the community had been hit by a dart like that when they were young, for example, Warra and Catrìona Ruadh. That really was scary. None of us wanted to end up like Warra or Catrìona Ruadh, both of whom were bent over double with arthritis, like a couple of staples!

Owing to our fear of getting a dose of arthritis, we children never again plucked up the courage to go 'swimming in the corn-field' on Cnoc nan Arbh – a favourite, forbidden pastime among children, all over the island. Indeed, from the day that Mòr MacIver let the cat out of the bag, by sharing with us the secret of her discovery, I doubt

* Standing oats and barley.

if a single child ever swam the fields on the hill between No. 11 and No. 15.

Now my friend, I'll let *you* in on a secret – a secret I have never shared with a living soul. It will be a secret only between ourselves. I told you the story of my service in the 'Malishy'. Well, shortly after I came home from that painful experience, I wandered down the crofts one golden, moonlit evening. It was the autumn and the fields of barley and oats were ready for the scythe. Well, a strange thing happened that evening. I arranged that Mòr MacIver's 'pin-kellans' had their annual ball in the barley of No. 15. Yes, no harm in admitting it, now that the grand old *cailleach* with the Second Sight is long since gone! I will never tell anybody who the belle of the ball was that night! But she was a 'beautag'!

Strange as it might seem, the 'pin-kellans' of my childhood followed me to the United States of America. While I was in that country, I wandered over to the City of Brotherly Love – Philadelphia. Myself and a few of my pals went to a circus there. They had all sorts of strange and wonderful things on show: a man who was 'bigger than Solomon', passing his time in front of crowds, tearing huge big copies of J.D. Williams's catalogues in half! There was the Fattest Woman in the World, who was as fat as a September bullock and had a voice like a foghorn! At another booth, we were invited in to see three pygmies from Africa.

As soon as I saw those three little fellows sitting on the floor with half a dozen darts in their mouths, I recognised them at once as being members of the tribe living in Mòr MacIver's barley field. Their skin was painted green and they wore mottled green clooties, so that they were well camouflaged against the forest painted on boards behind them. Each of them had a blowpipe. With his eyes closed, one pigmy after another blew a dart that hit a bull's-eye on the target with every shot. You just wouldn't believe the talent they had. Everything fitted Widow MacIver's description exactly, except that the Philadelphia 'pin-kellans' were about three feet taller than those living in Cnoc nan Arbh! That did not surprise me a bit! In America, everything has to be bigger and better!

The booth-master offered a dollar to anyone who could hit the bull's-eye using the blow-pipe – even with his eyes open. No-one who tried was able to hit the target, never mind the bull's-eye.

The booth-master told the audience that, back home in Africa, anyone hit by a pigmy's dart has only a few minutes to live. It was obvious to me that Widow Marion was understating the damage that could be done by a dart from a No. 15 'pin-kellan'!

If I could, I would have boxed up those three pigmies in 'Filly' and posted them home to my sister Lydie.

Chapter Four

The Downward Spiral

In 1917, with the First World War still raging throughout Europe, Lord Leverhulme purchased the Isle of Lewis and soon afterwards began to draw up ambitious plans to improve communications and create new industries which would transform the lives of the islanders. The war ended in November 1918 with the signing of an Armistice, but for the people of Lewis and Harris the Armistice did not end their suffering. Within the first few hours of 1919, more than 200 Royal Naval Reservists returning frpm active service lost their lives when the yacht Iolaire *foundered on the Beasts of Holm when less than twenty minutes' sailing from the pier at Steòrnabhagh.*

Many of the soldiers and seamen who had fought in the war came home strongly opposed to the wealthy ruling classes, whom they blamed for the huge loss of life and misery that the war had brought. When Lord Leverhulme began to put his plans into operation, some of the ex-servicemen became increasingly opposed to his declared aims of uprooting the islanders' identity as independent crofter-fishermen.

The recession that was to become the Great Depression began to threaten Leverhulme's industries worldwide. Resistance to his plans for Lewis was unabating and, having already spent huge sums in the island, Leverhume decided to call a halt to his development schemes. In 1923, he abandoned his Lewis enterprises altogether, and gifted his estate to the islanders, to be administered by an elected body called the Stornoway Trust.

The collapse of the Leverhulme schemes in Lewis resulted in widespread unemployment for hundreds of workers. In the mid-1920s, more than a thousand young men and women emigrated to Canada and the USA. It is not known whether, at that time, Soolivan re-entered Canada as someone already holding a Canadian passport. In those days, it would have been comparatively easy for him to 'jump ship' at Halifax and, during the next two chaotic and lawless decades, to pass reasonably freely between Canada and the United States. What we do know for certain is that, during the Prohibition era of the 1920s and the Great Depression of the early 1930s, he spent several years in North America, moving from place to place as the proverbial 'rolling stone', occasionally earning a living on the edge of the law. In the late 1920s, he served as a seaman on an American cargo-ship out of San Francisco. Through no fault of their own, he and his non-American shipmates were abandoned at Sydney to fend for themselves.

THE USA

After the First World War, laws were passed prohibiting the manufacture, transportation, import, export and sale of alcoholic drink in the United States. This was the era of Prohibition, which lasted nationally from 1919 to 1933. Even after the Prohibition laws were repealed, some states continued to enforce them. Oklahoma, Kansas and Mississippi were 'dry' until 1948.

While Prohibition did much to reduce the consumption of booze, illicitly distilled 'moonshine' continued to be widely available at speak-easies and other underground drinking-dens. Large quantities of booze were smuggled in from Canada and from the French islands of Saint-Pierre and Miquelon situated at the mouth of the St Lawrence River. Home-brewing became popular and 'Malt & Hop' stores popped up across the country. Criminal gangs became active in the 'bootlegging' (importation), manufacture and distribution of booze. Al Capone, whose parents were Sicilian immigrants, became the most ruthless and infamous bootlegger of the Prohibition era. Organised along the lines of a feudal Italian criminal society, his gangsters behaved violently and became increasingly daring due to new inventions – the machinegun and the motorcar. With alcohol production largely in the hands of criminals, the quality of the product varied widely. There were many cases of people going blind or suffering from brain damage after drinking 'bathtub gin' made with industrial alcohol or various poisonous chemicals As a result, tens of thousands of victims suffered paralysis of their feet and hands. The considerable revenue that accrued from the sale of alcohol before Prohibition was no longer available to the American treasury. So much government money was spent trying to maintain law and order that the country's coffers were being seriously depleted.

In October 1929 the stock market crashed, wiping out 40 per cent of the paper value of common stock and triggering a worldwide depression. By 1933, the value of stock on the New York Stock Exchange was less than one-fifth of what it had been four years earlier. Business houses closed their doors, factories shut down and banks failed. Farm income fell by some 50 per cent. By 1932 approximately one out of every four Americans was unemployed. The core of the problem was the disparity between the country's productive capacity and the ability of people to consume. Great innovations in production methods during and after the First World War raised the output of industry beyond the purchasing capacity of US farmers and wage earners. To add to the misery of thousands of farming households, the very soil on which they raised their crops became sterile for, throughout the 1930s, and in particularly from 1935 to 1938, a severe drought hit the Great Plains states and violent wind and dust storms ravaged a huge area and turned it into what became known as the 'Dust Bowl'. Not until President Franklin D. Roosevelt became president in 1938 did the USA begin to recover from its economic and social malaise. Realisation of the industrial potential of the USA began during the Second World War and its economic strength has continued to grow ever since.

Owing to the special and intimate relationships that had been forged between the United States and European economies after the First World War, the Great Depression quickly turned into a worldwide economic slump. The United States had emerged from the war as the major creditor and financier of postwar Europe, the national economies of which, had been greatly weakened by the war itself. The Depression hit hardest those nations that were most deeply indebted to the United States – particularly Germany and Great Britain. In Germany unemployment rose sharply so that, by early 1932, it had reached 25 per cent of the workforce. Britain was less severely affected, but its industrial and export sectors remained seriously depressed until the Second World War.

The Democrat Franklin D. Roosevelt, who became president of the USA in 1932, initiated massive public-works projects to promote a recovery. Despite that intervention, mass unemployment and economic stagnation continued, though on a somewhat reduced scale. In 1939, unemployment dropped rapidly as American factories were flooded with orders from overseas for armaments and munitions.

Australia

In Australia and New Zealand, the Great Depression caused widespread unemployment and poverty. It hit the New South Wales economy with great severity, and not least in the city of Sydney where Soolivan and other members of the crew of an American freighter became stranded.

By 1932, unemployment in New South Wales, Australia's most populous state, reached a third of the workforce and factory output fell by nearly 40 per cent. Mainly because of social services payments, the state government, which had borrowed heavily for public works, had the highest level of public expenditure in Australia. Many people struggled on part-time work, or depended on charity or the dole. For thousands, unemployment also meant eviction, with the result that shanty towns of homeless people sprang up in many areas. Foreign seamaen such as Soolivan became sundowners, an underclass living by their wits.

Governments throughout the world found it difficult to solve their social and economic problems. One result of disillusionment was the rapid growth of radical or extremist political organisations which claimed that they could defend the interests of the workers where democratic institutions had failed. In New South Wales, a number of left-wing groups emerged advocating direct action, particularly in relation to opposing house evictions. On the right, nationalist and fascist-style organisations rapidly gained in membership.

In 1933 or 1934, Soolivan managed to return to the USA and, in due course, found himself in trouble with the law once more. On this occasion, he was given a short jail sentence in Jacksonville State Penitentiary, Florida. Short though the sentence was, Soolivan found himself in the company of convicts jailed for murder and other heinous crimes and planning to break out of 'the Pen' within hours. Terrified that he was being forced to participate in the break-out, Soolivan managed to alert the prison authorities. The cells were searched and a huge cache of arms was discovered. Knowing that his life was in danger, the prison authorities rewarded their informant with immediate release.

Soolivan began to travel through Texas and Mexico bound for the Panama Canal where, by hook or by crook, he intended to board a British ship and escape North America, never to return. Unfortunately, he was delayed in Mexico much longer than he intended.

Mexico

In the 1820s and 1830s, Mexico, newly independent from Spain, needed settlers in the under-populated northern parts of the country. An invitation was issued for people who would take an oath of allegiance to Mexico and convert to Catholicism, the state religion. Thousands of Americans took up the offer and moved, often with slaves, to the Mexican province of Texas. History was to prove that the Mexicans had invited a Trojan Horse on to their territory. Many of the new Texans were unhappy with the way the government in Mexico City was administering the province. In 1835, Texas revolted and, a year later, after several bloody battles, the Mexican President was forced to sign a treaty giving Texas its independence.

With skirmishing between the Republic of Texas and Mexico continuing, many people in the United States openly sympathised with the Texans, most of whom had been born in their country. In the end, the young Republic of Texas decided to join with the United States, and on 4 July 1845, the annexation gained approval from that country's Congress. Understandably, Mexicans were furious that its breakaway province had chosen to become an American state, and the undefined and contested border then became a major international issue. Both nations sent troops to enforce their competing claims, and in 1846, they went to war. With superior forces, the Americans pushed southwards and, in spite of suffering heavy casualties, entered Mexico City, their enemy's capital.

In February of the following year, a treaty was signed annexing the northern portions of Mexico to the United States. In return, the United States agreed to pay $15 million as compensation for the territory seized. The war cost the victors over $100 million and around 14,000 men killed in battle.

In Mexico, Soolivan found a country no more stable politically or economically than that from which he had departed. It was a poverty-stricken nation, which continued to feel bitterly resentful of the fact that, some ninety years earlier, the United States had annexed huge areas of its oil-rich land. In spite of the costly conflict between the two countries in the nineteenth century, there was a certain amount of cross-border traffic of people and goods between them in the twentieth. Nevertheless, English-speaking foreigners were not welcome in Mexico and were contemptuously called 'Gringos' – men who could not be trusted.

As Soolivan discovered to his cost, 'Gringos' broke the law at their peril! He became involved in an escapade that resulted in his being thrown into a large, overcrowded cell in the notorious Tuxpan Jail, where men and women were frequently degraded and held without trial, in conditions of appalling squalor.

Attacked by Frogs

When we reached Port Jackson near Sydney and unloaded our cargo of grain, there wasn't any cargo waiting for us to carry back to the States. The ship was docked there for about a fortnight, and we were fed-up awaiting word from Frisco. The agents came on board every second day but they had nothing for us but bad news. Depression had set in between the trading nations of the world. Eventually the ship's master paid off all his non-American crew and set off home 'light ship', leaving the five British members of his crew on the dockside watching our ship departing. It was a terrible situation to find yourself in. We didn't have much money in our pockets, no work, and nowhere to go. We were desperate to find a way of getting home and to avoid becoming destitute on the wrong side of the world. The Federated Union of Australian Seamen didn't show any interest in helping us to get on to an outward bound ship, for there was not enough work even for their own members. It seems that the Australian government didn't know how to handle the situation and ignored the hundreds of seamen left high and dry in the country's ports.

There was nothing for us to do in Port Jackson but bum around in waterfront pubs in the hope that a British ship would dock there and agree to give us a berth. British, or any other nationality! My money ran out – every last penny – so I was without lodgings, without booze and often even without bread. *A Dhia gléidh mi*, I never felt hunger like that. Talk of deprivation! I remembered the poverty back home when I was a child, right enough. During the black months of winter and spring, our families sometimes went hungry, but when they were really hard pushed, they could sneak down to the shore for seaweed or shellfish to stop the rumble in their bellies. They hated doing that, mind you, and felt humiliated doing it. Of course, it was different back home in the summer and autumn when you could feast on as much food as your belly could take: fish and turnips and potatoes and milk – everything of the best. But, in Australia, when

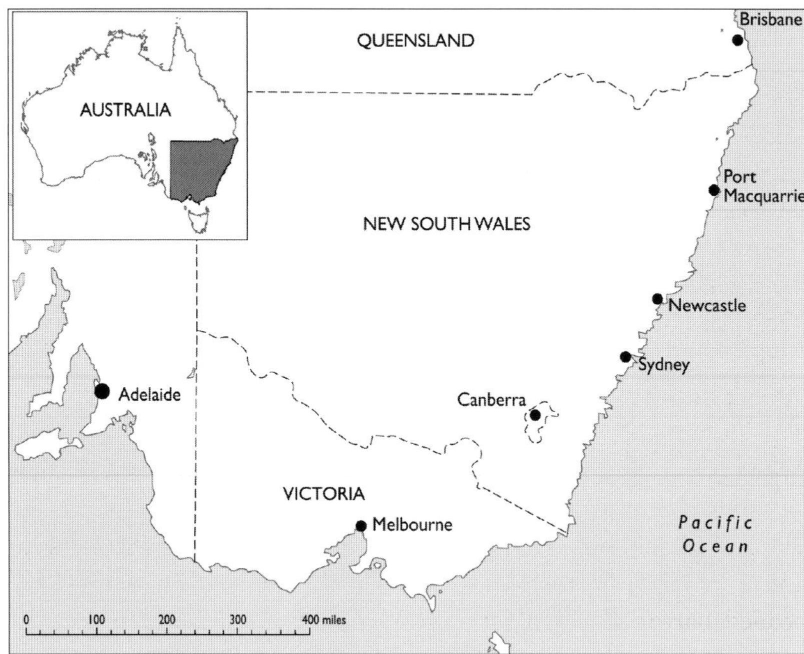

Map of Eastern Australia, showing the positions of Sydney and Newcastle

you were thrown on the rubbish heap, as we seamen were, there wasn't even a fistful of dulse or a mug of winkles that you could gather on the foreshore.

It was a depressing time for old Soolivan, I can tell you. A lot of thinking time and just sitting about wondering if you would ever escape the hunger and the loss of everything that you once had.

Though we didn't know it at the time, the Great Depression was affecting people all over the world and not just the east coast ports of Australia. Knowing that millions of people were suffering like us wouldn't have made much difference to me. When you're in a jam like that, you can only think of your own survival. Before two months were up, I had become an unshaven, bedraggled sundowner, a hobo, a tramp, a down-and-out living by my wits. Without work or income, and without home or prospects, I was forced to beg, scrounge and steal. I was a *cù gun urra* – the homeless dog of the old proverb, alive on a diet of hope! Socks were no more, and even the soles of my shoes were worn through, trekking round the back streets of Sydney pleading at every door for work or for charity. I carried all that I owned in a swag-bag no bigger that a Lewis duff!

The first real step forward came when the Australian government decided to build a new highway between Sydney and Newcastle – a city-port about one hundred miles to the north. There was a notice in the paper that unemployed men in New South Wales and Victoria were being offered work on the scheme. The wages offered were pretty poor but the most attractive part of the deal was that navvies were to be given three good meals a day. Three good meals a day, mind you! It sounded like the Relief of Lucknow!

For months my sundowner friends and I slept under the Woolloomoloo Rocks on the outskirts of Sydney. When news of the road-building scheme got around, everyone who was able to move took up his swag-bag and set off. You have never seen such an army of down-at-heel scruffs, all of them trudging north to report for work! As soon as we signed on, we got a meal of broth and meat and, after that, tea and buttered bread. Well, it's hard to believe it, but a lot of the fellas couldn't eat more than a few mouthfuls. Our stomachs had shrunk so much for lack of food that they just couldn't cope with a proper meal.

After dinner, work! Picks, shovels, sledge-bars, wheelbarrows and crowbars. Aye, and sweat and aching limbs! We hadn't exactly come to a schoolgirls' picnic, I can tell you! Far from it. Not a cloud in the sky and the sun beating down on you from early morning until late in the afternoon. Everywhere you looked, men hammering, pushing loaded barrows, shovelling – all in a stoor of clayey dust. After a week, we began to get the hang of it. My appetite improved and I began to put on muscle. The gangs of workers slaving away pushed the highway steadily north. A hard slog! By George, it was that! Once seafarers like myself began to feel better, our eyes began to wander to the east and to the horizon of the distant ocean. The further away from Sydney we moved, the further removed we became from the kind of life we knew and craved for. The seamen became discontented, for seafarers are never happy unless they have the cool salty breeze of the sea on their cheeks and the motion of a hardwood deck under their feet.

Navvying in an Australian desert in summer is every bit as hard as navvying in the frozen wilderness of the Canadian winter. On the New South Wales highway scheme, life was no different for the navvy than it had been on the Trans-Continental Railway. Get the hell out of here Soolivan, says I to myself! Well, that was the way of it, in the end. The seamen in the gang debated whether to remain with the scheme or to return to Sydney in the hope that, sooner or later, the deep-sea trade would return to normal. Having heard of our dissatisfaction, the gaffer came to us and we explained to him our feelings. He says, 'Don't be so daft as to give up your work here unless you have other work lined up. The Depression will be over in a few months and, by then, you will be within shouting distance of the port of Newcastle. But in the meantime, you've got to remember that you signed on to work here for a period of eight weeks. If you leave without a doctor's line, you won't be allowed to sign back on.'

What the man was saying was reasonable enough, and after listening to him, I thought that I would be crazy to go back to mooching around Sydney. As the old sea-dog saying goes, 'He who walks with head-no-eyes will fall in the mire!'

We were having our mid-morning smoke-o and, like most of the lads, I was sitting in the shade, behind one of the big canvas tents. Next to me was a Cockney – a lad of about nineteen. He had fallen asleep and was moaning – and no wonder! His back was sunburnt as red as a boiled lobster. When he woke up, we started to chat.

'Look,' I says, 'if you stand on tiptoe, you can see the Tasman Sea from here. How I envy those fellows who are out there right now, fifty miles off the coast, outward bound for the islands of Polynesia.'

'I'd give anything', he says, 'to be on a ship, a thousand miles from here, with the moon shining on the deck and watching the phosphorescence turning in the tide! Imagine being on a City-boat leaving here and not stopping until we docked in Tilbury!'

We were both pretty homesick. The two of us decided there and then to make a break for it. We agreed to make our way to the sea, then to follow the coast back down to Sydney. At our midday meal, we ate as much as we could. I managed to steal a loaf and the Cockney lad stole a leather water-bottle which was half full. We didn't even take our swag-bags. Off we went into the bush, heading for the shore. We figured that we were three or four miles inland, but between us and the seashore was a wilderness of rocky hillocks and dips covered in thorny bushes. It may have looked like three or four miles to the seashore as the crow flies, but we soon learned that the trek was going to be much longer than that.

Big clumps of thorn and boulders forced us to zigzag, making our way through where the scrub was thinnest. Looking as attractive as heaps of barbed wire some of the bushes seemed to be lying in wait for us. And once they managed to get hold of you, they were very reluctant to let go.

My Cockney friend says, 'Hell's a-cooking, Soolivan! I've already lost half my clothes to these blasted thorns! At this rate, I'll be bollock-naked before we reach the seashore!'

He made me laugh. In front of us, we saw two almighty rocks, each of them as big as all the *Trusachan* of Calanais put together. That gives you an idea of the size they were. When we got up to them, we threw ourselves down beside them in the shade. We were exhausted. No sooner had we sat down than we heard a noise like the sound of an approaching train. I swear that the earth began to tremble as the noise grew louder and louder.

The Cockney shouts to me, 'It's a bone-crushing earthquake, mite!'

Scared? I don't mind admitting that I was scared! We stood away from the rocks and immediately realised that the noise was made by hundreds of huge beasts stampeding in our direction. Big ugly beasts they were, jumping ten feet or more off the ground as they travelled.

'Holy Mother of God!' says the Cockney, 'Let's get back under the rocks or we'll be crushed to death!'

We dived for shelter and the beasts passed by us in a cloud of dust. As soon as the noise ended and the dust settled, the Cockney and I looked at each other. Not a word passed between us. We just started running as fast as we could, back up in the direction of the highway. Through the scrub we ran, as best we could, ignoring the hooks and barbs scratching our skin and tearing at our clothes. At last, we reached the road about two hundred yards apart, and a quarter of a mile from where our gang was working. We were exhausted.

When our workmates noticed us clambering on to the road, they rested on their picks and shovels. We arrived with them, stumbling along the road and half dead with fright and exhaustion.

'Where have you two beauties been then?' inquires the gaffer.

'We were in the bush,' says I, pulling thorns from my flesh. 'And we were attacked by a swarm of huge frogs. Six feet tall they were and they were jumping ten feet into the sky as they passed over us.'

'We were lucky not to be squashed flat by them!' says the Cockney, his face and chest like my own, criss-crossed with scratches.

When the gaffer heard our explanation, he belly-laughed, and his laughter was echoed all along the line.

'Frogs!' he shouts. 'Frogs! You ignorant Pommies! Have you never heard of Australian kangaroos?'

Now, the Campbell boys down the road there won't believe a word of what I'm after telling you. They're an ignorant bunch that lot! But, I tell you here and now, and it's the truth, I hadn't seen animals as big as that ever before. Sure, I had seen wallabies on the outskirts of Sydney. Those are smallish animals no more than three or four feet tall. But until that day, I had had no idea that kangaroos were bloody giants. But come to think on it, how was I to know what kangaroos looked like? I had never seen one before!

After that unfortunate incident, I was looked upon by the Australian navvies as a kind of village idiot. They no longer called me by my nickname 'Soolivan' but by the insulting name 'Froggy'. I didn't care for that much and, even if there had not been any other reason, I would have moved on. But of course, there were plenty more important reasons. I just hated the heat, the thirst, the dust and the fact that there did not seem to be any prospect of my ever seeing the ocean again.

Next time I decided to return to Sydney, I did it the easy way. I went to the gaffer and told him that I was resigning my commission. We shook hands and that was that.

Jock Tamson's Bairns

We followed the road back to the city of Sydney and were overjoyed when we sighted the ocean. The sun shone every day and, even at night, it wasn't too cold. I had become quite used to living in the open, without a roof over my head and without a bed to lie on at night. That didn't really bother me but, owing to the lack of food, I had become thin and pretty weak compared to the way I was in my heyday.

Having made it to Sydney, my mates and I made several journeys away from the city, sometimes south, sometimes west. It wasn't unusual for us, first thing in the morning, to be walking between five and ten miles from our base, trying to find somebody willing to give us chores to do about their houses. Sometimes folk took pity on us and gave us meals and other handouts in exchange for a few hours of labour. Seldom were we given money.

After those sorties into the countryside, we always returned to Woolloomooloo, our headquarters. Though we were alive by the skin of our teeth, there was a feeling of companionship amongst us and an almighty grudge against the shipping-line that had dumped us on the far side of the world.

For a time, our staple diet was hard-tack biscuits gifted by a bakery which used to supply ships but which was nearing bankruptcy because of the collapse of the maritime trade. News reached us that a couple of cargo-ships had docked at Newcastle. God knows how the news got to us and there was no way of finding out if the news was true. True or not, it suddenly offered us a beacon of hope and was enough to set us off on a hundred-mile trek to Newcastle.

We went along the banks of the Hawkesbury River, walking mostly at night but also part of the day. Padding through unknown territory under the stars reminded me of my lovesick days back home. As a teenager, I used to travel the fifty miles to and from Tolastadh, in the hope of seducing a night owl! *Bu dìomhain dhomh*! [A futile exercise!] Nothing ever came of my efforts there. It was all a boyish pipe-dream.

Some of our group were faster walkers than others. A Cornish fellow and I got in front and, after a few hours, lost sight of the others altogether. On the third day of the trek, we came across a farmhouse. A woman was outside it on a porch beating a rug. We were so hungry that we felt we had to ask her for something to eat. Who would have believed that Harry Lauder, the most famous Scot of our generation, helped us that day!

Harry Lauder wasn't in Australia at that time, but even in that remote place, his name was to the fore.

'Ahoy, lady!' cries the Cornishman. 'Excuse me, but can you give my friend and me a sandwich or even a piece of bread? We'll do any work you want.'

The woman looked in our direction, sized us up, then continued to beat the rug. You couldn't blame the woman for wanting to ignore us. By no means could you blame her! The couple of dirty vagabonds standing in front of her house wasn't a pretty sight. I walked right up to her.

'Please, lady-of-the-house!' says I with a broad smile. 'We've come all the way from Sydney to see you! We're on our way to ship out of Newcastle and we're starving. I mean real, rumble-belly starving.'

The woman's eyes lit up.

'A Scotsman, ain't ye?' Come on here so that I can have a dekko. Are you carrying your kilt in your tucker-bag?'

What a sight I must have been, unshaven and scruffy. She went round me, inspecting me just as my dog Diamond used to inspect a visiting tinker.

'Do you know Harry Lauder?'

'No,' says I. 'If you're looking for a good song, there's no better singer in New South Wales than "Cornish Harry" and he's standing right there!'

Cornish Harry (whose right name I have forgotten) had a go at singing a verse of 'Keep Right on to the End of the Road'. It was awful to listen to. The woman had a good laugh but clapped anyway. She showed us into the washhouse, then went to the house to get us something to eat. We could hear her singing beautifully, 'Keep right on to the end of the road'.

There were bars of soap and a water-pump in the washhouse and when the farmwife returned, she found us sparkling clean and shaven.

'Fair dinkum!' she shouts. 'In twenty minutes, you have peeled off twenty years!'

She had brought us a plate piled high with mutton sandwiches. Cornish Harry and I made short work of them, washed down with home-made lemonade. What a treat! The lady's name was Lindi. She told us that her brother had been killed serving with the Anzacs at Gallipoli. Her husband was also wounded there and, since coming home, had become housebound. We didn't see him. Lindi wasn't interested to hear our reasons for wandering about New South Wales. All she wanted to talk about was her hero, Harry Lauder, how his only son had been killed at the Front and how there was talk of the great man coming to Sydney to sing his famous songs. We kept on chatting to her on her favourite subject but our minds were only on filling our bellies, for we had no idea when we were likely to eat again.

A few miles on from the farm, we entered a little valley and found workmen there rigging a new camp. I think the camp was meant for workers before the opening of a silver mine. I'm not quite sure of that. It is such a long time ago! Anyway, we looked reasonably clean and respectable when we reported to the foreman's office and we got a couple of days' work there. Again we ate well at meal-times and, on the morning of the third day, we hit the road.

During our trek to Newcastle, I saw some strange animals and birds. Of course, we saw cattle and sheep, and the occasional horse. We also saw mean-looking, wild-dogs called dingoes which were light-brown in colour and went about in threes and fours. We were leerie of those animals, for some of them followed us for a time, skulking about in the bush. Sometimes they seemed to be sizing us up, and considering how they could get the better of us. On the other hand, they might have been hoping to come across scraps left over from our meals. If that was the case, then they chose to follow the wrong humans! Cornish Harry and I ate every scrap of food we could find. Anyway, as you can imagine, I sent quite a few stones whirring in its direction whenever any of the dingoes came within range.

There was one strange-looking creature that took our fancy. It was called a koala. It lived in the trees and moved slowly, as if it had all the time in the world. Watching it stretching its fore-paw to grasp a leaf on a tree was like watching a sleepy old *cailleach* getting out of bed to search for the *poit* under the bed! Not that I've ever watched an old *cailleach* doing any such thing!

We arrived at Newcastle, foot-sore, hungry and exhausted. Pretty lean we were too. Lean, unshaven, unkempt, and tattered! Strange though it might seem, we did not stand out in the crowd. The place was full of battered old sundowners like ourselves!

We discovered that ships did sometimes visit the port – a hopeful sign. But for Cornish Harry and me, there was no prospect of our getting a berth aboard one. The Australian Seamen's Union saw to it that the stranded foreigners didn't get a look-in. The money we had earned at the camp-site quickly trickled away through our fingers. Things looked really desperate and my friend was very downcast. One day, he says to me, 'Soolivan, we had better get back to Sydney.'

'By all means, you go back, old son,' says I, 'but Soolivan's feet will never walk that wilderness again and his ears will never again have to listen to that cackling kookaburra!'

Every day, twenty or thirty stranded seamen hung around at the waterfront, hoping to get a break. One day, Cornish Harry and I were standing behind sheds at the docks, watching a British ship coming in to berth at a wharf. A fine looking P&O boat she was, and I felt in my bones that she was the lady that was going to carry me away from Newcastle! I caught my friend by the sleeve.

'That ship was built on the Clyde,' says I, 'and it would take a good man to keep Soolivan and his friend from boarding her!'

'Stowaway?' says Harry. 'You're loco! We'd spend a year in jail.'

'Better the peace and quiet of a prison cell than hanging about here. Now you come with me,' says I, leading him by the arm towards the gatehouse. 'You keep your mouth shut and let your pal Soolivan do the talking!'

The gate policeman came out of his box as soon as he saw us two sundowners approaching. He stood with his hands on his hips and says, 'No-one is allowed inside here but dock employees, ship's crew and passengers.'

'And that includes us!' says I.

He laughed at my comment and smirked inwardly at our tattered appearance.

'The old story,' says he, 'And now you're about to tell me that you were wounded in the war and Australia owes you a berth on a ship!'

'Wounded in the war – yes, sir! Spot on!'

I continued to speak, but as I did so, I drew up my trouser-leg to reveal that there was a chunk missing out of my knee. 'But a berth on a ship – no, sir! I was at the Dardanelles and I'm sure a brave fellow like yourself was there also along with the Anzacs. And if you were, I know that you can understand why I wouldn't sail again on a ship even if you paid me a king's ransom. Landlubber I am, and landlubber I'll die!'

The man was a bit flummoxed. I reached into my shirt pocket and brought out an old letter which I had gotten from my sister, Màiri Kate, and which I carried to show who my next of kin was, in case I should kick the bucket unbeknowns.

'My brother sails on that P&O boat,' says I. 'His name is Alex MacLeod and he's Third Engineer. He sent me this letter asking me to look him up when he comes into Newcastle. Have a read of the letter yourself. Now would you like to come down to the gangway and verify what I'm saying with Alex himself? By the way, this gentleman here is our cousin Norman MacLeod.'

'How do you do?' says Cornish Harry solemnly.

I knew that the policeman was not permitted to leave the gate unattended. He was tempted to, but in the end, he thought better of it.

'Mind,' says the policeman, 'I'll be here until you fellows come off the ship and quit the dock!'

So far, so good! On we went. Cornish Harry and I started climbing the ship's gangway. A sailor stood at the head of the gangway, and when he saw us two ragamuffins approaching, he presented his baton.

'No need for a weapon, son,' says I, smiling for all I was worth.

My Cornish friend kept quiet as a mouse.

'Where are you from, mate?'

'Liverpool, but that's no business of yours!' he replies. 'What is more to the point – what do you want?'

Oh, the fellow was naturally quite edgy and suspicious. I told him that we were from the Old Country – sailors marooned on a foreign shore.

'Our business with this ship is this. The policeman on the gate told us that there's a cousin of ours on board here, serving as a crew member. He suggested that we try to see him before the ship sails.'

'The policeman told you that?'

You could see that the fellow was betwixt and between.

'You can see the policeman at the dock gate from here. You can go ask him if you don't believe us!'

'What's your cousin's name?' He brought out a check-list of crew members.

'Well, we have so many cousins sailing that I'm not sure who it is. It's probably Alex MacLeod, or perhaps it's John MacKenzie – that's my mother's sister's boy.'

'We haven't got any MacLeods or MacKenzies. We have a MacAllister, though!'

'No, I don't know anybody sailing of that name! Anyone Campbell?'

'We have an Alasdair Campbell.'

'That's him. That's my mother's Auntie Chrissie's boy! Lord save us, I haven't seen Alasdair for the past fifteen years. Great to see him again.'

A deck-hand was called to take us to my 'Aunt Chrissie's boy' and, as we trooped through the ship, I prayed that Alasdair Campbell was a Gaelic speaker. Thankfully he was. As it turned out, he was a lad from Gairloch, and when he returned my Gaelic greeting, I knew that he would agree that we were *càirdean* [kinsmen].

Alasdair Campbell arranged for me and Harry to get something to eat, but when I confessed to him my plan to stow away on the ship to Sydney, he refused to have anything to do with it. And who could blame him! To be honest, I was only interested in saving my own skin. During the Great Depression, it was a case of dog eat dog. And for sure, there was nobody going to look after anybody's skin but the guy living in it!

Well, Alasdair and a young deckhand showed us a big locker in which we could hide. The locker, full of blankets and other bed-linen, was normally kept locked when the ship was at sea. The Chief Steward, who was responsible for the key, was persuaded to leave the door unlocked and slightly ajar. Harry and I promised the lads who helped us that we would remain inside the locker for twenty-four hours until the ship was securely berthed at Port Jackson.

But, *a Thighearna*, within an hour of going into that hell-hole, surrounded by all those blankets, the place became like an oven and Harry and I thought we were going to suffocate for lack of air. We came out of our hidey-hole and started to make our way toward the deckhands' mess where we had eaten with Alasdair Campbell.

As luck would have it, the Second Officer coming off duty nabbed us. He bellowed into the crew's mess and, very soon, two strapping lads appeared and were told to march us up to the Captain's office. As we walked, I turned to the Second Officer. 'Before you put us in front of the Captain, do you think I might have a word with you in private?'

'I don't want to hear a word out of you!' he says.

Well, those were not the actual words he used, but you get my drift! No two ways about it, the man was only doing his duty. We reached the officers' quarters. The Second Officer hesitated as we passed one of the cabins – his own. He opened the door and told me to step inside. Cornish Harry flanked by the two crewmen, was left quivering outside.

'You have less than one minute!' says he.

'What I want to say will take less than that.' says I. 'Just imagine yourself in my position! Three months ago, I was a bosun on the *Santa Rosa*, a 15,000-ton American ship out of Frisco. The Depression hit us and all non-American crew were dumped in Port Jackson! Now, here I am, destitute and forced to wander all over this god-forsaken country, alive on charity. All I want from you, my friend, is to be allowed to hitch a lift down to Sydney!'

'You know that as the Second Officer I have to do my duty,' he says. 'It's the Captain who will decide the next step.'

A decent lad he was and I could see that he was sympathetic. I had one more go at him.

'This Depression', says I, 'is going to destroy the little maritime trade that's left! Within the next week or two, you might be made a sundowner just like me and, when that happens, no-one will give a tinker's cuss whether you live or die. But thank God for the kindness of the lads below decks there! Hearts of gold they have, even willing to share their food with us.'

He didn't say a word.

'For goodness's sake,' says I, 'we're all Jock Tamson's bairns! Just let us continue down the coast without a word to the Captain and once you berth at Port Jackson, we'll vanish into thin air!'

To cut a long story short, Cornish Harry and I were returned to life in the dark, airless locker to sweat it out among the blankets. By the time we arrived at Port Jackson, Harry and I were as thin as rakes and as weak as water. We had a thorough wash, and went ashore wearing clothes which Alasdair Campbell had left us before he went on duty. No-one gave us a second look as we passed through the dock gates.

Now, that experience taught me a lot. It taught me that when the going gets really tough, you must be bold and take every opportunity to ease your situation. You've got to be cunning to survive – especially when the full moon isn't shining over Port Mholair Bay! And so, my friend, if you should ever find yourself in a tight spot, try reminding the fellows in authority that we are all Jock Tamson's bairns. It works to your advantage sometimes. Not very often, in my experience. I would say maybe about once in a lifetime!

The Bonnie Girls of Suva

Every ship coming into Port Jackson raised my hopes that I might escape my poverty. I heard of an occasional vacancy right enough, but the place was hoaching with fellas desperate for work and I never managed to be at the front of the queue. Och, they were there from all over – Scots, English, Irish, Swedes, Dutch, all wanting to get away.

By chance, I met a Filipino who had been with me on a ship out of Los Angeles a couple of years back. A handsome lad he was too, with chocolate-coloured skin, friendly and down-to-earth, like most seamen you meet. He and I had always got on well together. As soon as he saw me on the other side of the street, he shouted a greeting, and very shortly we were exchanging news over a beer in a waterfront pub. It was the first beer I drank in many weeks and I didn't have any money to pay for it!

Life had treated the Filipino boy better than it had me. He was bosun on a tramp steamer trading between the east coast ports of Australia and the islands of the Pacific – New Hebrides, Fiji and Samoa. His ship, the *Island Freighter*, was an old tramp of less than 6,000 tons. She had just docked and was one man short. Funnily enough, I wasn't the first to be invited to join her crew. A couple of other fellows had turned the job down. They weren't interested in working the islands, they said. All they wanted was a ship that would travel westwards and carry them home to Blighty! Beggars can't be choosers, I thought, and within an hour of meeting the Filipino, I was introduced to Captain Dow, an old Geordie, who was glad to sign me on. I became a crew member of what deep-sea sailors of my generation would refer to as an old 'rust bucket'.

Well, you are over twenty and, although you probably would not admit it, I'm sure that you are practised at *caithris na h-oidhche** just the same as I was. Yessir! You would not be a true Gael if your hand had not reached no-go places by the time you were eighteen! But, *a bhalaich,* if you had been born on Viti Levu in Fiji, you would have frolicked before you had reached the age of twelve!

They were a handsome people, the Fijians. The men were big, strong, muscular fellows with rows of glinting white teeth on them, and jaws so powerful that you could imagine them to be able to crack a coconut! The women also were good-looking, with curvaceous bodies, bare breasts and come hither smiles. Oh, I'm telling you the truth! Fiji was the place to be – but only if you were a young Fijian! The people of Suva had only one thing on their minds. I suppose their friskiness had something to do with the kind of food they ate. Anyway, you could see them at it in doorways, behind tree-trunks, on the shore, both little and large, old and young. Now, although I was worldly wise and familiar with the habits of the human race, I had never been to a place where that kind of ploy was not played within walls, and with a certain amount of modesty. The Fijians did not bother with the white man's ways. Just got on with what came naturally.

We were met by canoes when we were still more than half a mile from Viti Levu, the biggest island of Fiji. They were full of young men and girls who were offering us coconuts, shells and other trinkets. As soon as we berthed, Captain Dow called the crew together and warned us not to have anything to do with the women of the island. He says, 'The men are so jealous and barbaric here that they wouldn't think twice before killing you if you so much as touched any of their females!'

The Captain told us about an incident that happened a couple of years previously, when two European sailors off his ship had frolicked with local girls. They were dragged to a secluded spot and there put to death. According to Captain Dow, their chests were crushed by men jumping on them with their bare feet.

As you know, I was not good at taking advice when I was young. However, on this occasion I did listen to the Captain, not only because of what he had told us but because of another very good reason. Long before I entered that part of the world, an old Lewisman I had come across in Sydney had told me that, less than fifty years ago, the people of some islands of the New Hebrides were practising cannibals. I believed the fella, for he had been in the Colonial Service and seemed to know what he was talking about.

Cannibals or not, the Fijians were very good-looking. How I

* Night-time courtship activities.

envied those broad-shouldered, mahogany-coloured lads who had free rein among the island's bare-breasted beauties! But the thought of being eaten, or my chest being flattened under the weight of their heels, made me resist temptation. Unfortunately, my Filipino friend did not. It all went wrong for him on the morning of the second of our three days at Viti Levu. After a couple of hours on deck, soaking with sweat and bothered with the flies, we got a ten minutes' break – a 'smoke-o', as it was called. The Filipino whistled at three girls who were on the quay, making eyes at us. They smiled up at him and one of them accepted his invitation to come on board. Now, the stevedores working in the hold were well aware that the girl was on the ship but they didn't let on, just continued handling the cargo and chattering among themselves. While we were up top among the flies and the heat, we could hear the girl and the Filipino giggling and carrying on, in the cool darkness below!

Uill, a bhròinein! At sunset, did we not see the two lovers appear on deck, holding hands and making for the gangway. Although I saw the two walking off the ship, it never crossed my mind that the Filipino was walking straight into danger.

It is a known fact that it is difficult for a white person to know a Filipino from a Polynesian. That is not the case in Polynesia, for the natives there don't have difficulty in knowing the people of one group of islands from those of another. Come supper-time and the Captain called us to the bridge and asked us where was the Filipino. We told him that he had gone ashore with a 'beautag'! Well, I can tell you that the Old Man just lost the rag: 'Don't you clowns realise that you probably allowed your shipmate to go to his execution!'

The Captain ordered six of us to go ashore with him to look for the Filipino. He issued us with axe-handles and armed himself with a loaded pistol which he hid in his inside jacket pocket. The mate was left in charge of the ship and our posse traipsed ashore. We had travelled little more than a hundred yards beyond the wharf when we stumbled on the body of our shipmate. He lay stone cold on the beach.

The dead man was carried to the ship while the Captain went to the shipping-office to see if there was anybody still working there. He must have managed to make contact with someone in authority, for, within a couple of hours, three Suva policemen came on board. They were half-clad, big lads whom I would not have wished to offend! They said that the Filipino had broken his ribs falling off the ship. They were talking rubbish, of course, and they well knew that we knew how the poor man had lost his life. Strange to admit it, but the Filipino's death affected me deeply. I realised for the first time that trying to get off with girls in a strange port can get you into real deep water. Having said that, the scantily clad maidens of Viti Levu remained no less attractive to my eyes. And I will not deny that when the ship next visited Suva, I did accept my fair share of their favours!

'Cleeks' MacKenzie, 'the Horse'

Calum (known as 'the Horse') was the son of Tarmod Thòmais [Norman MacKenzie] of the Àird. He was known as 'the Horse' from early on in his life. He enlisted in the army as a Regular and there was no-one there from any quarter of the globe who could stand up to him in a fight. You don't have to take my word for that! If you have any doubt at all on that claim, you can see it for yourself if you go to Fort George and look up the Seaforth records. Yes, that son-of-a-gun deserved the name 'the Horse' right enough, for he wasn't just a hard scrapper. In my day, you could find hard scrappers in the Rubha, ten to the penny! Calum was hard as nails but the difference with him was that he proved himself to be a first-class athlete and boxer. While the Lewis boys were proud that he came from our island, a lot of them including me, felt jealous of him.

I hadn't seen the Horse since he was a carter's assistant working for Innis Uilleim, the Merchant, down at the corner there. I'd heard snippets here and there in different corners of the world about how durable the Horse was and how hard a puncher. He was army heavyweight champion of the Middle East while he was stationed in Egypt and heavyweight champion of the Far East when he was stationed in India. All that in spite of the fact that he weighed just under twelve stones. He fought in the army under the name 'Cleeks' MacKenzie and all the island boys in the army looked up to him and admired him.

I never expected to meet Calum, for I was a sailor and he was a soldier. But as it happened, our paths did cross on one occasion when I was on my way home from the sailing.

I had stopped off in Glasgow to visit my three spinster sisters, Màiri-Kate, Annie and Effie, who were living in the Gorbals. One evening, I went down to MacKenzie's Bar at the Broomielaw, hoping to meet up with Gaels on their way home from the sailing, or about to ship out. The bar was jam-packed with punters and as soon as I entered, three or four fellas came over to say hullo. We shook hands, bought a round of drinks and sat down blethering about the news from home and, most importantly, about bullying on board ship – a perennial problem. At the far end of the bar, another group of lads was creating a bit of a stir, laughing loudly and singing in Gaelic. I stood up to have a deco and who did I see in the middle of the huddle

'Cleeks' MacKenzie, 1938, while stationed at Maryhill Barracks, Glasgow

but the famous son of Tarmod Thòmais of the Àird – none other than the Horse, the famous 'Cleeks' MacKenzie! The sailor lads sitting with me told me that, earlier in the day at Maryhill Barracks, the Horse had been fighting in a tournament and had knocked out three opponents on the trot.

The din coming from the far end of the bar got louder and louder and the fellows at our table began to suggest that, with a reputation like mine, I 'could flatten the army champion, nae bother'! Of course, in those days, there was nothing that boys liked better than to witness a scrap. And it's amazing how soon a couple of double whiskies can allow flattery to swell a man's opinion of himself!

'Och,' says I, 'if I was a bit younger than I am and in training for a few weeks, I'm sure that I could give the Horse a run for his money!'

At that, the boys began to tease me, saying I was never as young or fit enough to tackle the Horse, and not to make excuses for not going over to where he was and provoking him into a fight. The conniving blaggards! In the end, they bet me a bottle of Johnny

Walker (whisky) that I wouldn't go to the Horse and challenge him to fight me there and then.

A bottle of Johnny Walker meant a lot in those days, so, to cut a long story short, I accepted the bet. I pushed my way through the drinkers to where the Seaforth Highlanders were carousing and I says to the company in general, 'Which of you bums is the mighty man they call the Horse?'

Of course, I recognised immediately that the strapping lad with the graze over his eye was the Seaforths' famous Cleeks MacKenzie.

Calum smiled. 'Come on in, Soolivan, and draw up a chair. You know very well that I am the son of Tarmod Thòmais from the Àird and that, for some unknown reason, they call me "the Horse" back home!'

'They're telling me that there's a fella amongst you', says I, 'who is known as 'Cleeks' and that people are fed-up of him boasting about his fighting ability.'

'Och, no!' says Calum. 'There's no-one like that here! There are one or two boxers in our company but not a single fighter!'

The rest of the fellas smiled but didn't say a word.

'Boxing! That's not real scrapping! That's prancing about like a couple of duchesses with gloves on.'

'Well,' says Calum, 'See these two fists of mine? They could lay you flat on your back whether you were wearing gloves or blundering about in the nude!'

By this time the whole bar was listening to the exchanges and roared with laughter at Cleek's put-down. Oh, the fellow didn't turn a hair – a real cool customer!

'Gloves are for pansies,' says I. 'Have you ever fought a real fight without gloves against someone who doesn't give a toss for your reputation?'

Calum got up and I prepared for him to come for me. All he did was to tip what was left of his pint down his throat. That was the signal for the whole company of Seaforth Highlanders to stand up and walk out of the bar. As they did so, they were loudly jeered. Before Cleeks disappeared through the doorway, he turned round and says, 'Good night, boys! You and I will meet again, Soolivan – and much sooner than you think!'

My drinking companions were very impressed by how I had driven the famous army boxing champion out of the pub. Of course, I knew very well that Calum had not left because of fear of me. But, even so, I enjoyed my moment of glory. And I enjoyed it even more when I was presented with a bottle of Johnny Walker which I had earned without so much as throwing a punch.

By the time my mates and I had polished off the contents of the bottle, they had convinced me that the famous Cleeks MacKenzie, the Lewisman known back home as 'the Horse' was a yellow-belly who had fled rather than face me, man-to-man.

When the celebration was over and the pub was closing, I parted with the boys and tottered off to my room in the Sailors' Home along the Broomielaw. At the reception desk, the register-boy said to me that my cousin was waiting for me up in my room. I had no idea which of my cousins it was, for I had three or four whose home ports were on the Clyde.

When I got up to my room, who was there sitting on my bed, reading a news-paper, but Calum the son of Tarmod Thómais – the Horse!

'Soolivan, you black-hearted rogue!" says he. 'It's amazing that no-one bumped you off, long ago! Perhaps this is a good a time as any for me to knock the stuffing out of you!'

'What's your news from home, cousin?' says I, pulling up a chair.

'You know fine well,' says he, 'that you would have ended up being beaten to a pulp, if I had fought you in MacKenzie's Bar. But because I didn't want to show you up in front of your friends, I decided not to give you what you deserve – a beating! Now, if you have any doubts about what I'm saying, you could have a go at me right here. Or if you would prefer a proper arena, let's walk together up to the Kelvingrove Park.'

'Calum,' says I, 'if I were sober, I daresay I could re-shape that ugly face of yours. And there again, if I were sober, it's possible that I would run a mile! As it is, I'm as drunk as a lord, thanks to the fact that you turned tail in the pub – and by doing so, won me a bottle of Johnny Walker!'

Calum enjoyed hearing about that! We sat down together like two old buddies and spoke about scraps we had seen or had been involved in, in different parts of the world. We parted with a handshake and the old Gaelic farewell, *'A h-uile latha a chì 's nach fhaic!'**

I admired Calum,** the famous Horse, for the way in which he had handled the situation in the pub and for coming to sort me out later. He had left my reputation intact when his was on the up-and-up, and mine on the downward slide. His record of wins in the ring speaks for itself. But I'll tell you this: I wasn't afraid of Calum, not even when he confronted me in the Sailors' Home. And believe you me, if he and I had fought each other when we were both in our prime, there would have been a fight to remember.

* A traditional lighthearted valediction: 'Good wishes for the days we have together and the days we have not!'

** While being held as a POW in Germany, Calum was tragically shot dead by a prison guard in the last days of the Second World War.

Paradise Elusive

When I was in Kalamazoo

Kalamazoo is a town south of Lake Michigan, and a fair distance east of Chicago. I spent three days in jail there, on account of my having sided with a poor Native Indian who had been beside me getting served in a store. My ploy in those days was doing odd jobs here and there, and moving about without a care in the world. Earning, spending, getting drunk twice a week, sobering up and then moving on. Like thousands of bums all over the civilised world, I was a proper rolling stone!

I smoked a pipe in those days and couldn't sleep properly unless I knew that there was a couple of ounces of strong Virginian tobacco about my person! There was this general store that I used to visit for my tobacco, and one morning I made my way there and gave the usual cheerful 'Good Morning!' to the storekeeper. He was a right friendly fella, always ready for a crack – but only if there were no other customers in the store. We had started yarning, when this Native Indian guy came in with a list of the things he wanted to buy. Well, being in no great hurry, I let the Native go in front of me.

A minute or two later, who entered the store but three local farmers along with their wives. I said 'Howdy!' to the farmers but they didn't want to know. Well, if you live long enough, you develop an instinct for when trouble is brewing. Fool that I was in those days, I never ran away from trouble!

Now, as soon as the ladies made their presence felt, they began to whisper among themselves and, at the same time, eyeing up the Native. They continued in that vein for as long as the Native was being served. Meanwhile, their men-folk seemed to ignore all their twittering – just went about the store looking at farming tools and general hardware, not letting on that there was anybody in the store but themselves. However, their mood changed when the youngest of the women approached the Native and asked him to give her the wampum-belt which he had suspended from his trouser-belt. Naturally enough, the fellow refused to oblige and, boy, as if someone had rung a bell at the beginning of a fight, all hell broke loose!

The husband of the lady whose request had been refused came storming over and delivered the Native a thunderous punch to the body and felled him. Oh, the fellow knew how to throw a punch all right, and he also knew where a punch would do the most damage. The poor Native on the floor was nursing his ribs while the farmer, red-faced with anger, stood over him, accusing him of insulting his wife. Unsure of what he should do next, the *truaghan* just lay on the floor trying to figure out what his course of action should be. In the end, he rose to his feet, took a few coins from his purse and, as he began to gather his purchases together, offered the money to the store-keeper. So far as the farmers were concerned, his doing that was like showing a red rag to a bull! The farmers tore into the store-keeper for selling merchandise to a person who was 'too dumb to show respect to white folk'. *A bhalaich ort,* those big, red-faced guys wanted everybody to know that they meant serious business! They warned the store-keeper that if he went ahead and closed the deal with the Native, they and all their neighbours would boycott his store.

Now, as I told you, I had only come into the store to buy a few ounces of tobacco, and had not expected to come across a set-to like that. The store-keeper, poor fellow, was in a dither and began to take the supplies he had given to the Native back out of the fellow's canvas hold-all. You could see that he was very afraid, for his hands were shaking. Back on to the counter came all the sugar, beans and other groceries the man had ordered. I have always thought that, in some ways, the natives of North America are just like the Gaels of Scotland used to be. For centuries, they got the same kind of raw deal from grabby, loud-mouthed folk who came into their land, robbed them and then treated them as if they were inferior.

Soolivan, says I to myself, isn't it time you said a word or two to the guys throwing their weight about?

And that is what I did!

'Excuse me,' says I, 'for butting in like, but this fella is my friend and he's in here buying vittals for the two of us!'

The big-punching farmer came straight over to me, stuck his finger in my chest and says, 'If you don't want to end up on the floor like this trash, you'll keep your mouth tight shut, fella!'

'I don't want to be hurt, no-how,' says I. 'I hate conflict of any kind and my religion won't allow me to fight! Having said that,' says I, 'I wish to speak on behalf of my friend here, and that's all there is about it!'

A ghràidh ort, my speech didn't go down well. The guy behind the prodding finger looked as strong as an ox and he was furious! And no wonder, when you consider all the maize, barley grain and beef those farmers were fed on.

'You keep your lip tight shut, preacher,' says he, 'or you'll regret it!'

There was a time when conduct like his would have met with a ready response from my right fist. But the years had taught me that the softly-softly approach is often more effective than the head-to-head – and especially if you are facing overwhelming odds. I explained to the company that I was a God-fearing man who would never dream of courting trouble. No, siree! My religion, says I, did not allow me to handle money, and so they had to understand that it was essential that they allowed the Native to buy supplies for us both.

'If that is so, you lying son-of-a-bitch,' shouts the trouble-shooter, 'you'll get the same treatment as he did!'

A furious brawl began. The ladies screaming, the big, red-faced fellow and I were throwing full-bodied punches at each other. What a shindig! Before I got a proper crack at my opponent's chin, two arms, as strong as iron bars, folding themselves over my chest from behind. You won't believe what happened next – that treacherous Native whom I was trying to help had sold me down the river. Hard to believe that he would do a thing like that! But there he was, holding me in a vice-grip and offering me to the farmers. I just couldn't believe that he was doing that.

'Hold him there,' shouts one of the farmers, 'I'm going to fetch the Sheriff!'

What was a man in my position to do? At the time, I felt that the only thing left to me to do was to let off steam by cursing the lot of them to kingdom come, in Gaelic, English and in a language of my own making!

'Some preacher!' shouted the ladies above the din.

The Sheriff arrived and the farmers' wives, all coy, told him that I, a total stranger, had starting brawling with their peace-loving husbands. The store-keeper agreed. The Native stayed silent. When the Sheriff began to refer to the farmers as 'these decent folk' and refused to listen to my side of the story, I knew that I was up to my neck in the *sitig* [mire].

It was not my first time in handcuffs and, unfortunately, it was not my last. On the following morning, I was sentenced to three days 'in the calaboose'. During those three days, I tried to figure out why the Native had turned on me the way he did, but also why he had not tried to stand up for his rights. I just could not make sense of it. At four o'clock on the third day, the door of my cell was opened, and a young deputy told me to leave.

Now, in those days, Kalamazoo was not a very big town and I have been told that it has changed a lot since then. But when I was there, the streets were busy with a few early motor-cars and lots of men on horseback and horse-drawn buggies of every description.

There was a pub near the jail and, as soon as I was released, I steered my course in the direction of the saloon where I planned to sit down in peace, enjoying a long cold drink of beer. Believe it or not, who did I see padding down the street towards me but the low-down treacherous Native who had sold me down the river! He didn't try to avoid me. No, siree! Even though my face must have shown him how much I hated him, he made straight for me.

'I want nothing to do with you,' says I. 'You're a treacherous skunk, so leave me alone, skunk!'

To be honest, I can't remember what I called him, but you get my drift! He took hold of my arm and he began to talk to me. It was difficult for me to understand what he was murmuring at me, but I understood enough to keep me from walking away. The most loud-mouthed of the farmers was known as a very dangerous man as he always carried a hunting-knife and was not loath to use it. The Native said that he didn't want me, a total stranger, to get hurt fighting his battles. And there was another reason why he objected to my getting involved. Natives had learned not to trust white men who said they wanted to represent them against injustice.

I walked with him right to the end of the street, and when I made to part with him, he indicated that he wanted me to continue along a path.

'Not far!' he says. 'Not far!'

His home was a log cabin beside a river. To my surprise, his wife was a white woman. They had a string of kids – poor-looking, under-fed little things. When the wife spoke, I knew at once that she was English and, all of a sudden, I began to understand what was upsetting the farmers. A white woman living with an 'Injun' was more than the local gentry could bear. That's how I read the picture anyway and, if that was the case, you might say that it was because the Native's wife was white that I spent three days of my life sitting without tobacco in the calaboose in Kalamazoo.

Moonshine and Cotton-fields

Although there was a lot of money to be made in Texas, I did not at all enjoy working at the oil-wells at Galveston. From there, I went to work on a huge cattle-farm but that didn't suit me either. I stole a ride on a freight-train and travelled through some beautiful scenery, full of cotton-fields and orchards along the banks of the Mississippi. My seat was an apple box, but I can clearly remember the rhythm of the freight train as she blew her way through a warm summer's night. Along with me were another three drifters and we shared the wagon with huge barrels of either tar or molasses.

The day was beginning to dawn. As soon as the train began to slow down on its approach to a station, my three companions and I leapt out. In those days, you had to be very careful stealing a ride on a freight train. A whole bunch of hobos were on the move everywhere you went, and the transport police and the city cops came down hard on anyone they found travelling the rail without paying their dues.

Understandable enough, I suppose, but in those days keeping to the letter of the law was not something that bothered me very much.

Having jumped off the freighter, I found that we had arrived at a place called Memphis. The other three fellows disappeared into bushes. I crossed the track and went straight into town. The sun came up around seven in the morning and the day was already hot and sticky. That's what I enjoyed most about places near to the Tropics. You didn't need to have piles of clothes and wellington boots on you all the time. In fact, dungarees, a singlet and a shirt was all that you could bear to have on you. And when it rained – you'll probably not believe this – the rain was warm falling from the sky! Your clothes steamed for a bit, but within an hour or so, you were completely dry. Now, you'll have to mind that this was in the 1920s, during Prohibition. The government had passed a law that banned the making and the drinking of booze. That's right! You were not allowed to make booze, sell it, buy it or drink it. That's what the Prohibition was. In those days the law-makers were lunatics. Still are.

At that time, there was nowhere in the world as unsettled and lawless as the USA. The police were at war with the thousands of folk making and drinking 'moonshine', which was the American name for illicit spirits. Mafia gangsters were in control of whole areas of the big cities and the newspapers were full of stories of shootings, murders, gang fights and police raids and corruption. Mayhem! Even so, travelling about in America was exciting, but you just had to watch your step. Sometimes, if you had a deep-down craving for a drink, you had to go looking for it. And, of course, there wasn't a pub on every street corner as there is today. No pubs, and still there was probably as much alcohol being sold on the quiet as there was before the Prohibition laws came in.

Up in Galveston, you couldn't get a beer for love nor money. Not even a whiff of a hangover! But who wants to go through life hoarding money, and as sober as the Reverend George MacLeod who never even tasted whisky! How daft can you get! I had a few dollar bills and I felt on top of the world. I wandered into this town at Memphis and after buying a coffee and a trencher of cowboy hash, I asked around where the nearest shebeen was in town. There wasn't one! Nobody in town would admit that there was a shebeen or a speak-easy in town. The three drifters who had been with me on the freight train met me coming along the street. They also had their tongues hanging out.

Just when I was on the point of collapsing for lack of booze, an idle-looking coloured fellow came up to us and told us that there was a shebeen at the edge of town. He gave us directions, and off we went. We passed by the last of the houses and gardens and entered a wood and, almost at once, came across a couple of punters 'sleeping it off' by the side of the track. 'A bhalachu,' says I to myself, 'I'm beginning to have a sore head already!'

Now, let me tell you that I was on the side of the country people who were making the 'moonshine'. Like most of the other fellows of my generation, I always hankered after making my own. My great-grandfather was famous for making the best *treas-tarraig** in Lewis. But all the country people everywhere had a go. And in my book, they must have had a lot of ploy doing it!

When I was a boy, long before the Great War, Iain Uilleim 'ic Tharmoid, a neighbour of ours, used to tell me how he had seen his own grandfather's brother making whisky down by Allt Shinigeadh in our own village. It wasn't a difficult thing to do. The people used to take turn about to hide the *poit-dhubh* – that is what they called the illicit still. Of course, the authorities were dead against ordinary folk making the whisky and punished anyone found in possession of a 'worm'. The most difficult part of the operation was having to sit by Allt Shinigeadh all day, feeding peat into the fire and attending to the still as it wept its precious liquid into stone piggies. It must have been a first-class pastime! Knowing a bit about making the stuff, I reckoned I could make a tidy fortune. I needed plenty of running water and that wasn't too difficult to find. As for the grain, there was enough of that around in the USA to sink a battleship! All I needed was to find folk who already owned a *poit-dhubh*.

We followed the track winding among the trees and came to a wooden bothy well hidden behind tall bushes. The shebeen, run by a black family, was full of people, black and white, all merry and doped up with the alcohol!

'C'mon in, man!' they shouted. Big, laughing, sweaty men, without a care in the world and all holding mugs of the 'moonshine'. The black lady in charge told us that, for two dollars, she would give us enough booze to 'set our bellies on fire'!

'Ain't gonna get a thing in this world without payin'!' she tells us and then laughed heartily as if she had told us a joke. Once you had paid your two bucks, you could drink until you keeled over. The woman took a stopper out of a jar and filled mugs for us.

'Black man whisky!' she laughs. 'Powerful good! Better than white man's whisky!'

'That remains to be seen!' says I. 'You can't teach old Soolivan nothing about whisky, lady, for we used to drink it by the pint back home in Scotland!'

The woman got a kick out of that and she shook with laughter. I

* Thrice-distilled whisky.

raised my mug of 'moonshine' to my lips and it was so rough that it grazed my tongue at the first sip. Nobody sober could have enjoyed it but, having paid two dollars each, the four of us bums decided to make the most of it. After a few gulps, you got a glow on and the taste didn't matter.

'Go on!' says I, 'fill us another noggin of your fire-water!'

Half-way through the second mug, my stomach felt as if it had come to the boil. My head was beginning to pound. I had the third mug in my hand when whistles started to blow outside, the door flew open and, in a few seconds, the place was flooded with cops with their truncheons drawn. Like the rest of the guests, old Soolivan was steaming. A cop came at me and snatched the mug out of my hand. I threw a punch at him, but long before it made contact, I was floored by his truncheon. What a mess Iain, this son of Tarmod Uilleim, was in! I woke in a small room and, for a moment, I thought that I was in the lamb-closet in the byre at No. 11. It didn't take me long to realise that I was lying on the prison floor, surrounded by stone walls and iron grilles. There was another prisoner in with me, all huddled up crying like a child. I left him to it.

The warden appeared at the door, opened it and motioned me out. We were on our way to the courtroom which was above the cells. I was invited to tell the judge my name and I told him, 'John MacLeod, sir!'

A black family of a century ago in the Deep South of the USA

'Occupation?'

'Sailor, sir, marooned in Memphis!'

There was a mouse of a man beside the judge taking notes. He wore spectacles and a hair-piece. When he heard my reply to the judge, he said, 'Just answer the questions, MacLeod. You don't have to volunteer anything more than straight answers!'

The judge says, 'Did you drink any alcohol yesterday?'

I took a breather before I answered, for I was not sure of which day I had been to the shebeen – yesterday or the day before.

'Answer the question!' demands the mouse-man.

'Now you had better be quiet, little fella,' says I, 'and let me speak direct to his Honour! I did take a liquid that made me drunk, right enough.'

'Did you assault a policeman?'

'No, sir, but that son-of-a-gun cop sure did assault me!'

Cousins John Murdo (left) and Kenny Campbell, who pretended to reject many of Soolivan's stories

Thinking back, I must have been drunk to be talking like that in court. I started making jokes about the little mouse-man, who turned out to be the clerk of court. Nobody was amused by my antics. I thought I might be fined a few dollars which, for a change, I would have been able to pay. Instead, I was sentenced to six weeks of hard labour in the cotton fields. The little mouse-man nodded to me as the policeman led me out.

No wonder I was down in the dumps, thinking of the price I had to pay for three mugs of 'moonshine'. Two dollars and six weeks' hard labour!

About thirty fellows who had broken the Prohibition laws arrived at the prison that day – a prison right in the middle of cotton fields. Later, I learned that only those found guilty of resisting arrest were given harsh sentences and I was considered to be one of those.

Every man-jack there was issued with a sort of pointed hoe which looked very like the *croman* used by crofters in the old days to hoe the potato crop. Every man jack, that is, except for the guards. They had the best job of the lot! They strutted about with their guns at the ready, hoping that some fool would make a break for it! As I remember them, they were all big, rough-spoken men, always chewing tobacco and bullying anyone whom they thought was swinging the lead. The inmates were expected to stay crouched over, working the *croman* for hours on end. At home on No. 11, I was never keen on hoeing the potatoes and always made some excuse to get out of doing it. You can imagine my feelings when I saw all those acres of cotton waiting for attention, under a blazing Tennessee sun. After only half a day's work, I felt sure that I would die before I had finished serving my sentence. The work was very monotonous – just raising earth round the foot of the cotton plants.

One day, after working about a week of my sentence, a big barrel-chested guard with a beard on him from ear to ear came sauntering over in my direction, holding his gun in the crook of his arm. He looked like the kind of fellow who was bored with not having somebody to kick. While I was giving him my attention, I accidentally uprooted a couple of cotton plants. He bawled at me at the top of his voice, 'Watch out there, you clumsy bastard!'

Those were his very words. 'There's a dollar fine for what you've just done!' he says.

I straightened up looking at him, 'I'm a sailor, my friend, not a farmer. If you could put me in a boat now, I'd show you how to row in the calm and tack in the breeze.'

He was taken aback by my answer and allowed himself a half-smile, 'Well, sailor boy', says he, 'if you have problems with your conditions of employment here, go see the prison boss. But until then, bend that back of yours and keep your mouth shut!'

As soon as the inmates were herded back to the prison, I did exactly as the barrel-chested guard had suggested. I asked to be allowed to speak with the prison governor – urgently!

I was surprised at what happened next. Within an hour, a warden came to the cell I was in, and says, 'No problem, MacLeod, the governor will see you before the week is out!'

You ask me how a normal person doesn't go mad confined for a long time inside a prison? Of course, many convicts come out scarred for life. But not me! And I'll tell you how I was able to hold on to my sanity while I was doing a stint of hard labour down in Memphis. I used to sing to myself the witty songs the Seisiadar boys used to compose for the girls of Pabail. And I used to repeat to myself some of the insults Ishbal Tharmoid used to throw at Iain Beag, her brother-in-law – something that happened at No. 7 regular as clockwork. That woman's wit and tongue were as sharp as a razor – and sharpest of all when she had an audience! The boys of the Sràid used to go down to listen to her and she never failed to give us a laugh. Sitting in my cell entertaining myself in Gaelic and making myself laugh must have made my cell-mates and guards think that I was crazy!

In a prison, many of the inmates are bad, dangerous people. Others are just plain loco and should be in an asylum or hospital. I was in the caliboose, though I was neither dangerous nor loco – just plain unlucky to be caught in a shebeen. Now that is the truth! That was the way of it!

On my very first day 'at my Uncle Sam's', I noticed one poor soul, sobbing in the corner of his cell. He had spent most of the day slavering, after being badly beaten up by one of the many thugs in the place. He couldn't stop crying, even when trying to eat his food. One of the inmates told me that the poor *truaghan* was doing time, after having been caught taking a drug called hemp. I became specially interested in him after I was told that he was a Scot.

One day, the fellow appeared out in the cotton-field, holding his *croman* and looking the worse for wear. When I got the chance, I approached him and asked him where in Scotland he was from. Oh, he wouldn't answer until I spoke to him in Gaelic.

His eyes lit up. It was then that I realised he was only a young guy – no more than twenty-five, I'd say.

'God must have sent you,' says he, 'to talk to me in this hellish place!'

He wouldn't tell me where on the Gàidhealtachd he came from, though from his accent it wasn't too difficult for me to guess that he came from one of the Uists! I was told that his surname was MacAskill but he wanted to be known as 'Lex'.

'I was recovering from an addiction,' says he, 'that was driving me to near suicide. I was still taking a little of the drug when I was caught by the police and here I am, caught up in this madhouse!'

I used to sing him a Gaelic *luinneag* [ditty] once in a while to make him laugh. In due course, I was summoned to appear in front of the prison governor. Two wardens marched me to the interview room. We walked through corridors where stone walls shut out all sounds except those of our boots. The governor was not at all the kind of man I expected. He was only about thirty years of age – on the surface, a nice, easy-going, friendly sort of fella, sitting in his swivel-chair with his shirt open, smoking a cigar.

'Now what can I do for you?' he says.

Though I was dying to take one, I refused to take a cigar from the open cigar-box which he pushed in my direction.

'I've asked to see you, sir,' says I, 'to tell you, sir, that I have no skill at all at the hoeing. I've accidentally broken the stem of a couple of cotton plants, which worries me a great deal. After all, I am a sailor, sir, and am more used to the marlin-spike than to the hoe!'

The governor made a face and shook his head.

'And no doubt,' says he, blowing out cigar smoke, 'like all the inmates of this prison, you are totally unsuited to hard labour. Not only that, you are innocent of the crimes that brought you here, eh?'

'No, not at all, sir, ' says I. 'I am guilty of having had drink taken, and deserve to be punished for that unforgivable crime! All I am asking, sir, with all due respect, is that you consider giving me a job, sir, more fitting to the skills of a man who has spent his life in a position of some authority on the ocean wave.'

The governor gave out the sigh of a man who was hearing the same speech several times a week.

'It's amazing,' says he, 'how often cons like you come in here, thinking that the guys running the jail are plain stupid! With your phoney accent and your Old World courtesy, you think you can out-fox me and out-fox the system. Let me tell you here and now . . . '

O, chuir e as a bhroinn!* The fellow goes on giving me a dressing-down until he and I were both in a sweat. I stretched forward and took a cigar from his cigar-box and he lit it for me. Oh, you could see that he was no push-over! After the telling-off, I expected him to signal the wardens to take me back to my cell. But no, the fellow sat back and relaxed for a minute, blowing smoke and not saying a word. He decided not to dismiss me there and then, and, as it proved, that was his big mistake!

'Where are you from?'

* Oh, he spouted forth at length!

'I'm from the Highlands of Scotland,' says I, 'and proud of it to the marrow in my bones.'

'You will have heard of Harry Lauder, then?'

'Have I heard of Harry Lauder!' says I. 'Well, I should know him – he's my mother's cousin!'

'The greatest entertainer to come out of Europe – ever.'

The governor told me that he had all of 'my mother's cousin's' records at home and played them at weekends. In fact, he was so taken by my kinship to the great man that I half-expected him to invite me home to hear Harry on his phonograph. Of course, the guy was just amusing himself at my expense. A gun-toting warden suddenly arrived at the interview-room with another prisoner and I was ushered out. As I was leaving, the governor told me that he would consider putting me on probation for a week as a trustee, 'to see how things worked out'.

Now, you have to remember that, in a prison, it's a case of dog eat dog. You'll do anything you can to make life as easy as possible for yourself. There are wardens with dogs and guns to make sure that your life is miserable. Anybody found trying to escape was in danger of being shot. That was a rule that all the prisoners were well aware of. Even though he knew the danger, Lex was so desperate to escape that he told me he intended to make a run for it while we were out in the fields.

'No, my friend, you'll do no such thing,' says I. 'Those tobacco-chewing guards would make target practice of you and you'd end up dead before you covered a hundred yards! Hold your horses and I'll see what I can do to help.'

As a probationer trustee (to which the guards referred as a 'PT'), I had a few privileges more than I had as a common or garden convict. One of these privileges was that, along with another half dozen trustees, I was given twenty minutes or so to do a few chores, after the rest of the inmates were locked in their cells – chores such as removing the swill-bins from the cook-house to an enclosure near the main gate. One evening, shortly after returning from the fields, I helped Lex to hide himself in a stinking swill-bin behind the prison kitchens. I told him that, to have any chance of escaping, he had to stay in all that stink until two or three in the morning.

You might think that what I did for Lex in the prison proves that I had a gentle side to my nature. As the old proverb says, *Is ionmhainn leis gach neach a choltas!* [All of God's creatures take to their own kind!] Lex was a Gael, so naturally I was inclined to be on his side. But, to be honest, I think that giving authority one in the eye was behind my helping him to escape. Now that I am sixty years of age, I look back and think how stupid I was to behave as I did. Although I was miles away from Lewis, perhaps deep down I was still fighting the old School Board!

Anyway, all hell broke loose when the lad failed to turn up for the evening meal. The inmates, including the trustees, were all confined to their cells. With the dogs on the leash, the wardens scoured the areas around the buildings but I believe it was because of the smell of the swill that even the dogs failed to pick up the scent they were looking for. The wardens seemed convinced that their man had not come into the compound after work, and spent most of their time out in the fields.

It was late in the evening before we were allowed to eat. The sweet-smelling Lex managed to get away, but we heard later that he had been captured a few miles from the prison. Whether that is true or not, I cannot say. But if he was captured, it was strange that he wasn't returned to his cell. Even after all those years, I think of him and wish I knew what happened to him. The upshot of Lex's escape was that I was summoned to the governor's interview-room. This time, I wasn't offered a cigar. Nor was there any mention of Harry Lauder. Instead, I was told that I was suspected of 'helping a fellow prisoner to escape'. The governor was fuming! He told me that if his inquiries showed that I was a friend of MacAskill and that if he discovered that I was involved in the escape, he would see to it that my sentence would be doubled. All through that one-sided *trod* [row], I kept my mouth shut.

When his lecture was coming an end, the governor says, 'MacLeod, you have let me down big-time and you have let yourself down by breaking trust with the prison authorities! You are no longer an acting trustee but will return tomorrow to the cotton rows where you will do as you are bloody well told!'

When he ran out of steam, he nodded to the wardens to return me to my cell. Just before I was led away, I says to the governor, 'Excuse me, sir, can I put you straight on one point before I go?'

'Sure.'

'Harry Lauder isn't the best entertainer to come out of Europe. Ishbal Tharmoid is!'

'Never heard of him,' says he.

Rat-tail in Miami

Long before I went up into the States, I had heard that the climate of Florida was the best in the world. *A dhuine bhochd*! I had only been there for a fortnight when I concluded that it was an ideal place to live. Long, warm sunny days and beautiful people. You didn't need a

jumper or wellies to live in Florida. You didn't even need a shirt or vest. After a few days there, I was convinced that I had found the Promised Land of the Old Testament. I was in the Paradise of the Hereafter! My skin turned as brown as the skin of a roast potato. Everything you could ask for grew in Florida. There were trees laden with apples, grapefruits, oranges, nuts – everything you could ever want to eat. I tell you the honest truth! If I had been Andrew Carnegie the millionaire I would have hired a Cunarder to take all the families in the Rubha over to Florida and housed them near to one of my favourite beaches at Key West. What ceilidhs we would be having! We would have had a 'four-and-a-half' keg whenever we felt in need of one! I would have brought Alasdair Dòmhnallach, the tinker, with his bagpipes and tin-whistles. I might even have brought over the School Board and Dòmhnall 'Ain Chaluim, the elder!

Soolivan was widely travelled in the south east of the USA particularly in Florida, which he described as Paradise

It was easy to make a living up there towards Miami. Sometimes

I was employed collecting trash from the houses, sometimes as a dogsbody in hotels. But the best jobs I had were working on fruit-farms. Strange as it might seem, even in that Paradise I was not completely happy. A man brought up by the sea has salt in his veins, and is always looking for the line of the distant horizon. The farm I spent most of my time on was about ten miles from the ocean – about the same distance, I would say, as the distance between No. 11 here and Steòrnabhagh. On my day off, I always spent my time over by the seaside, envying every man-jack who owned a sea-going craft, even if it was no bigger than a rowing-boat.

There were hundreds upon hundreds of boats of every kind along the Florida shores and, as I said, I spent much of my time watching them. All the well-to-do folk owned flashy yachts and even their flunkies owned sail-boats or racers. Rich folk spent much of their time gadding about, having parties on their yachts with their friends, and just showing off. Good luck to them, I say! *A Dhia*, if I could have afforded that lifestyle, nobody would have showed off more than old Soolivan! As it was, I was neither well off nor well connected, so I had to slave away on the farm. It wasn't that the life I was living was hard or without enjoyment – not at all! There were plenty of attractive young ladies working on the farm, all of them nicely rounded and friendly-like. Round about Miami there, the ladies were fond of foreigners, and this Gael here sure qualified as a foreigner! But that's another story.

I badly wanted to have a boat and told myself that even a twelve-footer with a sail would do me just fine – just so long as I could put to sea on my own, on my days off. Well, if you stick with an ambition long enough, you will succeed one day. As Fate decreed, I got a bargain of a boat, and the day I took possession of her was one of the happiest of my life. Bought her for twenty dollars at a boat auction and she was delivered by her previous owner to the farm on which I worked. Everyone told me that she wasn't worth twenty dollars – she had been that neglected. On the other hand, I knew that if I set my mind to it, I could make a nice job of her. The first chance I got, I sanded her down and then painted and varnished her. In the end, she was a real 'beautag'. Everybody who saw her all spruced up like that admired her. I was never so proud of anything I ever owned. In due course, who comes round to see her but Mrs Dysart, the wifie who owned the farm.

'Lovely job, John!' she says. 'Are you going to give her a name?'

'I'm going to give her a Gaelic name,' says I. 'I'm going to call her the *Faoileag Rubhach* – the Rubhach Seagull!'

'What kind of seagull is that?'

'It's not a bird at all. The place where I was born is called the

Rubha, and all the people there are wanderers and are referred to on our island as *faoileagan* or seagulls. Life can be very lonely for a wandering seagull, so this boat and I are going to be two *Faoileagan Rubhacs*, talking to each other in Gaelic every day!'

Mrs Dysart didn't know what I was talking about but I assured her that it made sense to the one who mattered – me. She offered to have the boat taken on the farm truck to the beach, on condition that she was allowed to be the first to sail with me after the launch.

'No problem!' says I.

Mrs Dysart's house was not a house as we know the word in Lewis. When you went upstairs, the staircase was as broad as the main road through the Rubha and the whole of it was carved out of stone. At the top of the stair, there was a broad landing with small palm trees and ferns growing there in big pots. In the middle of it all, there was a fountain which shot water four or five feet into the air when it was switched on. In the pool round the fountain there were fishes like coloured saithe swimming among lilies and water-plants. The ceiling above the fountain was made of pure glass and there were panels in it which were usually open to the sky. Now, I'm telling all that because many of the people living hereabouts think that they are real toffs because they have new Board of Agriculture houses with toilets in them and linoleum and carpets on the floor. Big bloody deal! They look down on poor old Soolivan for living in a felt-roofed ramshackle like this. By George, they would come down a peg or two if I could take them to see the mansion I was living in, in those days. Looking at me now, standing here in my old dungarees and old Crimean shirt, who could believe that I was, once upon a time, a well-dressed slicker, drinking brandy and smoking the best of cigars? In Florida, you hardly ever shut your bedroom windows, but there was a special netting on them to keep out the mosquitoes. On the morning that the *Faoileag Rubhach* was due to be launched, I woke up with a strong breeze blowing into the bedroom. The atmosphere was heavy and the sky was slate-coloured. There were no clouds, you understand – just a stony grey sky, with the sun reduced to a peep. I had hardly put my trousers on when I heard Mrs Dysart shouting that there was a tornado coming. I knew something terrible was in the offing. In those days I had no idea what a tornado was. It was just a word that I had heard somewhere. I knew what it was after asking Mrs Dysart, by God, for I got a tornado of words as an answer! She called me an ignorant something-or-other, so I gave her a kiss and told her there were plenty more where that came from!

It was then all hands on deck, boarding up windows and tying down everything on the farm that was in danger of being blown away. You can be sure that I tied down my precious *Faoileag Rubhach*! I anchored her down with every yard of rope I could find.

Ach, a charaid ort! That day in Florida, the sky looked so strange that I thought that the end of the world was just round the corner. I was sweating like a pig because I was not only running here and there but, looking back, I suppose that I was also pretty scared. The rain started coming down in big drops, a few at first, then as a downpour. All the farm-hands and everyone who happened to be on the farm took shelter in the basement – all except Mrs Dysart and me to keep her company. We opened a French window. The wind was whipping the palm trees at the front of the house, bending them over and tearing off their branches. What a din!

Mrs Dysart began to shout. She was pointing to something in the distance. I could hardly believe what I was seeing hanging from the sky. It was like an enormous spout, shaped like a huge rat's tail, suspended between the sky and the land and approaching us from the direction of the sea, sweeping this way and that and coming steadily our way. Half a mile from us, the spout hit a barn, whipped the roof off and the walls fell in, just as if you had kicked an old kipper box with your tackety boot. The barn doors went sailing upwards and disappeared.

'Dhia, gléidh mi!' says I to myself, 'if that spout hits this house we'll go straight up to heaven!'

As Fate saw fit, the spout went past the house a few hundred yards to the south with a noise as loud as a freight train given full throttle! We were very lucky. The noise got steadily less and less, but the rain continued to lash down for a good half an hour afterwards.

When the crisis was over, we all trooped out to see if there was any damage. The place looked like a battlefield. Demolished outhouses, orchard trees uprooted, the farm truck up against a greenhouse and palm-branches strewn across the road. One of the farm-hands came up to me grinning, and says, 'Mr Minos says that you've got two boats now!'

Mr Minos was the orchard manager. I hurried through the rubble, and came on half a dozen folk standing round my boat. Well, I swore like a Provost Sergeant when I saw the state she was in! Lying on top of my little *Faoileag Rubhach* was a cabin-cruiser with her back broken and her clinker sides sprung open like an old barrel. What a disappointment! My wee boat that I had never even sailed, with or without Mrs Dysart, was lying broken beyond repair.

The loss of the *Faoileag Rubhach* was like the loss of my only link with my homeland. Mrs Dysart offered me forty dollars to buy another sail-boat but I decided that there was never going to be a full moon for me over Florida. The place was not the Paradise that I once thought it was.

Mrs Dysart could not have been kinder to me and she shed tears when we parted. She smiled when I told her that as soon as I found the Promised Land, I would come back for her. Needless to say, I never saw her again.

Paradise Lost

Florida was the most beautiful place I was ever in. The Garden of Eden could not have been more beautiful. The peacefulness of the Keys did me a lot of good. Lying there with the blue sea breaking on the pure white sand, I used to wait to see the sky above me turn to gold and the sun set in a sea of fire. It is something I'll never forget and, if I could be granted one wish before I die, it would be that I could go off with Shonag to the Keys and spend a summer there.

Who knows why I left my job on Mrs Dysart's fruit-farm. The loss of my boat was just the excuse I had been waiting for to hit the road again. A real rolling stone I was at that time in my life. As it turned out, my decision to leave Florida was one that I have always regretted. With my wages from the farm in my pocket, I headed for New York. Within a fortnight of leaving the Keys, I was locked up in a cell in Jacksonville Jail. Today, it is difficult for me to believe that I got myself so often into deep water.

Many's the time I've been punished for my wrongdoings. In my bones I always knew that that punishment was just the result of my being discovered breaking some rule or other. But my ending up in the penitentiary at Jacksonville was really unfair, for I was innocent of almost everything I was accused of.

Like all young fellows of my age, I was fond of playing blackjack and pool – in other words, gambling. Lucky at it, too! But in Jacksonville, on the north-east coast of Florida, my luck ran out. I was unfortunate enough to be caught in a gambling joint playing blackjack, and was duly hauled off to jail. Associating with bootleggers and breaking the Prohibition laws were the two main charges brought against me. On top of that, they charged me with cheating, vagrancy, house-breaking, breaching the Immigration laws – the list seemed endless! Because I had served a couple of sentences in the States before, my references from Mrs Dysart and other employers counted for nothing. In the eyes of the Jacksonville law officers, I was a hardened criminal, and they tried to pin on me every unsolved petty crime in the county. Except for my being caught gambling and drinking hooch in the gambling joint, nothing else could be proved. In spite of that, I was sentenced to six months in the slammer.

Gléidh mise, what a mess my life was in! Jacksonville was a big,

big prison, many times bigger than the Tennessee, cotton-pickin' calaboose I had been in. It was a major prison even before the town was burnt to cinders in 1905. Since then, the prison was rebuilt bigger and more secure. There were several hundred prisoners there – black, white, Natives and Chinese. They were there having been convicted of every crime you can imagine – bootlegging, grand larceny, grievous bodily harm, murder – you name it! Many of the inmates were poor souls who weren't at all what you might describe as wicked or aggressive. In fact, some of them were very quiet, interesting, intelligent people. On the other hand, there were really dangerous, long-term convicts there, and the best thing you could do to save your skin was to keep well out of their road.

On condition that they played to the rules, prisoners working in the workshops were paid three dollars a week, and with that money they were allowed to buy cigarettes on Sunday. If they stepped out of line once, they lost their pay and other privileges for a week or more. The amazing thing was that the old lags – the long-term prisoners – imposed their own system of justice on the rest of the convicts. All new prisoners were made aware of that arrangement as soon as they arrived. The cell I was told to share with another two fellows was next to the cell occupied by a villain known to the rest of the prisoners as 'the King' – a huge black fellow, head and shoulders taller than the gangsters who flocked around him whenever we were allowed into the exercise yard. The rumour was that he was in for sixty years, having been found guilty of hiring a killer to drown his wife and three children.

The King and his pals made newcomers stand before them and answer the same sort of questions they had been asked at the time of their trials. Like a tribal chief, the King had given himself the power to fine them a certain number of cigarettes each week, depending on what he, the King, decided was suited to the severity of the crime. Nothing at all was taken from you if you had killed a law officer. Killing or abusing a child was reckoned to be the worst crime, and anyone convicted of that had to suffer a terrible existence.

My blood boiled to think that this horrible King fellow was allowed so much scope inside the prison. He got others to do his dirty work and made sure that he was never found doing anything that would bring him to the notice of the prison authorities.

Now, my friend, I have not got the education to write a good letter to the governor of Jacksonville Penitentiary in Florida, so I' m asking you to do so on my behalf. Write him as someone who has not got a prison record in the States. Ask him if there is still (in 1954) a system which allows the long-term lags in his jail to judge new prisoners in kangaroo courts and to confiscate part of their earnings. See what he says! He's likely to deny that such a ploy ever took place in the 'pen', but believe me, it did!

There was one law in the prison that no-one was allowed to break. After being locked up for the night, we were forbidden to communicate with any prisoners in cells other than our own. In spite of that, prisoners found a way of communicating with those in the cells adjacent. What they did was this. A prisoner would hold a mirror in his hand so that he and the fellow next door could see each other. Then the fellow giving a message would mouth the words without speaking out loud. A couple of light taps on one of the metal bars next door meant that we were being summoned to hear something the King had to say. He had an awful lot to say and he gave the signal every hour or two.

As I said, three of us shared the cell, but I was the one who seemed to be receiving more attention from the King than either of the others.

I was fed up seeing the King's thick ugly lips in the mirror, mouthing sentences which as often as not I could not understand. After four months, I was looking forward to getting out and immediately going off home to Lewis. Approaching midnight one night, long after lights-out, there was the familiar tap-tap and one of my cell-mates got off his bunk. After a spell at the cell door, he came back to tell me that the King wanted a pow-wow. *A Thighearna*, before I went to the door, did the messenger not whisper to me that there was going to be a big jail-break on the following night! My three

Communication with 'the King'

cell-mates and the King were in cahoots and wanted me involved in the break-out. I think that I was more scared that night than at any time in my life! With less than two months of my sentence to run, you can understand that I was not all that keen to break out of jail and risk spending years back in the 'pen' if I was caught. I told my three cell-mates how I felt and also that I didn't consider it very smart, in the circumstances, for me to risk death by gunfire. But those rednecks didn't care for that kind of thinking.

'The King's waiting for your answer, Scottie!'

The King's expression told me everything. My cell-mates had told me their plans and I was to help them break out of jail or else become dead meat. With a choice like that, there was only one way for me to go.

'Good choice, man!' says the face in the mirror.

The King brought into view a cleaver, then a bayonet, then, to crown it all, a revolver. When I retreated from the door, my two cell-mates brought out their own little arsenal – a small pistol, home-made knives, sharpened nails, and what the hoods in Glasgow called a 'Malky Fraser' (a cut-throat razor) – all of them lethal.

'Just remember, Scottie, that these will be ready to slit your throat, if you lose your nerve!'

After breakfast on the following day, I took a terrible fit. I fell down in agony, writhing and sobbing as I had seen Lex the Uibhisteach do, when he was having the shakes in Tennessee. My performance was so convincing that I developed stomach cramp and could hardly talk to the fellas who came to help me. A big black helping me on to a stretcher – a fellow I hadn't seen before – whispered in my ear, 'If you grass, you'll never live to see your mammy!'

In the prison hospital, which was partly run by trusties, I asked to see the doctor. After a while, the chief medical officer came and agreed to examine me in private. As soon as I told him of the plot, I was whisked off to solitary confinement, and after that didn't see a soul until the following morning. A guard came with my breakfast and, after a while, the deputy governor arrived to thank me for what I had done. He told me that, in the search for weapons throughout the prison, the guards had discovered dozens of lethal weapons. I told him that what I wanted was not thanks but my freedom.

'Surely I have now proved that I am a law-abiding citizen!'

'You haven't proved a damn thing,' he says, 'except that you weren't desperate enough to try to escape. But this I do know. If I were to put you back in your cell with those hoods, you'd be dead within the hour!'

I was given my clothes and my eighty dollars and driven twenty miles from the prison to a little railway station. I took the first train to arrive there, which, as it so happened, was heading for Texas. I stayed on it for a good few hours. When I got off it, I hired a room at the nearest hotel and went straight up to bed.

It took me a long time before I was able to sleep soundly at night. I saw the same nightmare time and again – a mouth as big as a skillet, mouthing words in a mirror, telling me that the King had discovered my hiding-place and was on his way to fix me up good!

Melancholy in Mexico

It wasn't hard to get into Mexico, the poorest country that I ever visited. The people there were much poorer than we were back home. Yet they were a beautiful people, especially the girls under twenty. Because the climate was so hot and dry, there was drought in places even on the coast and further inland. Much of the country was desert. For the people living in the driest of those areas, life was real, down-at-heel poverty. After I left Jacksonville Penitentiary, my life in the States was harder than you can imagine. Because of my record, the only jobs I could get were dead-end jobs. Oh, there was plenty of work, if you didn't mind becoming involved with the underworld – burglary, running hooch, thieving warehouses or broaching cargoes. But I had had enough trouble with the law. Jacksonville had taught me a lesson and I swore that I would never again spend time behind bars.

I wanted to go home to Scotland but, without money, I couldn't go anywhere. The food that kept me alive was what was left from the plates of others. Folk in Texas told me that it was easy to cross into Mexico, so I thought I would work my way down through Mexico and get to the Panama Canal, where I could board a British vessel by hook or by crook. That was my plan, but it was not fated that I should reach home that way. It wasn't drought or heat or lack of anything that delayed me in my travels through Mexico. The climate was warm and there was something in the air that made people as content with their lives as *crodh an Taobh Siar*.* Hurrying had not yet been invented! Apart from that, the girls were truly beautiful. I spent several weeks with a crowd of wasters, drifting from place to place. There were lads there from all over – good company for one who had just left prison. Half a dozen of us drifted into a small town full of adobe buildings. Behind the town was the biggest building in the neighbourhood. We found out that it was a bonded warehouse belonging to the government – the biggest warehouse of its kind in the country. It was

* The cattle of the west side of Lewis, said to be perfectly content.

said that there was enough alcohol in its vats to keep the population of Mexico in a stupor for twenty years! It was also rumoured that there were so many armed guards around it that it was impossible for anyone to get anywhere near it. Two of my mates decided to have a dekko and came back to tell us that there were a lot of armed guards around it right enough. Armed guards or no armed guards, nothing was going to stop Soolivan in those days, especially when the lads bet me twenty US dollars that I would not bring them back a bottle of whatever liquor was inside the warehouse. Twenty dollars sounded like a lot and the challenge also sounded like good fun.

'Show me the dollars first, and then I'll have a go!' says I.

After a whip-round, the boys showed me a twenty dollar bill.

'OK,' says I, 'I'll need another volunteer to come with me and, if we succeed, I'll share the money with him, fifty–fifty!'

Getting inside it was no more difficult than getting inside Iain Mac Anndra's house at the time that I was frolicking with Shonag. An American Chinese, by the name of Jimmy O, came with me – a fellow who was as agile as a cat. One evening, he and I got on the roof, no bother. We entered through a small skylight. Looking down on the

During the Great Depression, few ships used the Panama Canal

warehouse was wonderful from that vantage point. The aroma of tequila filled us with an almighty thirst. From floor to ceiling was about twelve feet. Our plan was that I would stay up top, catch a couple of bottles thrown up by Jimmy, then by using the length of rope we had brought, I would haul my friend back up.

Would you believe it! Once Jimmy landed on the floor and had a look-see, he came back to report that there weren't any bottles in the place. Next thing, I was down beside him looking for a bucket or something with which we could steal some liquor. We took the bung out of a glass pitcher and decided that the liquor was tequila. There were hundreds of casks piled one on top of the other, piled up to the ceiling – all full of Mexico's national drink. By George, if Mexico was suffering the worst drought in years, there was none of it affecting

Uilleam ('Kellan') with wife, Anna Anndra, and their family

Soolivan that night. The stuff we drank was the very best and we became stoating very quickly. Nobody has ever accused me of not being street-wise, but what Jimmy O and I did that night was plain stupid! He and I sat in a dark corner of the warehouse joking and yarning away, just as if we were in a cosy corner of the Star Inn in Steòrnabhagh. With our unlimited supply of booze, we were in a boozer's heaven. Not since I had drunk the rum from the Bloody's cask had I enjoyed myself so much!

A pale blue glimmer of daylight began to filter in through the heavily grilled windows high in the walls. By then, we could hardly stand, never mind jump twelve feet up to our roost. With him standing on my shoulders as we had planned at the start, Jimmy tried to reach the skylight through which we had entered. No way! We were both so drunk that we wobbled and weaved and fell in a heap of laughter on the floor. Och, we were having fun all right, until panic set in – the kind of panic that hits you when you are half-crying and half-laughing because the problem facing you is beyond your ability to solve it. We wandered round inside the building trying to figure a way of getting out.

As Fate would have it, we got one last chance. About six feet off the ground, there was a small hatch covered by a small wooden door which was bolted from the inside. We stood on a chair, drew the bolts and looked out into a narrow lane. The drop to the ground was about fifteen feet. No matter – even if it had been a hundred feet, I would have jumped!

'Hey, Jimmy,' says I, 'let's have one for th'e road!'

Would you believe it? We went back to our mugs, filled them and drank enough to sink a battleship.

A guard coming on duty for his early morning shift found the two of us in the lane asleep in a drunken stupor. We awoke to find policemen swarming around us. It is said that the Mexicans are hospitable people. They are that – so long as you don't cross them. But, I tell you, we got some rough handling from those Mexican cops. When I sobered up, I found myself in Tuxpan Jail – a filthy black hole of a place. Men, women and children were all there together. The rats in the jail were fearless and almost as big as cats. I spent months of my life rotting in that hell-hole before I even saw a judge. If you could see the way the women and children were treated in that place, it would make you sick. The behaviour of the men, both guards and prisoners, was disgraceful.

I managed to get one of the guards to give me a paper and pencil, and with these I wrote a letter to my brother Kellan pleading with him to help me. The guard said that he would give the letter to the prison governor and that he might post it for me. Don't hold your breath,

Soolivan, I told myself. Eventually, the day came when I was told that they had released me, but I was no sooner outside the prison gates than they arrested me again. Apparently, the Mexican authorities had contacted the British Consul and requested that I be repatriated. While they were waiting for reaction from Great Britain, they kept me locked up in Tuxpan Jail for another three months.

As the old Gaels used to say, *B' fharsainn mo lion-sgoradh a' cosnadh mo lòin.** In the brave New World, the land of opportunity and boundless wealth, I had landed flat on my face in the gutter! I returned to Lewis shamefaced and an embarrassment to my family and friends. I didn't have enough saved up even to feed, far less to clothe myself. I was totally dependent on their charity.

'You suffered nothing but what you deserved to suffer!' That is what my relations said. Fair do's! Insults were heaped on my head, even though it was obvious to everyone that what I had suffered in Mexico was more punishment than most humans could bear. I got back home in 1935, hurt in mind and in body.

Opposite.
Neighbours welcome the Prodigal's return

Above.
Shonag and Bellanne, Soolivan's wife and daughter

* Wide had I cast my net to earn myself a living.

Against the odds, there was one person who remained faithful to me and treated me with kindness and devotion. She was the sweetheart of my young days who had borne me a child, by then a good-looking young lady. Shonag was always there! It was her own idea that, as soon as I got on my feet, we should marry. At long last Fate decided to smile on me. I reckon that I'm a very lucky son-of-a-gun.

Rehabilitation

Chicken and Cremola

As you know, the front of our house is only a step away from the edge of the main road. The only advantage of that is that we can hear and see every car, cart and *ceàrd* [tinker] that's coming or going from our village. One day, Shonag and I were sitting down at the table having our *diathad** of salt herring and potatoes when we heard the rumble of cart-wheels approaching. Only, when we looked out, it wasn't a cart at all but a wheelbarrow being pushed along by a young fella. He was crying out that he had something for sale. I rose to the scullery window and saw that the cadger there was a lad of about fourteen – a broad-grinned lad – who winked at me while he was trundling his barrowload past our window.

'Whose balach is he?' says I to Shonag.

'They call him 'Chirpy'. He's Coinneach Beag's son from the Buaile.'

'Cremola custard at half price,' yelled the lad. Like a swarm of hungry locusts flying to a paddy-field, all the housewives on the Sràid, were scurrying from all the nearby houses to buy Chirpy's Cremola custard. Of course, in those days, Cremola custard was something that all the country folk had taken to as part of their Sunday dinner. Scoffing Cremola, red jelly and milk after a dinner of broth, meat and potatoes was all the rage – one of the few things that brightened up the Sabbath. All the rest of the day was devoted to keeping quiet and looking forward to the freedom that Monday brought!

Well, Chirpy went all the way down the Sràid selling the packets of Cremola at a penny ha' penny a packet, and by the time he reached the far end of Ceanna-loch, he had got rid of his entire barrowload!

'Where did Chirpy manage to get that heap of Cremola?' says I.

Stacking her newly-bought six packets in the press, Shonag said, 'According to himself, it came off a ship that was bound for America. She ran aground on Sgeir nan Ràmh and they are after selling her

* Early afternoon meal.

cargo of Cremola everywhere between Barra and the Butt.'

''S an cac!' says I. 'The Americans are going to be broken-hearted if they can't have their Cremola custard next Sunday!'

On the following morning, the Poolivar (the postman) told us that somebody had stolen a cardboard box containing twelve dozen packets of Cremola from the back-door of Mell's shop and that Chirpy had actually tried to sell a few packets to Mell's own daughter. The fat was in the fire! Mell went to Chirpy's father and explained the situation. No argument. Chirpy and his pals had to go round all the houses with the money they had earned, asking the housewives to sell back all the packets of custard that they had not cooked. Unfortunately for Chirpy and his mates, much of the stolen goods had been consumed overnight, so that their furious fathers had to fork a few bob out of their own pockets to pay Mell back for the loss of his stock.

Now, everybody had a lot of sympathy with two out of the three of the parties involved. They felt sorry for the boys' parents for the embarrassment that their sons had caused them. They felt sorry for Mell, who was a very popular fella, related to everybody in the Rubha because he was one of the Barantaich – an old-established family in Lewis. Nobody but me felt sorry for the boys. It was just the kind of stupid thing that I would have done when I was their age.

A few days after the families of Port Mholair were prevented from having the feast of Cremola custard, who did I see walking down the

Shonag (left) with Bantrach Iain and Bellanne

Sràid with a half-ladder on his shoulder but Chirpy. As jaunty as ever, he went by our scullery window, whistling.

I hurried to the door.

'Where are you going with that half-ladder, a bhalaich?'

'None of your business!' was the reply.

Cheeky rascal! I thought. After walking a few yards, he turned round grinning, winked and continued his jaunty carefree walk down the Sràid. You just had to laugh at him.

In the evening, I was on the lookout for Chirpy on his return journey and, in due course, saw him coming up the Stràid carrying his half-ladder on his shoulder.

'You look tired, a bhalaich!' says I. 'What were you doing with that half-ladder?'

'None of your business!'

'Och,' says I, 'it's no grand secret that you were out at Ceann a' Loch all day, helping to thatch your seanair's house. Why don't you come in and share a cuppa char with myself and Shonag?'

To my surprise, Chirpy accepted my invitation. And what a mischievous, witty guy he turned out to be. He was full of funny stories about village worthies such as Corrody, Cochaly and Barabal. He took five spoonfuls of sugar in his tea and ate a big slab of *aran-coirc*. No flies on this fella, I thought to myself.

'Did you really think', says I, 'that you were going to get away with your Cremola adventure? Going about in broad daylight, selling a barrowload of Mell's property, was bound to get you into trouble.'

'I enjoyed it while it lasted,' says Chirpy. 'The thought of all the *cailleachan* in Brocair and Port Mholair making pans of custard on Wednesday instead of on Sunday was so funny! It was worth doing it for the laugh!'

'How bad do you want to make money?' says I. 'If you like, I can share with you a little secret way that earned myself a few bob in my time.'

In those days, the big English trawlers from Fleetwood and Grimsby had begun to sweep up all the big fish that we had in the Minch. Although it was against the law, these *trustairs* used to come into Broad Bay at night and sweep to within a few hundred yards of the shore. Local people were so upset that they could have throttled the necks of every trawlerman out of Fleetwood and Grimsby. Real ill-feeling there was. And when a Tolastadh gentleman started shooting his rifle over the heads of the trawlermen who came in too close, the fat was well and truly in the fire.

The last of the summer herring was gone. No more *spealtragan**

* Gutted herrings minus the backbone, opened out, fried and eaten with new potatoes.

or fat flounders from Bàgh Phort Mholair. It was now November time and the weather was bleak and blustery and we had to live off the salt herring in the barrel and the potatoes in the *cùil bhuntat'* [potatoes bunker]. It was the same every year since the world began. Tons of fresh fish in the summer and autumn and then six months of salted food. Oh, how we used to crave fresh fish just pulled out of the sea. Tomsh with his fish-lorry would occasionally pass down the Sràid shouting, 'Iasg ùr!' [Fresh Fish]! Shonag and the rest of the housewives would rush out with their enamel basins and sporrans and buy whatever fresh fish was on the lorry: flounders, ling, coalfish, skate – that sort of thing. In the 1930s, the herring fishing was very poor and the weather 'coorse' and, because of that, we only managed to get fresh fish once in a while. It was the craving for fresh fish that led me to suggest to Chirpy that he and his mates go out into the bay at night and do some petty bartering with the Sasannaich. I says, 'Why don't you go out with a few hens new throttled and watch how their tongues will hang out!'

Chirpy scratched his head and says, 'Where would I get the poultry and where would I get the boat that would take me out to a trawler?'

'Chruthaigheir,' says I, 'isn't Port nan Giùran full of rowing-boats!

Inshore fishing-boats of the early twentieth century

At night, you could hijack one of Innis Uilleim's little cobbles and you could easily take 'a while' of a pair of oars from his stables where he keeps them.'

'And what about the poultry?'

'No problem there either,' says I. 'See here! The trawlermen are sick to death of eating fresh fish and potatoes. Halibut, ling, turbot, cod at every meal. Well, anybody in his right mind would get sick of that kind of luxury – especially if he doesn't speak Gaelic. Lord only knows what a hungry Fleetwood trawler-man would be prepared to give you, if you went out to him with, say, half a dozen fat hens!'

Oh, I had Chirpy going all right. You could see it in his eyes. I pointed out that every average *cailleach* in the Rubha owned a flock of thirty or forty hens. If one hen happened to go missing from a flock here and a flock there, the average *cailleach* wouldn't even notice. Chirpy was definitely interested. He could see that my idea was a good one.

Trawlers sheltering in Village Bay, St Kilda

'I'd get my mate to help me,' says Chirpy. 'He's as strong as a horse and loves to go on escapades.'

By this time, the lad himself was like a hen on a hot girdle.

I says to him, 'One thing now before you leave. You will, I hope, remember to drop by a bit of ling or cod to old Soolivan and Shonag here – I mean if you get a good haul from the Sasannach.'

'Och, don't worry about that,' says Chirpy, putting a heaped spoonful of sugar in his mouth. 'If we get fish you'll get your share.'

'S an cac, says I to myself, as I watched Chirpy go striding up the Sràid with his half-ladder on his shoulder. Oh, the fella looked so cocky, he reminded me of myself when, as a youngster, I first began to feel the strength of manhood seeping into my muscles. Game for anything I was.

The following day was really rough with a roaring gale blowing from the south-east. The Minch was full of heaving white horses. As I stood in the shelter of the scullery, looking over to Port nan Giùran, I watched four trawlers ploughing their way round the Rubha Meadhanach and into the shelter of the Loch a Tuath. Two of them dropped anchor less than half a mile from Port nan Giùran pier. Anyways, I sort of forgot about Chirpy for the rest of the evening – and there was a reason for that. The wind was in danger of carrying away our haystack and Shonag and I spent a good hour in the dying light of the day, binding the stack with *sìoman Theàrlaich* [coir rope] and anchoring it with boulders. Last thing Shonag did was to count her dozen hens and cock into the hen-shed, shut the door and roll the usual big stone against the door.

The wind died down in the night and I suddenly awoke thinking of the lads who had gone out to the trawlers. Lord, how I envied them the excitement of it all – the stealing of the hens and the oars and then the excitement of rowing out in the dark to barter goods with the trawlermen.

When we got up in the morning, Shonag went to let the cat out. Of a sudden, she began to shout. And no wonder! When she took the bolt off the door, she saw, lying there on the door step, a sack containing the biggest fish you ever saw in your life. Man alive, that cod had a head on him as big as the one on the Bonach's brindled bullock! Not only that, but it had not been gutted, and when I put the knife on him, his belly was bulging with liver. I was so excited that I wanted everybody to see the gift that had been delivered in the night.

I says to Shonag, 'Go on out and ask anybody who happens to be passing to come in and have a dekko at this. Today, we're going to have the biggest ceann-cropaig* you ever saw in your life!'

* A traditional dish consisting of fish livers kneaded together with oatmeal and seasoning to the consistency of dough; then, boiled in the head of a cod or similar.

Oh, Shonag was fair smiling, right enough. She was that. But who would have left us the gift of a man-sized cod?

'Lord knows,' says I. 'One thing is for certain, he wasn't left for us by Tomsh or Narrow. Them rogues would have demanded at least a couple of quid for him.'

After our porridge, we began to cut the cod into chunks – some to be salted and some to be sent out to the neighbours. It was as good as the best tonic I've ever had to see all that lovely fresh fish. It made my mouth water to see it and smell its freshness. Going on for midday, Shonag suddenly put down her knife and said, 'I forgot to let the hens out this morning and to give them their taois [dough]. I'm afraid that they won't lay us any eggs today.'

'Aye,' says I, 'I'm sure the cock will bring them all out on strike because he didn't get his early-morning taois!'

Off she went with her basin, and I could hear her crying, 'Joog, joog, joog!' as she rolled away the stone from the door of the hen-shed.

After a minute or two, she came hurrying in to report that only five birds had come out to their breakfast.

'Come out here yourself and see if they are hiding inside the bothag.'

I went out as Shonag had asked and pretended to be peering into the darkness of the shed. Of course, in my bones, I knew that the cock and six members of his harem were, by that time, some distance from their safe haven at No.11 Port Mholair.

Oh, Chirpy! *Mac an t-Sàtain* – a lad after my own heart!

Note*

In 1937, Chirpy became a regular in the Seaforth Highlanders. By the age of seventeen, he was an excellent piper and a marksman with the rifle. A few months after the outbreak of the Second World War, the German armies overran France and the Low Countries. Retreating towards Calais and other Channel ports, Chirpy was among thousands of British soldiers captured by the Germans. He escaped twice from POW camps but was recaptured on both occasions and threatened with death if he should attempt another escape. But he did escape a third time and, on that occasion, managed to avoid capture. He walked westwards for many hundreds of miles through Germany and then south through France to Marseilles. With the help of the Rev. Donald Caskie (the 'Tartan Pimpernel') and the Maquis, he managed to cross into

Spain and, eventually, returned to Scotland. After the war, he settled in New Zealand and died in 2002.

The names 'Chirpy', 'Coinneach Beag' and 'Mell' are pseudonyms.

Primo the Bull

Almost every household in the Rubha was known to me, and even though the children I knew before I went on my travels were grown into men and women, they were all kind and willing to talk to me. Right enough, some of the women were standoffish but, apart from the very religious ones, the men treated me as a long-lost friend. My brother Kellan was my mainstay, for without his help, I would probably have died in Mexico.

Once Shonag and I got married, her mother gave us all the support she could. Of course, she was only a poor widow but she was far-seeing and wise. Bit by bit, we managed to build a house – the one that I call my 'Ramshackle'. It's a bit old-fashioned now, but when I built it in the 1930s, it was no better or worse than the majority of houses in the island. What was important to me and to Shonag was that we had a roof over our heads and that it was ours – mine and Shonag's – and I was happier than at any time in my life.

One day, Bantrach Iain, my mother-in-law, said to me, 'Do you think you could handle a bull to serve the cows at this end of the Rubha?'

It was a strange question for an old woman to be asking a man first thing in the morning!

'Come on, Soolivan,' she says. 'Isn't it time for you to start earning yourself and Shonag a living? Would you like to own a bull?'

Not taking into consideration that I was a physical wreck, I said yes. She promised me twenty pounds and left it to me to go to Manor Farm to buy a bull that was advertised in the *Gazette*.

'You can pay back this money when the bull starts working,' she says. 'You'd better move on it right away or the animal will be sold to someone else.'

Kellan went with me on the bus, and when we reached the farm, we were in luck, for the bull had not been sold. I had as much experience of judging bulls as I had of flying aeroplanes – and that amounted to none. The animal looked fit enough – a solid brown brute with wicked-looking black eyes. He kept snorting through his wet nostrils whenever I laid my hand on him. I asked the farmer how much he wanted for him and he says, 'The price was given in the *Gazette*. Twenty pounds and that makes him a real bargain.'

I decided to haggle, went round the animal examining him from the stern and full frontal, looked at his undercarriage and then had a dekko at his *rùsan* [nose], which had a metal link bored through his nostrils from one to the other.

'Och,' says I, 'that animal is fit only for the knackers' yard.'

'That's probably true,' says he, 'and there's a cove from the slaughterhouse coming in an hour to take him away if you don't want him. I've bought a champion Ayrshire bull that should be arriving on the *Loch Ness* tonight.'

'I'll give you ten pounds for him and that's all I'm willing to give you.'

Without another word, the farmer turned away and led the bull towards the byre. Perhaps I realised when I saw the size of the animal that it would be beyond my strength to keep him under control. Anyways, I didn't like the way the animal was looking at me and kept snorting as if challenging me to take him on. In spite of all that, my brother was determined that I would buy him.

'Don't be a fool!' says Kellan. 'You have twenty pounds to spend on him, so why don't you give the man the price he wants?'

'Because', says I, 'I would need to have ten pints of beer in me to take on a beast that size. Come on,' says I, 'let's go to Taigh MhicChaluim to give the matter some thought.'

'Taigh MhicChaluim, my arse!' says Kellan. 'I'll buy the bull on your behalf and you can go and get drunk if you want to.'

I suddenly remembered that I didn't have a penny in my pocket and no amount of pleading would make Kellan surrender a quid. Wisely enough, Bantrach Iain had given the £20 to Kellan for safekeeping, and the result was that my brother and I arrived home in Port Mholair – us like a couple of Texan cattle-barons sitting in the front of the Manor Farm truck and the bull caged like a tiger in the back.

I decided to call the bull Primo after the Great White Hope of American boxing in the 1930s. Primo Carnera was an Italian American, a huge fellow and as strong as an ox. He was quite a good boxer until he came up against the champ – Joe Louis, Heavyweight Champion of the World. When they met in the ring, Joe flattened Primo in a few rounds. Even though he proved to be the second best heavyweight boxer in the world, I admired Primo for showing his face outside the door with a surname like Carnera! *Dhia,* I'd rather be called Campbell than Carnera!

My bull Primo was a good enough bull in the bull business! He may have been a has-been just like Carnera but he was a game old son of a gun, and whether cows came to frolic with him by day or by night, he never turned his back on any of them. Folks came with bellowing cows from all over the outer end of the Rubha and, after Soolivan was handed five shillings, Primo silenced them, one after the other. To everybody's surprise, I was able to pay Bantrach Iain her twenty pounds in less than a year.

You have to look on a bull as a kind of steam engine. He needs an awful lot of coal fed into his boiler when he's working. Fortunately, there was enough grass in the croft to keep Primo munching in the summer and autumn but, when it came to the winter of 1939, we didn't have enough oats stacked to keep him in tip-top condition. He began to show signs of temper when he was hungry and one day trapped me between his shoulder and the wall of the stall. Fortunately, Kellan heard my calls for help and pulled on the chain that was through the link in the brute's nose. I said, 'Right, mate! If you're not happy with the conditions in this here hotel, you can go up to SY to entertain the troops!'

At that time, the population of the island was getting bigger and bigger because of the numbers of soldiers, airmen and sailors quartered here to defend us from Jerry. Finding enough grub to feed them was a permanent problem for the Ministry of Food. That caused the price of beef to improve like billy-o. So I said to Primo that the time had come for him to make a contribution. I got Kellan and some of the local gals and boys to help me to load Primo on to Narrow's fish-lorry and off we go!

At the slaughterhouse, I got nearly thirty pounds for Primo. Boy, was I in clover! I repaired to my favourite public house Taigh MhicChaluim,* and got drunk. While I was there in the pub, I treated everybody to a dram and when I came home to Shonag here, I had only about twenty-five pounds left. Mind you, she was happy enough with that payout, for she thought that it was a fair price for Primo. She was even happier when I told her that, while I was in Taigh MhicChaluim, I had got myself a job as a labourer working for Simms, Sons, & Cooke, the civil engineers.

That's where I spent the Second World War, labouring most days at the aerodrome at Mealabost – doing as much as I was able with a shovel. I was so full of arthritis that my body didn't allow me to do much towards the war effort. However, Simms, Sons & Cooke were pleased enough with my navvying and kept paying my wage. A lot of my old pals were working there with me – Sandy Phàdraig, Hoddan, Neilly Grant, Dollan Ishbeil, Cailean a' Ghosjee. Oh, I remember them all. Fine boys but, och, by that stage, all the steam had gone out of me. I couldn't even get drunk properly or contribute to any kind of hell-raising!

* MacCalum's Bar in Cromwell Street, Steòrnabhagh; now O'Neills.

The 'Four and a Half'

I had come back to Port Mholair with less money than I had leaving to go to Canada as a young lad. The big world out there humbled me and taught me to treasure my little share of the world here in the back-of-beyond. When you come to think on it, there isn't that much difference between our lifestyle here and the lifestyle of the richest toffs in Miami or London. We eat three good meals a day as they do; we have clothes on our backs and we have a weather-proof roof over our heads. What else does a fella need?

Shonag married me and nursed me back to health. What a wonderful gal she is – she with her one eye! When I had a minor accident a few years back and lost my eye, hers came out in sympathy! Shonag lost her eye after grit got into it, when we were carting home the peats. A great shame for her! But that's OK! Economy all round. We have a half-decent pair of eyes between us. Shonag is my Marilyn Monroe, but not a woman without fault, mind you. She has a mighty sharp tongue on her at times, but as everybody knows, Soolivan needs someone to trim his sails and keep a steady hand on the helm!

I love company. In my young days, swapping yarns in the ceilidh-house was a way of life. Hundreds of stories are stored on my memory. Some things still haunt me, though, and I have dark remembrances of which I cannot talk to anyone. Never will.

The *Sràid* crew of Angus Sheonaidh's peats tractor

In the years after we got married, I earned enough at the navvying to see us through. Before Hitler's war, our home was the ceilidh-house. One thing that Shonag did was to ban the four-gallon beer-keg from our home. That is something that I miss very much. For about three years after we got married in 1936, the young men of the village used to pool their money every second week, so that they could buy a beer keg in Steòrnabhagh. John Murdo Campbell's charabanc used to bring the keg home and drop it off at the Brocair road-end. The lads would then carry it down the road, singing for all they were worth and set it up on our living-room table. Sipping from their jeely-jars, they would sit here for hours, listening to my stories and pretending to doubt everything I told them! They used to tell folk that they were 'going up the Street to listen to Soolivan's tall tales'! The Campbell boys used to rile me when they argued to my face that what I was telling them was lies. I often got on my high-horse – especially if I had drink taken! They enjoyed that – the conniving buggers! But don't misunderstand what I'm saying. The boys' company was a tonic to me. We laughed all evening. Well, our Marilyn Monroe banned the keg and Hitler scattered the boys, and that lifestyle was gone for good. Since the war ended, old-timers, college students, and friends from all over, take the time to visit Shonag and me.

Shonag is happy enough to go off to bed at eleven o'clock as she did tonight, and to leave me here sitting by the fireside, yarning. She's

Soolivan (left) and Donald MacVicar, son-in-law (right): Shonag and neighbours

OK so long as I keep off the booze. Make no mistake. I have spent the happiest years of my life sitting here with 'Marilyn Monroe'! There is no place on earth that I'd rather spend my final years than here with her on the croft on which I was born. Though our island is poor in many ways, it is the most civilised place on earth.

If what the ministers say about sinners holds water, then I am heading for the Everlasting Lake of Fire when I die. But I think on this quite often and, as God is my witness, I am telling the truth: I never harmed anybody who didn't deserve to be harmed. Well, maybe one or two right enough, but that's to be expected considering the kind of nature I was born with and the way I was thrown in at the deep end from the start.

Tell everybody that Soolivan was hospitable, not particularly talented and, alas, totally unschooled. Oh, I was quite good at sea, at fishing and sailing, but I cannot say that I could navigate a boat from London to Buenos Aires. Tell them that I was strong and self-confident and, until I was thirty years old, that no one ever dared raise a fist to me. Tell them that I was never at a university! No, sir, never was! But I spent my whole life at the Academy of Hard Knocks! Maybe, because of that, on Judgement Day, God will go easy on me and forgive me my many sins.

Soolivan died at his home at No. 11 Port Mholair on Wednesday, 22 August 1956.

Soolivan and Shonag in the 1950s

Appendix One

No Angel!

Ewen MacKenzie [Eóghann Mhurchaidh Eóghainn]

In 1937–8, I went 'deep-sea' on a ship called *Matakama*. I was then in my late teens, a little scared of the unknown, yet thrilled to be visiting countries on the far side of the globe. On that first trip, 'Bob' Ferguson, my brother-in-law, had me under his wing.

It was a wonderful time in my life. The *Matakama* visited Sydney and, within a few hours of the ship docking, I happened to see a distinguished-looking gentleman striding along the wharf. He was wearing a white cap and had some kind of official insignia on his jacket. As he advanced towards our gangway, I noticed that a foreman docker and a ship's officer going ashore saluted him. Next thing, the fellow climbed the gangway and made his way to the bridge and I felt in my bones that some member of the ship's crew was in dead trouble. I nearly fainted when a message came from the ship's Captain that I was to attend to him on the bridge immediately. In fear and trembling, I followed the messenger and duly stood before the Captain and the stranger. Of course, as I think on it, I must have appeared very shy and embarrassed as I stood there.

'Ewen MacKenzie?' said the stranger. 'You needn't answer, lad, for I'd know you among a thousand. I'm your great-uncle, Ruairidh Mhurchaidh 'ic Dhòmhnaill!'

Known in Australia as Roderick MacDonald, Ruairidh had left Lewis in his twenties and had risen through the ranks in the Sydney police. My mother had been in correspondence with him over the years and, as I discovered while I was in his company, he had been aware of the prospective arrival of the *Matakama* for weeks.

My newly discovered great-uncle asked the Captain if Bob Ferguson and I could be released from our duties for forty-eight hours, so that we might spend that time with him at his home. Permission was granted, and Bob and I trooped ashore with my distinguished kinsman.

Ruairidh's home was in a leafy suburb of the city – somewhat different from the sooty black-house in which he had been born and reared. As one would expect of a Lewisman born in the 1850s,

Ruairidh was a fluent Gaelic speaker and he scarcely spoke a word of English while Bob and I were in his company. Our two evenings together were spent as one might spend winter evenings back home. After dinner, the céilidh with plenty of stories and songs. Ruairidh told us about his police work but his most memorable anecdote was not one about crime but about his amazing encounter with a distant relation of his: a man whose reputation had already travelled as far as Sydney – a man called Soolivan.

The encounter took place one day as Ruairidh was walking along the waterfront in Port Jackson. I understand that he used to go for a stroll down to Port Jackson, hoping to meet up with Gaels off the ships newly berthed there. On a particular day, he was sauntering past a Russian ship when he heard loud shouting and swearing coming from the forward section of the ship. He paused to listen, and realised that the swearing was in Gaelic! Boarding the vessel, Ruairidh found his way to the Captain and, having introduced himself, he asked if there was a British citizen held prisoner on board.

'Yes!' replied the Captain. 'I have a UK citizen imprisoned in the chain-locker. I took him on as a crew-member in Odessa but, over some grievance he had concerning conditions on board, he went fighting mad and beat up the First Officer.'

Ruairidh told the Captain that he had a special interest in the prisoner and asked if it would be possible to see him. In due course, Soolivan was brought out of the chain-locker, handcuffed and looking the worse for wear. Having established whom the prisoner was, Ruairidh asked the Captain if he would consider surrendering the man into his charge.

Roderick MacDonald [Ruairidh Mhurchaidh 'ic Dhòmhnaill] of Sydney

'I am only too willing to do that, but first you would have to find the means to pay for the damage done by the prisoner while he was employed on this ship!'

The amount of the wages due to Soolivan was only part of the sum required to meet his debt. Ruairidh immediately went ashore to fetch the amount of money demanded, and also to explain the situation to the Immigration Authorities. The conditions imposed by Immigration were that before Soolivan could be disembarked, Ruairidh had personally to guarantee Soolivan's good behaviour for four weeks. After that time, the situation would be reviewed. It was hoped that, in that time, employment could be found for him on board a British ship outward bound.

After agreeing to take the prisoner under his wing, Ruairidh began to worry that Soolivan might not be the kind of fellow who would toe the line while ashore in Australia. As he pondered the situation, Donald MacDonald [Dòmhnall 'Ain Phortair] – another Port Mholair man living in Sydney – appeared on the scene. Closely related to Soolivan, Donald immediately paid the sum owed to the Russian. That done, Soolivan was taken from the chain-locker, his handcuffs were removed and he was released into Ruairidh's care.

Once settled into a room in Ruairidh's home, Soolivan was treated as any guest would be – with courtesy and with hospitality. He was taken to a clothiers and measured for two new suits. After that, he was presented with shoes and underwear so that, within a few days, he was transformed into a well-dressed, respectable-looking young man. Relaxing with Ruairidh and his friends, it was discovered that Soolivan had lost count of the days and nights he had spent in the heat and darkness of the ship's steel prison. Suffice to say that, by the time the ship had berthed at Port Jackson, he had become very confused and thought that the ship had been abandoned and that he had been left to suffocate or starve to death.

Gradually, Ruairidh became more and more confident that Soolivan would not do anything that would cause him embarrassment. After a week or so, Donald MacDonald asked him if it would be OK for him to invite Soolivan to spend a few days at his home. Ruairidh was quite agreeable, for he felt sure that his guest was back on the straight and narrow.

Soolivan appeared to be enjoying the hospitality showered on him. He packed his newly acquired clothes and was transported to Donald's home, where a number of expatriate Gaels attended an informal ceilidh in his honour. All went well until the third morning after Soolivan's arrival. Mrs MacDonald called to her guest to come down to join the family at breakfast. There was no reply from upstairs. When she went to investigate, she found that her guest's bed had not been slept in. Soolivan had disappeared in the night. The city police searched high and low for him but failed to find him. He had somehow managed to slip away and, so far as was known, he never again returned to that part of Australia. *Cha robh cuimhne air an aran-eòrna ach fhad 's a bha e anns an sgòrnan.**

Strange how those three men met in Sydney, on the far side of the world: Donald from Croft No. 4 Port Mholair, Ruairidh from No. 6 and Soolivan from No. 11. Two of them acted as Good Samaritans and, in the end, felt badly let down by the down-and-out whom they had done so much to help.

It would probably be going too far to say that Soolivan never had much of a conscience about anything. Yet I think it would be fair to say that he was in the habit of doing whatever suited him at the time. From what he told me many times, I'd say that that was how he behaved for most of his life – accepting or stealing and constantly fleeing from one crisis or other, and trying to keep a couple of steps ahead of the 'bogey-man'!

* The gift of barley-bread was forgotten as soon as it passed his gullet! [proverb].

Appendix Two

Rascal, but Made of Iron! An Obituary

'Bob' Ferguson [Iain Chaluim Alas' 'ic Uilleim]

Soolivan was a compulsive lawbreaker and drunkard. He was not a man to be admired. On the other hand, no-one could deny that he was intelligent and charismatic and that he was an extraordinary Lewisman. When his brother saved him from ending his days rotting in a Mexican jail, he returned to Port Mholair and became a kind of folk-hero. Unfortunately, he was anything but a hero. He was an incorrigible rogue who always put Number One first!

I happened to be working for a season on the *Prestige*, a small fishing-boat owned by *Balaich na Sràid* (the 'Street' lads). It was in the very year that Soolivan returned from Mexico – a pathetic shadow of his old self. Everybody felt sorry for him and *Balaich na Sràid* decided to give him a berth on the *Prestige*. He joined her in the spring when winds from the north and nor'-east frequently swept across the fishing-grounds with cold, sleety gusts. While the rest of the crew were well clad in woollen ganseys, moleskin trousers, oilskins and thigh-length waders, Soolivan sat on a thwart, kitted out only in dungarees, cord jacket and worsted shirt. On his feet, deformed by osteoarthritis, he wore calf-length boots. I remember it well: rain and sea-spray lashing us and Soolivan with his bony knees showing through his sodden trousers sitting with another crew-man gutting fish and all the while singing softly under his breath. He was resilient and durable and seemed able to adapt to any kind of situation in any kind of climate. I would agree with his own claim, that from his childhood, he was 'as hard as nails'!

On the *Prestige*, Soolivan proved to be the least competent of the crew. On the other hand, he was excellent company. Once in a while, he would look up from his work to give us some interesting snippet of information about his experience in some distant part of the globe. He had panned for gold in the Blue Mountains of Australia; had seen 'a giant of the deep' overcome by killer whales; had worked on a sheep-farm in Patagonia; and, by the skin of his teeth, had narrowly escaped from a couple of alligators in Florida and from a pack of wolves in Manitoba. He claimed to have had extraordinary experiences 'in his own back yard'. He had 'discovered a gold seam in Cnap Cìleag' near Tiumpanhead Lighthouse; had seen a ghost in a cave in Geodha Mille Gruaman where, as a schoolboy, he had lived for a day and a night; had found stalagmites 'like Mexican church statues' in the sea cave of Geodha na Sgalaig, near Goitealar; and so on.

He didn't seem to suffer any sense of embarrassment while telling us of his numerous misdeeds and punishments. Only one subject was *verboten*! He would clam up as soon as anybody mentioned his prison experience in Mexico.

How much of what he claimed was true I cannot say, but, if the passion and the amount of detail with which he told his stories was anything to go by, he had been everywhere and done everything that he described. The crew of the *Prestige*, including me, believed all that he said. The last time I saw him he was seated in the open, by the scullery door of his 'Ramshackle'. His *lèine chrimean* [Crimean shirt] was unbuttoned at the throat and his cap, as usual, was slightly askew on his head. Peering through his one eye, he lifted his gnarled hand and pointed to the Siùmpan, which happened to be lit by a bright afternoon sun.

'I sure am glad to be sitting here,' he declared, 'and that, at the end of my life, I am back home in the land of my forebears and able to see my Hills of Joy – Cnuic an Àigh!'

Appendix Three

Soolivan and History

At the time of Christ and for several centuries thereafter, the land of the Highlands and Islands was occupied by tribes which were collectively known to the Romans as Picti, a name said to mean, though some might not agree, the 'painted people'. During the sixth century, Gaelic-speaking inhabitants of Dalriada in the north of Ireland began to migrate to the mainland of Argyll and the Inner Hebrides and, in due course, made those places part of their kingdom. At that time, Ireland was dominated by monastic leaders who were devoutly Christian. Their missionaries travelled abroad and converted much of Northern Europe to Christianity. Having already set up many churches and monasteries in his native country, Columba, who was a prominent preacher and aristocrat in Ireland, landed with twelve followers on the little island of Iona, off Mull, in the year 563. There he established a monastery dedicated to training bearers of the Gospel. In due course, Columba's missionaries succeeded in converting most of Scotland and the north of England. (Christianity had been introduced to Scotland earlier by Ninian at Whithorn.)

Although various churches on Lewis were dedicated to him, it is likely that the island was not Christianised until long after the death of St Columba. It is interesting to note that Lewis is not mentioned in Adamnan's biography of St Columba, written in the seventh century.

In the last decade of the eighth century, the Viking* hordes from Norway, Sweden and Denmark burst quite suddenly into European history, conducting a series of savage attacks on the coastal communities in Britain, Ireland and Francia. For centuries, their homeland had been a remote region about which other Europeans knew little. In the generations that followed, people throughout western Europe were constantly terrified of seeing the distinctive square sails of the Viking long-ships on the horizon, each vessel with a carved dragon's head raised tall above its prow.

In AD 795 the Vikings landed on Iona and, as they were heathens who did not respect the sacred artefacts of the Christians, they carried

* *Vikingr* – 'sea-rover or pirate'.

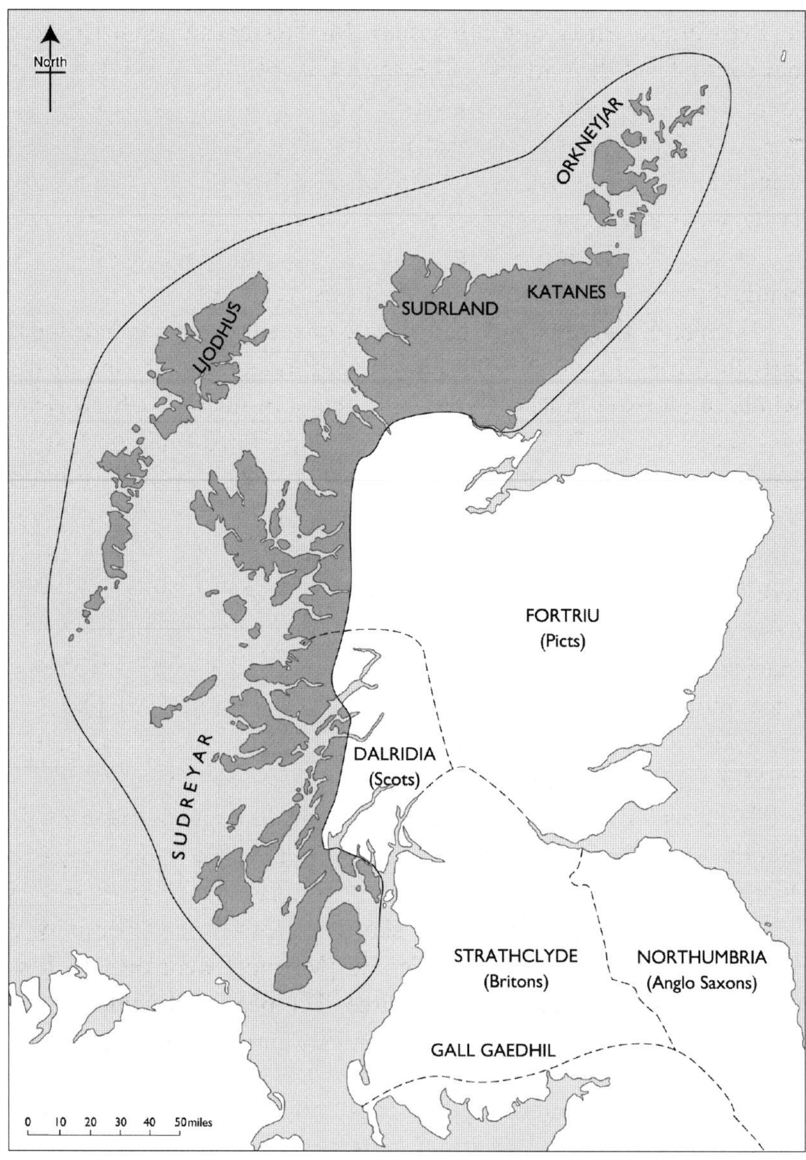

Map showing the Norse Earldom of Orkney, c. AD 1000

off the items which they thought might be valuable, destroyed the rest and killed many of the monks. In the decades that followed, the Vikings continued to raid Iona and other coastal settlements. About 890, long before Scotland had become one kingdom, a king of Norway called Harold the Fair-haired came with a great fleet and conquered Shetland, Orkney and the Western Isles. Not long afterwards, Norway took possession of Sutherland and Caithness. Until that time, the northern half of the country now called Scotland, including the Western and Northern Isles, was occupied by Picts. Few if any of the place-names that existed before the Norse colonisation of the islands survive.

The geographical range of Viking activity was enormous, spanning most of the then known world and going some way beyond it. Even North Africa and the eastern Mediterranean countries were not secure from their attacks. In eastern Europe, they sailed down the great rivers such as the Danube to cross the Black Sea and the Caspian Sea to attack Constantinople. In the west, they settled in the uninhabited Faroe Islands, Iceland and Greenland. Under the leadership of Leif Erikson, they discovered North America, but failed to settle there. From the ninth century, successive kings of Norway claimed the Outer Hebrides as part of their empire.

In spite of the resistance from some of the country's independent jarls [nobles], Harold the Fair-haired constituted himself king of the whole of Norway in 875. As a result, many of the jarls left Norway and sailed to the Outer Hebrides to set up a state independent of Norway. Harold pursued the disaffected jarls and conquered Shetland, Orkney, the Outer and Inner Hebrides and the Isle of Man. However, in the year following that conquest, the Isles rose in rebellion against Harold, who responded by sending his cousin Ketil to restore order. Having put down the rebellion, Ketil exceeded Harold's instructions and declared himself King of the Isles. In the generations that followed, the people of the islands continued to agitate against their conquerors. In the end, they rose up against them and slew their Norwegian overlord and all his supporters.

Magnus Bareleg* (1060–1103) reconquered the Northern Islands and the Outer and Inner Hebrides in 1098. In translation, the Saga of Magnus Bareleg states that he '. . . fell straightway to harry and to burn the builded country and to slay the menfolk . . . Fire played fiercely to the heavens over Lewis. He [Magnus] went over to Uist with flame. He harried Skye and Tiree. The people of Mull ran for fear. There was smoke over Islay. Men in Cantyre bowed before the sword.'

The oldest reference to the Isle of Lewis is in this Saga of Magnus Bareleg. There, the name is given as 'Ljodhus', the pronunciation of which is very close to the Gaelic 'Leódhas'.

Whereas the Vikings had come for plunder, their later descendants, known to us as Norsemen, came with their wives and families and settled on the land. They spoke a Germanic language similar to an early form of English. How ironic that our Norse ancestors of a millennium ago – the ancestors of, for example, the MacLeods, MacDonalds and MacAulays – should have seen their Germanic language being gradually eroded and replaced by a 'foreign' language that originally emanated from Ireland – a foreign language called Gaelic.

Towards the end of the thirteenth century, the Outer Hebrides

* So called because he had adopted the dress of the Gaels, the kilt.

were known to the Gaelic-speaking Scots of the Mainland as Innse Gall – the Islands of the Foreigners. Like his father before him, Alexander III, King of Scots, sought to negotiate with King Hakon of Norway the sale of Innse Gall, but Hakon steadfastly refused to come to terms. When the Earl of Ross, one of Alexander's nobles, started a military campaign against them, the chiefs of the islands appealed to King Hakon for help.

In July 1263, Hakon responded by setting sail with the largest fleet of long-ships that ever sailed from Norway. His own galley, made of solid oak, had a gilded dragon-head at its prow. It had twenty-seven benches for the rowers. For a short time, the fleet anchored at Orkney, then rounded Cape Wrath into the Minch. Looking forward to the showdown, many of the chiefs of the Outer Hebrides joined Hakon with their retainers.

The Scottish king and his nobles strengthened the castles near the coast and prepared the army to meet the invaders in battle. Spies sent to watch for the approach of the enemy reported that Hakon's fleet was off the coast of Argyll. When at last the squadrons of long-ships sailed into the Firth of Clyde, Alexander sent messages to Hakon, saying that he wanted to solve their disagreement amicably. Messengers travelled to and fro between the kings but the parleying was brought to an abrupt end on Sunday, 30 September when a violent storm arose and raged for forty-eight hours. During that time, some of Hakon's ships foundered near Largs on the Ayrshire coast. On Tuesday morning, Hakon ordered men ashore with rowing-boats to rescue those whose ships had sunk. While that was being done, the Scottish army, including 500 horsemen in armour, attacked. In the fighting, many men on both sides died. The Norwegians fought bravely, but in the end the survivors were driven back to their boats. After a few hours, the Norse fleet weighed anchor and began the voyage back to Norway. The reason for the fleet's withdrawal has been a subject for debate for centuries. One theory is that Hakon became ill before or during the battle and was not well enough to direct the disembarkation of his main force. In any case, while the ships were being provisioned at Kirkwall in Orkney, the king lost consciousness and died.

After the so-called Battle of Largs, Alexander had little difficulty in subduing the Outer Hebrides. King Magnus, Hakon's successor, agreed to cede the islands to Scotland on payment of 4,000 marks and 100 marks 'every succeeding year for all time to come'. This treaty ended the power of the Norwegians along the western seaboard of Scotland. Lewis then became part of the Earldom of Ross but the principal possessors of the island were MacLeods, descendants of the Norsemen.

A long time passed before the islands of Orkney and Shetland became part of the kingdom of Scotland. For almost 1,000 years, the language of the Orcadians was a variant of Old Norse known as Norn. By the late eighteenth century, only a handful of older Orcadians still knew the language and when they died, Norn went with them.

Remnants of the Old Norse language are to be found in numerous place-names throughout the areas of Scotland which, at one time, belonged to Norway. In Gaelic, our vocabulary relating to sailing and fishing is strewn with borrowings from Old Norse: for example: akkeri [*acair*] – an anchor; bithring [*birlinn*] – a galley; batr [*bàta*] – a boat; hlunn [*lunn*] – a launching roller; dorg [*dorgh*] – a trailing line; styra [*stiùir*] – a rudder; langa [*langa*] – a ling; skata [*sgait*] – a skate; and thorsk [*trosg*] – a cod. Apart from words relating to sailing and fishing, one finds in the Old Norse dictionary, numerous words that the Gael will find familiar: for example, deila [*deilich*] – divide; fel [*féileadh*] – a folded skirt; brak [*brag*] – a sudden noise; broddr [*brod*] – a spike; bara [*bara*] – a hand-barrow; sura [*sùrag*] – sorrel; ljos [*leus*] – a burning light; and knapp [*cnap*] – a knob or protrusion.

In 1609, Hebridean noblemen meeting at Iona under the presidency of Andrew Knox, Bishop of the Isles agreed a series of measures aimed, inter alia, at improving education in the Islands. The measures, known as the 'Statutes of Icolmkill', required that 'every gentilman or yeaman within the saidis Ilandis or ony of thame having children maill or famell and being in goodis worth thriescoir ky, sall putt at leist thair eldest sone, or having no children maill, thair eldest dochtir, to the scullis in the lawland . . . And bring thame up thair quhill thay may be sufficientlie to speik, reid and write Inglische.'

In 1616, the Privy Council of Scotland passed an Act that may be regarded as the first compulsory Education Act that applied to the Highlands and Islands. Its preamble attributes the 'barbaritie, impietie and incivilitie within the Yllis' to the neglect of education, particularly because the children were not sent to the mainland to be trained in 'vertew, learning and the Inglis tunge'. The Act required that the 'haill chiftanes and principal clanit men of the Yllis and every ane of thame send thair bairns, being past nyne yeiris of age, to the scoolis in the Inland to be trained vp in vertew, learning and the Inglis tunge'. It was further enacted that 'no personis quhatsomevir in the Yllis sal be seruit (h)air to their father or vtheris predicessouris nor ressauit nor acknowlegeit or tennentis to his Majestie vnless they can write, reid and speake Inglische'.

Later in that same year, an Act of Parliament was passed for the establishment of parish schools in Scotland. Among the objects aimed at was the extinction of Gaelic: '. . . that the vulgar Inglish toung be vniversallie plantit and the Irishe language, which is one of the chief and principall causis of the continewance of barbaritie and incivilitie among the inhabitantis of the Illis and Heylandis, may be abolisheit and removeit'.

The Patronage Act of 1712 conferred on a landlord the right to appoint his own nominee to be minister of a church, even if the appointee was unacceptable to the congregation. A century later, the iniquity of this privilege led to serious repercussions within the Established Church. During and after the Napoleonic Wars, which ended in 1815, many of the indigenous people of the Highlands and Islands were being driven off their land to allow landlords to develop sheep-farms or sporting estates. In effect, the eviction of the native people – the Clearances – amounted to ethnic cleansing. Fearful of being deprived of their homes and livelihood, the majority of ministers of the Established Church refrained from offering comfort to their parishioners who were under threat of eviction. On the contrary, they preached that their congregations should not resist the regime imposed upon them, as their suffering was the will of God and resulted from their wickedness. In 1834, the Lewis Presbytery resolved to petition both Houses of Parliament for the abolition of lay patronage. Dissension within the Established Church reached fever point, and in 1843, a new Church was formed to become known as the Free Church of Scotland. The severance of the Free Church of Scotland from the Established Church of Scotland became known as the Disruption. In the new Church, ministers were appointed by the will of the members of the congregation.

The Free Church regarded education as being of prime importance to the population it served. In the second half of the nineteenth century, it provided funds to enable young men to attend universities and to become graduate preachers. It also established schools in most districts to augment the work of other agencies which, over the years, had been active in that field of education. Parochial Schools had already been established, as were Industrial Schools and Spinning Schools (promoted with great zeal by Lady Seaforth). Also active in the field were the Society in Scotland for Propagating Christian Knowledge (SSPCK) and the Gaelic Schools Society.

Several reports written at the beginning of the nineteenth century suggest that Lewis parents regarded education as a threat to the welfare of their families and their way of life. A report on 'Agriculture in the Hebrides' (1811) claimed that the great mass of people in Lewis believed that 'If we give them education, they will leave us'. Before a Select Committee of the Houses of Parliament, Thomas Knox, Chamberlain of Lewis, believed that '. . . The country people are not fond of their children being taught the English language; they think that if they were taught English, they would leave the island'. In 1883, John Munro MacKenzie, Chamberlain for Lewis, reported to the Napier Commission that '. . . parents who did not keep their children at school were dealt with but to no avail, as they often told me, they did not want to give their children wings to leave them'.

A report on the 'State of Education in the Hebrides' (1865) stated that, at that time, there was a population of 2,159 in the Rubha. Of those, 403 men and 463 women could read Gaelic, while only 208 men and 46 women could English. The number who could write was 170 men and 26 women. Although girls were taught to read the Bible in Gaelic, they were not sent to school in any numbers. 'Of 2,697 scholars on the school rolls in Lewis, there were 1, 590 boys but only 1,107 girls; in attendance, 922 boys and 684 girls. Yet the female population of the island, in 1861, was in excess of males by 122, the numbers being respectively 11,089 and 9,967.'

The first census giving the number of Gaelic speakers in the population was that of 1891 (when Soolivan was two years of age). Out of a total population of 27,590, 14,015 spoke only Gaelic. Persons speaking both Gaelic and English numbered 11,254.

> *Extract from the Crofters Commission report to the Secretary of State for Scotland, 1902:*
> It has often been said that of all parts of the crofting area, that portion which presents the most difficult questions is the Island of Lewis. Not but that some at least of the problems existing there, are to be found elsewhere; but in Lewis they are more pressing, as they affect a wider area and a denser population . . . Our inquiry as to the Lewis of the past proves that the inhabitants of that Island are worthy of all the attention they have received. Although they occupy a remote and, in some respects, a sterile Island, they are men of strong physical development, of tough moral fibre, and of undoubted intellectual capacity. The defects now to be found in the Lewis-man are mainly of insufficient education, and of too limited experience of the world – not defects of character or mind . . . An Island which can produce the ancestors of Lord MacAulay, as also Sir Alexander Mackenzie (the Arctic explorer from whom the Mackenzie River in North-West Canada takes its name) and Colonel Colin Mackenzie, Surveyor General of India, cannot fail to compel attention. The physical and moral strength of the Lewis-man is partly due to his surroundings. These compel simplicity of life and foster powers of endurance. They nerve him to face privations before which men brought up in more favourable circum-

> stances would succumb. The cynical critic might indeed urge that Lewis is an earthly paradise, for there is to be found an exceptionally high birth-rate, an exceptionally low death-rate and, notwithstanding insanitary conditions, a striking immunity from many complaints. But little argument is needed to show that, in spite of these facts, Lewis is still far behind the condition of development to be found among the better class of crofters in most quarters of the Highlands, notwithstanding the efforts made for their amelioration in recent years. Thus to take one example, in the matter of housing and sanitation, Lewis may be said to stand alone. It is the sole place left where the custom of only one byre cleaning in the year prevails.
>
> For a considerable period after passing of the Education Act, thirty years ago (1872), the progress of education in Lewis was slow and unsatisfactory. . . But soon after the issue of the Departmental Minute of 21 December 1888, a great change for the better became apparent. Exceptional relief was granted to the Lewis ratepayer; educational matters generally were placed on a sound and progressive footing.

The Education Act of 1872 ignored Gaelic as a living language. Thus, teachers in state schools were discouraged from educating their pupils through the medium of their native tongue. The result was that for two generations following the passing of the Act, children beginning their schooling as monoglot Gaels were physically and psychologically abused by teachers whose perceived duty was to 'beat English into them'.

The past two millennia have witnessed three linguistic revolutions in Lewis. Pictish was replaced by Norse, and then Norse by Gaelic. Today, one sees the modern juggernaut of English and Americanese in danger of obliterating the ancient and expressive language of the Gael. After centuries of sustained pressure from different agencies of government, the Gaelic language was brought to within a few generations of total extinction. Today, thanks to the efforts of modern educationists (many of them on the Continent) the language is recognised as part of the European cultural heritage. Considerable efforts are under way to regenerate the language and to make this and future generations aware of our people's history and rich linguistic heritage.

Towards the end of the nineteenth century, there were further schisms within the Protestant churches in the Highlands and Islands. In 1900, the majority of congregations in the Free Church of Scotland joined with the United Presbyterian Church to form the United Free

Church of Scotland. Most of the people of Lewis were against this union and remained in the Free Church. Whole communities were divided in their allegiance to different ministers and denominations. The changes gave rise to a great deal of bitterness and the spirit of unity and co-operation on which the crofting communities relied so heavily suffered accordingly. In some cases the sense of brotherliness among boat-crews was lost.

From his earliest years, Soolivan was aware of the tensions between the various religious individuals in the community. In his later life, he could remember the consternation caused when church ministers preached sermons from the pulpit that included sharp, uncompromising criticisms of their own peers. It is impossible to say whether Soolivan's unruly conduct as a boy was influenced by the tumultuous and divisive events in the local churches – institutions claiming to be founded on the gospel of love, humility, tolerance and forgiveness. To a certain extent, his lack of discipline and waywardness may have been exacerbated by the premature death of his father. As he himself admitted towards the end of his life, he did nothing to help his widowed mother to keep the wolf from the door. On the contrary, he was a constant source of worry to her because of his 'wild, rebellious ways'.

> *Extract from a Crofters Commission report, 1902:*
> To the present day, the poor in Lewis largely depend on the charity of their neighbours. This may be inferred from the statistics received from the Local Government Board which show that the proportion of paupers to the whole population of the island is little more than half the corresponding figures applicable to the mainland of Ross and Cromarty. Having regard to the general poverty of the inhabitants a different result might have been expected, but when the circumstances are considered, it is of easy explanation. A considerable proportion of the ratepayers are very poor and the existing rates higher than they can well bear. Accordingly, a large number of applications for parochial relief have to be refused and the applicants are then obliged to have recourse to the bounty of their neighbours who, though often unable to help them with cash, are usually able and ready to afford help in kind. Their charity assumes various forms. A feeble or infirm person who is not a recipient of parochial relief gets land tilled and seed sown for him or her. In like manner, aid is given in casting and curing and carrying home peats. When boats arrive with fish, the poor who have no male relative to fish for them are seldom forgotten; and when crops are reaped in the autumn, those

> who have not sown often receive quantities of potatoes, etc. from neighbours . . .

The convulsions in the churches notwithstanding, the spirit of compassion and the sense of clanship described in that Report of 1902 was equally in evidence in the 1930s when Soolivan was allowed home from Mexico. That was a decade before the inception of the Welfare State, a time when families had to work together as a community to allow them to survive. Tarmod Uilleim's 'Prodigal son' returned to his homeland during the Great Depression, when hundreds of Island seamen were unemployed and many households were in dire straits. Perversely, the herring industry slumped: the herring shoals that had brought a measure of prosperity to many in the 1920s, all but disappeared from the Minches in the 1930s. In spite of those hardships, the Port Mholair community rallied to Soolivan's assistance and rehabilitation.

Today, the security provided by our social and medical services has resulted, to a large extent, in a loss of community spirit and co-

A black-house family of a century ago

operation. Like virtually every township in the Highlands and Islands, Port Mholair has been transformed. The inception of the Welfare State, the improvement in housing and advances in transport links and other means of communication have immeasurably raised the standard of living of the people living there. The indigenous families cling to the tenancy of their crofts but the crofting way of life has become a distant memory. Soolivan and his contemporaries, who were persecuted at school for speaking their native language, would be astonished to discover that in the twenty-first century there are State-funded classrooms throughout much of Scotland – indeed, to within a mile of the Scottish Parliament in Edinburgh – in which all teaching is done through the medium of Gaelic.

The majority of houses in Port Mholair are now occupied by incomers – Lowland Scots, English and German families – so that only a handful of people continue to remember Soolivan and where his once famous Ramshackle stood.

Chan eil duine gun dà latha ach duine gun latha idir! He who lives long will find himself in a world beyond his ken!

Old croft houses modernised – reminders of the way things were

Appendix Four

Clockwise with the Ancestors

According to Soolivan, all Lewis children of his generation were brought up on the *cladach* [seashore]. In that, his generation differed little from every generation of islander since the world began. For the inquisitive child, the seashore remains a place of mystery and discovery. Resident mussels, limpets, hermit-crabs, winkles, blennies, eels, green-crabs and sea-urchins are constantly there to draw the attention. The *cladach* is covered and uncovered by the tide twice every day and, at an early age, the island child learns how to anticipate the time of the full ebb, which advances by thirty minutes every twelve hours. After he learns where to look, he will often discover new creatures that have ventured in from deep water and become marooned in the rock-pools. Apart from the familiar *crùbag* [edible crab], lobster, starfish or sea-urchin, he might discover a rare exotic visitor: an anglerfish, a sunfish or, perhaps, a John Dory.

For the island children, the *cladach* was their first experience of exploration, and what they learned of that wonderful ever-changing world left an indelible impression. Early in their formative years, they learned the names of each rock, boulder, outcrop and gully within half a mile of their croft end. In his beloved 'Hills of Joy', Soolivan and his contemporaries were familiar with every foot of the braes, knaps and dells in hills such as Foitealar, Goitealar, An t-Siùmpan and Cnap Cìleag. They also knew of 'secret places' hidden behind the hills: the sea-caves, trenches, ravines and overhangs where they could shelter from the weather or spend hours in exploration or solitude.

In the Rubha, most shore-land names are Gaelic and their meaning obvious: Clach na Muilne [The Mill-stone], Geodha na Muic [The Whale Gully], An Carragh Bàn [The Whitish Outcrop] etc. However, there are others whose origins and meanings were hidden by the mists of time: Ocabhaig, Millim Goile, Gréinigeadh and so on. Many believed that such place-names belonged to the language of a primordial race of people who lived on the island at the dawn of time. In this chapter, we aim to show that that 'primordial people' were the islanders' own ancestors of, perhaps, a thousand years ago.

During his many months in jail, Soolivan kept his mind alert by playing *Duan a' Chladaich* [The Shore Recital] – a memory game that, up to the time of the Second World War, was a popular form of entertainment in the fishing communities of the Gàidhealtachd: that of recalling the names of more than one hundred rocks and gullies round the coast. In Port Mholair, the challenge was to recite the names, starting at Sgeir nan Ràmh in Port nan Giùran and finishing at the Rubha Deas in the Àird. According to Soolivan, he was in the habit of reciting *Duan a' Chladaich* every day to two appreciative fellow-prisoners who spoke neither English nor Gaelic!

From the events described in the foregoing chapters, it is not difficult to view Soolivan as a throwback to the age of the Vikings, when travel, adventure and lawlessness were accepted as the norm. He was a MacLeod and, as such, carried the genes of the fearless, adventurous Vikings who swarmed through the known world and beyond. Surely a man so durable, self-confident, pugnacious, and given to regaling audiences with his personal saga, would have been accepted as worthy of a berth in one of the marauding longships of Magnus Barelegs or Leif Erikson!

The following pages record the shoreland names with which the indigenous Gaels of the townships of An Rubha are still familiar. It is a treasury of words that provides us with a linguistic link with our ancestors both Gaelic and Norse.

The different kinds of indentation or intrusion in the shoreline

Soolivan with his dog, Dìleas, at the door of the 'Ramshackle'

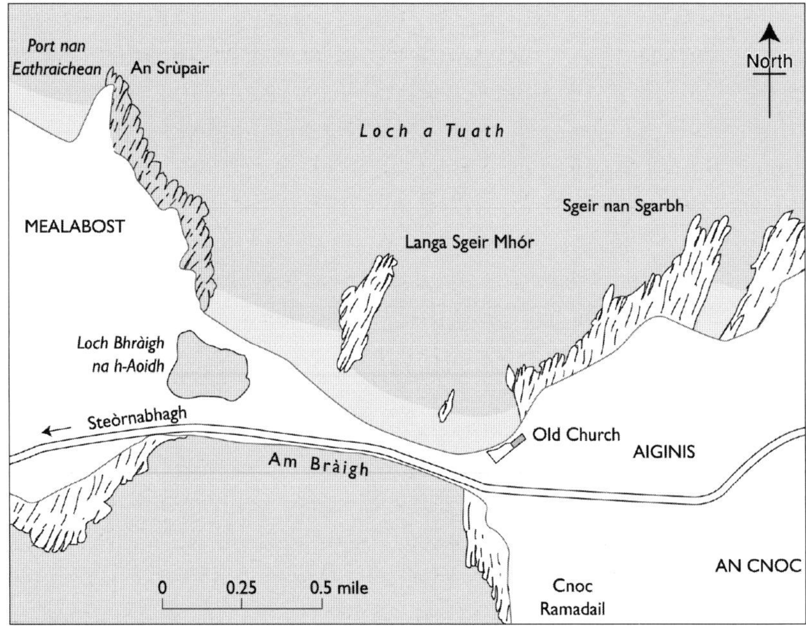

(clefts, creeks, rifts, coves etc.) are here given under the generic term 'gully'. Abbreviations used are as follows: BMK – Bridget MacKenzie; DW – *Dwelly's Dictionary*; Eng. – English; G. – Gaelic; McI. – D. MacIver's *Placenames of Lewis & Harris*; N. – Norse.

Mealabost

Sandbank Farm: N. 'mel' – a sandbank; 'bolstath' – a farm'.

Port nan Eathraichean The Boats' Beach G. 'nan eathraichean', gen. plur. of 'na h-eathraichean' – the boats.

An Strùpair The Spout: G. 'strùpair' – a spout or protruding point.

Tràigh Mhealaboist The Mealabost Shore: G.'tràigh' – a shore.

Am Bràigh The Causeway; a narrow neck of land, a half mile long, joining the Rubha to the mainland of Lewis: N. 'brú' – a bridge.

Aiginis

The Promontory of the Ridge: N. 'egg' – a ridge; 'nes' – a promontory. Once a farm, the township occupies an area of about 280 acres, bordering the Loch a Tuath.

Beginning at Mealabost, we cross the isthmus of the Bràigh and continue clockwise along the shore of An Rubha

An Aoidh (also spelled **Uidh** and **Ui**) The Isthmus: N. 'eith' – an isthmus. Nowadays, the term is applied to the land occupied by the cemeteries for the Rubha.

Langa-sgeir The Long Rock, an outcrop of conglomerate rock, protruding through the sandy beach on the north side of the Bràigh: N. 'lang' – long; 'sker' – a rock.

Langa-sgeir Bheag is a much smaller outcrop, about 100 metres to the east: G. 'beag' – small.

Sgeir a' Ghàrraidh The Wall Rock, situated at the shore end of the township's drystone wall. Separating the arable land from the rough grazing of the common; a drystone wall is a feature of many crofting townships: G. 'a' ghàrraidh' gen. sing. of 'an gàrradh' – the wall.

Sgaraisgeir The Cormorant Rock: N. 'skarf' – a cormorant; 'sker' – a rock.

Huisgeir The Seabirds' Rock: inaccessible from the shore, this rock is revealed at low tide: N. 'ufa-sker' – seabirds' rock.

Sròn an t-Seann Eich The Old Horse's Ness: G. 'sròn' – a point/ness; 'an t-seann eich', gen. sing. of 'an seann each' – the old horse; 'seann' – old. The name recalls a time when it was customary to get rid of old horses by shooting them close to the edge of a cliff, thus allowing their bodies to be carried away on the tide.

Geodha nan Càirdean – The Friends' Gully: G. 'càirdean' – friends or relations. Originally, more likely **Geodha nan Ceàrdan** – The Tinkers' Gully; 'nan ceàrdan', plur. of 'na ceàrd' – the tinkers. The word 'geodha' is derived from N. 'gjá' – a gully.

Garrabost

The Walled Farm: N. 'garth' – a wall or fence; 'bolstath' – a farm.

Dìobadal Deep Glen: N. 'djúp'– deep; 'dal' – dale or glen.

Bun Allt nan Gall – Foot of the Foreigners' Burn: G. 'bun' – foot/outlet; 'allt' – a burn; 'nan Gall' – gen. plur. of 'na Goill' – the foreigners. This burn draining Loch Drolabhat, Suardail, is also known as **Allt Dìobadail.**

Gluma Dosag Dosag's Pool: 'Dosag', the byname of a woman from No. 3 who used to wash her blankets in Allt Dìobadal; died in 1941: G. 'gluma' – a deep pool.

Am Bogha Mòr The Great Reef, some little distance from the shore and stretching from Bun Allt Dìobadail to Roisinis A-muigh: G. 'bogha' (loan-word from N. 'bothi') – a reef; 'mor' – great.

Stac Bheag Gharraboist The Little Stack of Garrabost, a

columnar mass of rock detached from a cliff by the action of the sea: N. 'stak' – a stack; G. 'beag' – little. Further east, **Stac Mhór Gharraboist** The Great Stack of Garrabost: G. 'mor' – great.

Stiogha nan Cliabh, a path used for carrying fish in creels to the cliff-top: G. 'stiogha' (from N. 'stíg') – a cliff-path; 'nan cliabh', gen. plur. of 'na cléibh' – the creels, usually used by women to carry heavy loads on their backs; 'cliabh' also means 'a lobster-pot'.

Na Beathar The Pastures; two shallow inclines north of Gleann Dìobadail, each measuring less than a quarter acre and producing luscious grass: G. from N. 'beitar' – pastures.

Geodhaichean Dhùgaidh Dougie's Gullies; two in number and named after Dougal MacIver of the Buaile Chreadha, 1930s: G. 'geodhaichean', plur. of 'geodha' – a gully.

Mac Ille Dhuilich This N. name has been given a G. form, thus altering it almost beyond recognition. It is safe to assume that the name included 'bakki' (a bank or cliff); perhaps also 'gilja' – a ravine. See the identical name, p. 241.

Sruthan Mac Ille Dhuilich The Stream emptying into Mac Ille Dhuilich: G. 'sruthan' – a stream.

Rainnstir The Crooked Cliff-path: N. 'rang' – crooked; 'stíg' – a path.

Rubha nam Marbh The Headland of the Dead: G. 'nam marbh', gen. plur. of 'na mairbh' – the dead persons.

Clach an Ròin Seal Rock: G. 'clach ' – a stone; 'an ròin', gen. sing. of 'an ròn' – the seal.

Sloc Dhòmhnaill Chuil Donald Col's Hollow: G. ' sloc' – a hollow; Donald MacLean of No. 1, early 20th Cent. 'Chuil', gen. sing. of 'Col', a township in the parish of Bac, Lewis.

Roisinis a Muigh Outer Horse-Headland, a low, grassy promontory, at one time used for grazing horses: N. 'hross' – a horse; 'nes' – a point; G. 'a muigh' – out.

Cuibh an Dìob The Sheep-fold of the Dip: 'cuibh', G. borrowing from N. 'kvì' – a sheep-fold; 'dìob' – possibly borrowed from Eng. 'dip'.

Geodha Chuibh an Dìob also known as **Geodha Roisinis.** The children of Garrabost Uarach used to swim and play in this broad sandy cove stretching between Roisinis a Muigh and Roisinis a Staigh (see next page). Those from Garrabost Iarach did likewise in Sinigeadh; see p. 231.

Cuibh Làr Mares' Pen: an area immediately above Cuibh an Dìob, at one time used as an enclosure for mares. G. 'làr', gen. plur. of 'làir' – mares.

Na Sgeirean Dubha The Black Rocks: G. 'na sgeirean dubha', nom. plur. of 'an sgeir dhubh' – the black rock.

A' Gheodha Ghorm The Blue Gully: G. 'gorm' – blue/green.

An t-Sròn Ruaidh The Reddish Point: G. 'sròn – a point/protrusion; 'ruadh' – reddish; also known as **an t-Sròn Chruaidh** – the Hard Point: G. 'cruaidh' – hard.

An Lot Bhàn, seaward of No. 1, a fallow croft communally owned by the eighteen crofts of the original township. Until WW2, it was used for hay-making in the summer and later in the year for grazing. G. 'lot', a loan word from Eng. meaning 'croft'; G. 'bàn' – fallow.

Roisinis a Staigh Inner Horse Headland: N. 'hross' – a horse; 'nes' – a point. G. 'A-staigh' – in, inner.

Sùil na h-Uamha The Eye of the Cave: G. 'sùil' – an eye; 'na h-uamha', gen. sing of 'an uamh' – the cave.

Bealaichean na Gaoithe The Windy Gaps: G. 'bealaichean', plur. of 'bealach' – a gap or pass; 'na gaoithe', gen. sing. of 'a' ghaoth' – the wind.

An Iòrr Mhór The Big Lug, projecting from the cliff beyond the boundary of Croft No. 1, a flat, horizontal slab of some twenty square metres: G. 'iòrr' from N. 'eyra' – a lug or projection; G. 'mór' – big. **An Iòrr Bheag** The Little Lug.

Fuaran nan Cat The Cat Spring: G. 'fuaran' – a spring; 'nan cat', gen. plur' 'na cait' – the cats.

Sgor Seònaid Janet's Crab-crevice: G. 'sgor'- accessible at low tide, a deep crevice in rock giving shelter to an edible crab or lobster.

Sloc a' Bhàta The Boat Hollow: G.'sloc' – a hollow; 'a' bhàta', gen. sing. of 'am bàta' – the boat.

Geodha nan Calman The Rock-doves' Gully. In the interior of the gully, rock-doves nest in a cave created by the action of the sea; G. 'nan calman' gen. plur. of 'na calmain' – the rock-doves.

Sròn a' Chlamhain The Buzzard's Point: G. 'sròn' – a point; 'a' chlamhain', gen. sing. of 'an clamhan' – the buzzard.

Geodha an t-Searmoin The Sermon Gully: G. 'searmon' – a sermon; probably so named when, immediately after the Disruption (1843), congregations held open air services.

Allt Fhors Waterfall Stream: a Gaelic name based on an older Norse one: N. 'fors' – a waterfall; G. 'allt' – a burn.

An Stalla The Overhanging Rock: G. 'stalla' – an overhanging rock.

Nead an Fhithich The Raven's Nest: G. 'nead' – a nest; 'an fhithich', gen. sing. of 'am fitheach' – the raven.

Tobair Chùisdein Cùisdean's Well on No. 30: G. 'tobair' – a well (mentioned by Martin Martin, 1690s). **Teampall Chùisdein** Cùisdean's Temple: G. 'teampall' – a temple.

Eas Allt Chùisdein – The Cùisdean Burn Waterfall: G. 'eas' – a waterfall; at the shore end of No. 30.

Sgeir Healair The Rock of Heallair: G. 'creag' – a rock. Heallair, literally means 'Fishing-huts': N. – 'sel' – a fishing-hut; plur. 'seljar'.

Stac an Trìlleachan The Oyster Catcher's Stack: G. 'trìlleachan' – and oyster catcher.

An Dùn Mòr The Big Pile, a bluff at the foot of No. 37: G. 'dùn'- a large rock mass; also means 'fort'; nearby, **An Dùn Beag** – The Little Pile.

An Stiogha Ruadh The Reddish Path: G. 'stiogha' – a path; 'ruadh' – reddish; also known as **A' Ghil Ruadh** – The Reddish Ravine. The G. 'stiogha' from N. 'stig' – a path; similarly 'gil' from N. 'gilja' – a ravine.

An Fhaing The Sheep-fank: G. 'faing' – a sheep-fank.

An Cidhe The Pier: G. 'cidhe' – a pier. Both 'cidhe' and 'faing' are loan-words from Eng.

Bun Allt na Muilne Mill-Burn Estuary: G. 'na muilne', gen. sing. of 'a' mhuileann' – the water-mill.

Stac an Trìlleachan is between us and Roisinis a Staigh; the point of Healair juts from the left

Na Cìreanan Cama The Crooked Combs; three rows of serrated rocks: G. 'cìreanan', plur. of 'cìr'- a comb; 'cama' – plur. of 'cam' – crooked.

Bun Allt Ran-ìodar The Estuary of the Ran-ìodar Burn: N. 'rang' – crooked; 'oethra' – a shallow burn; G. 'allt' (a burn) is superfluous.

Hurraghal ('hurr-' pronounced as in Eng. 'hurry') The origin is uncertain. Local lore suggests the word is onomatopoetic: G. 'uraghuil' – a deep growling noise heard with certain states of the wind and tide.

Sinigeadh The Swimming Gully: N. 'synda' – swimming; 'gjá' – gully. Norsemen swam for pleasure and also as part of their training for manhood. Until recent times, the young of successive generations used this sheltered, sandy cove for summer swimming.

An Laga Dubh The Black Hollow – a large grassy hollow which, nowadays, is certainly not 'dubh'!

Some other place-names in Garrabost

Buaile a' Mhuilleir The Miller's Cattle-pen: G. 'buaile' – a pen; 'muillear' – a miller.

Earrainn na Croise The Cross Portion; having an ecclesiastical association, ground adjacent to Buaile a' Mhuilleir: G. 'earrainn' – portion; 'na croise', gen. sing. of ? 'a' chrois' – the cross.

Geàrraidh Teangainn The Grazing Enclosure on the Spit; the area of land on which the Garrabost water-mill is situated: G. from two N. words: 'geirthi' – a walled field; 'tangi' – a spit of land.

Allt nan Gall The Foreigners' Stream: G. 'nan Gall' – gen. plur. of 'na Goill' – the foreigners; compare 'Innse Gall' – The Norsemen's Isles (The Outer Hebrides). The stream, which at one time powered the Garrabost mill, is also called **Allt Diobadail**.

Crò Phàdraig Peter's Fold: G. 'crò' – a sheep-fold; 'Pàdraig' – Peter.

Poll a' Mhaighistir The Priest's Pool: G. 'poll' – a pool; 'a' mhaighistir', gen. sing. of 'am maighistir' – the priest/master.

Cnoc Bhaile-roth The Hill of the Circular Clearing: G. 'cnoc' – a hill; N. 'val' – round; 'roth' – cleared land.

Cnocan Biorach The Pointed Hillock: G. 'cnocan' – hillock; 'biorach' – pointed.

Gearraidh Teangainn with Allt nan Gall which at one time powered the Garrabost

Bota nan Aighean The Heifers' Bog: G. 'bota' – a bog; 'nan aighean', gen. plur. of 'na h-aighean' – the heifers.

Hòl The Hill, an eminence between Garrabost and Pabail Uarach: N. 'hóll' – a hill.

Cnoc Eòin Eòin's Hill: G. 'cnoc' – a hill; Eòin, a variant of the name Iain, John, etc.

Tom na h-Inghinn Ruaidh The Knoll of the Red-haired Girl: G. 'tom' – a hillock; 'na h-inghinn', gen. sing. of 'an nighean' – the girl; 'ruadh' – red-(haired).

A' Bhuaile Chrèadha The Clay Cattle-enclosure, nowadays known as 'Clay Park': G. 'buaile' – a cattle-enclosure/pen; 'chrèadha', aspirated form of gen. of 'crèadh' – clay. In the nineteenth century, this was the site of brickworks and chemical works established by Sir James Matheson.

Siulaisiadar

The name consists of two N. words, the second of which is 'saetr' – summer pasture. However, the meaning of the first word is uncertain. It may be from 'sula' – a standing-stone; but if such a stone ever existed, it has long since disappeared. Interestingly, there is a group of standing-stones (albeit depleted) on the summit of Cnoc nan Tursainnean, the hill immediately to the south. Also, on the moor and roughly half way between that circle and Siulaisiadar, is a solitary upright monolith known as A' Chlach Ghlas. There may have been a relationship between those stones and the postulated 'sula' at Siulisiadar.

Na Lagan Dubha The Black Hollows, a short distance from the shore, a long narrow trough which was a habitat of grey gurnet and flat-fish: G. 'lag' – a hollow; 'dubha', masc. plur. of 'dubh' – black.

Bun a' Ghàrraidh Boundary-dyke Foot: G. 'a' ghàrraidh', gen. sing. of 'an gàrradh' – a wall.

Port Shiadair The Siadar Berthing-place: G. 'port' (pron. 'porst') – a berthing-place or haven.

Geodha 'n t-Slacain The Gully of the Slacan, so called because of a roughly cylindrical cave in its interior: G. 'slacan' – a potato-masher; or 'a circular depression' (DW).

Unaisgeir The Seabirds' Rock: N. perhaps ' úfa-nes-sker'; 'úfa' – seabirds.

Geodha Mhór an Fhithich Great Raven Gully: G. 'an fhithich', gen. sing. of 'am fitheach' – a raven. **Geodha Bheag an Fhithich** Little Raven Gully.

An Cladach Dubh The Black Shore: G. 'cladach' – a shore; 'dubh' – black.

Bun an t-Sruthain Dhuibh The Estuary of the Black Stream: G. 'an t-sruthain dhuibh', gen. sing. of 'an sruthan dubh' – the black stream.

Millim Goile Between the Two Ravines – the shore area between the end of the Gil at No. 15 and the mouth of Allt Mór Shiadair at No. 4. N. 'millim'– middle; 'geilar', plur. of 'geila' – a ravine.

An Sgonnan The Stone Block: G. 'sgonnan' – a block of stone. It is also called **Rubha a' Ghràn** The Grain Headland, said to be so named because at one time grain was unloaded there for the local farm: G. 'a' ghràn', gen. sing. of 'an gràn' – the grain.

Stac a' Ghreimire The Climbing-iron Stack: G. 'a' ghreimire', gen. sing. of 'an greimire' – the climbing-iron or grappling-hook.

Geodha an Uillt The Burn Gully. The water from Allt Mór Shiadair (the Great Burn of Siadar) exits through this gully. G. 'an uillt', gen. sing. of 'an t-allt' – the burn.

Geodha nan Eathraichean The Boats' Gully, in which the community's boats were based during the fishing season: G. 'nan eathraichean', see p. 226.

Geodha na Ceothadh The Mist Gully: G. 'na ceothadh', gen. sing. of 'a' cheò' – the mist.

Geodha Bheag nan Calman The Little Gully of the Rock-doves: G., see similar p. 229.

Geodha Chaol an Sgadain The Narrow Herring Gully: G. 'caol' – narrow; 'an sgadain', gen. sing. of 'an sgadan' – the herring.

Geodha na Faing The Sheep-fank Gully: G. 'faing' – a sheep-fank.

Geodha na h-Eubhachd The Shouting Gully; so called because of an echo: G. 'na h-eubhachd', gen. sing. of 'an eubhachd' – the shouting.

Geodha na Cloiche or **Geodha a' Chleit** The Gully of the Stone: G. 'na cloiche', gen. sing. of 'a' chlach' – the stone; 'a' chleit', gen. sing. of 'an cleit' – the stone (from N. 'klètt' – a rocky eminence). Also, **Gob a' Chleit** Cleit Point.

An Cladach Iosal The Low Shore: G. 'cladach' – a shore; 'ìosal' – low.

Camas Shiadair – Shader Bay, stretching from Geodha na Ceothadh to Rubha Ghràn: G. 'camas' – a bay.

Gob Shiadair G. Shader Headland.

Port nan Giùran

O.S. Surveyor's notes (1848–52): *The name is derived from the quantity of whales which, from time to time, were brought ashore at this bay, where their livers were taken from them . . . hence the name, the Port of Livers.*

The suggestion that the name derives from G. 'grùthan' (liver), rather than 'giùran' (gill) is plausible. It appears that at some time in its history the name was changed from Port nan Grùthan to its present form. The shingle beach round which the original community grew and prospered has long since disappeared and has been replaced by a small modern harbour capable of accommodating small fishing-boats. Within the past hundred years, the population has increased mainfold and, within the township, three satellite villages have been created on land which, at one time, was part of Port nan Giùran's common grazing: Na Fleisearan, Brocair and An Ceann Beag.

Ocabhaig Auk Bay: N. 'alka' – an auk; 'vik' – a bay.

Geodha Bheag Ocabhaig and **Geodha Mhór Ocabhaig** The Little Ocabhaig Gully and the Great Ocabhaig Gully.

Caisteal MhicRiachail Nicolson's Castle (close to the sea-shore, a ruin in the care of the National Trust): G. 'caisteal' – a castle; 'MhicRiachail', gen. sing. of 'MacRiachail', a corrupt form of MacNeacail.

Geodha Leathann a' Chaisteil The Wide Castle Gully: G. 'leathann' – wide; 'a' chaisteil', gen. sing. of 'an caisteal' – the castle.

Geodha nam Boitneagan The Gully of Boitneags: G. 'nam boitneagan', gen. plur. of 'na boitneagan' – the boitneags (a variety of mollusc).

Bun Allt Amadail The Amadail Burn Estuary: N. Amadail from 'lamba' – lambs; 'dal' – a glen.

Geodha Chaol a' Chaisteil The Narrow Castle Gully: G. 'caol' – narrow.

Geodha an t-Soithich The Ship Gully: G. 'an t-soithich', gen. sing. of 'an soitheach' – the ship. Presumably, a ship ran aground here in the distant past.

Sgeir nan Ràmh Oars' Rock; so-called perhaps because, from a distance, the rock looks like a boat under way with oars: G. 'nan ràmh', gen. plur. of 'na ràimh' – the oars.

Geodha Tharmoid Aoidh Norman son of Hugh's Gully: G. 'Tarmod' – Norman; 'Aoidh' – Hugh. The subject of folklore tales of mystery and the supernatural, the cave here stretches well inland and is claimed by some to extend to the Seisiadar seashore.

Geodha Chailligeadh The Well/Spring Gully, a narrow gully and probably the longest on the coast of the Rubha: N. 'kelda' – a well or spring; 'gjá'– a gully. The G. 'geodha' is superfluous. **Allt Chailligeadh** – The Cailleageadh Burn which drains Loch an Dùin empties into Geodha Chailleageadh. **Rubha Chailligeadh** The Cailligeadh Headland: G. 'rubha' – a headland.

Geodha na Ciste The Gully of the Narrow Entrance: G. 'na ciste', gen. sing. of 'a' chist'– the pass or defile (not kist).

A' Gheodha Bheag Bhàn The Little Light-coloured Gully: G. 'bàn' – light-coloured. To the east, **A' Gheodha Mhór Bhàn** – The Big Light-coloured Gully.

Geodha Bheag nan Glainnichean The Little Gully of the Glass, possibly used as a refuse-tip in earlier times: G. 'nan glainnichean', gen. plur. of 'na glainnichean' – the glasses.

Na Fleisearan

The Splitting Rocks, a long line of shelving rocks which, by use of sledge-hammers and wedges, were split to make lintels: N. 'flysar' – splitters.

Cladach nam Fleisearan Fleisearan Shore: G. 'cladach' – a shore.

Sgeir an Tàilleir or Sgeir 'Ain Tàilleir The Tailor's Rock or The Rock of Iain, the Tailor's Son: G. 'Ain', an abbreviation of 'Iain'.

Geodha Chaol an Fhuarain The Narrow Gully of the Fresh-water Spring: G. 'caol' – narrow; 'an fhuarain', gen. sing. of 'an fhuaran' – the fresh-water spring.

Geodha an Eilein Gully of the Island: G. 'an eilein', gen. sing. of 'an eilean' – the island.

Sgeir Dhòmhnaill Màrtainn Donald Martin's Rock (D. Martin, No. 11 Port Mholair, 19th cent.).

Geodha a' Chait The Cat's Gully: G. 'a' chait', gen. sing of 'an cat' – the cat.

Geodha Bun-àrsdaidh. This has Gaelic overlying a N. name. It is likely that, many centuries ago, a stream entered the sea through this gully, which was probably used as a landing-place. BMK notes: 'I wonder if "-àrs-" of the modern name was originally *ár* (river) or *áros* (river mouth). It is possible that the "bun" was originally N. *buna* (a burn) with *stath* (a landing-place).' In that case, we would have a N. name *buna-áros-stath* – 'the landing-place at the Burn Estuary' to which the G. 'geodha' has been prefixed later.

Taigh an Stòir The Store-house; built in 1900 by Northern Light to house a boat, etc. Also built in 1900 for Northern Light, Cidhe Hannah Hannah's Pier: G. 'cidhe' – a quay; Hannah, wife of Donald MacAulay, living locally, early 20th cent.

An Rubha Dubh The Black Headland: G. 'rubha' – a headland.

An Sgeir Mhór The Great Rock.

Cladach Phort nan Giùran The Port nan Giùran Shore: G 'cladach' – a shore.

An Carragh Gorm Beag The Small Blue Rock: G. 'carragh' – a rock; 'gorm' – blue.

An Carragh Gorm Mór The Great Blue Rock.

Allt Fhorsainn The Waterfall Stream: N. 'fors' – a waterfall; G. 'allt' – a stream.

Bun an Uillt Stream Foot: G. 'bun' – an estuary; 'an uillt' gen. sing. of 'an t-allt'.

An Stèisean The Station: from Eng. G. spelling of 'station'.

An Cladhan The Boat Channel, blasted out of the rock to allow home-coming boats to approach their berths on the Shingle: G. 'cladhan' – a man-made channel.

Stalla Mór The Great Overhanging Rock: G. 'stalla' – an overhanging rock; 'mór' – great.

A' Gheodha Bheag The Little Gully: G. 'beag' – little.

Am Platform Eng. 'platform'.

Na Goban Bàna The Light-coloured Points: G. 'gob' – a point; 'bàn' – light-coloured.

Geodha an Duine The Man's Rock: G. 'duine' – a man: so-named, perhaps, because of its association with a 'Duine', one of the 'Men'; i.e. a church luminary.

Geodha 'ic Sheòrais The Gully of George's Son: G. '(mh)ic', gen. sing. of 'mac'; Seòras' – George.

Sloc nan Daoibhe The Dive Pool: G. 'sloc' – a pit; G. 'daoibhe', a borrowing from Eng.

Geodha 'n t-Simileir The Chimney-stack Gully: G. 'an t-simileir', gen. sing. of 'an similear' – a chimney.

An Ordag Bheag The Little Thumb: G. 'òrdag' – a thumb/ pointer.

Geodha an Eisg The Fish Gully: G. 'an éisg', gen. sing. of 'an iasg' – the fish.

Sgeir Geodha an Eisg The Rock of Fish Gully.

Geodha Bheag a' Chìrein The Little Gully of the Cock's Comb: G. 'a' chìrein', gen. sing. of 'cirean' – the cock's comb. Between this and **Geodha Mhór a' Chìrein** (The Great Gully

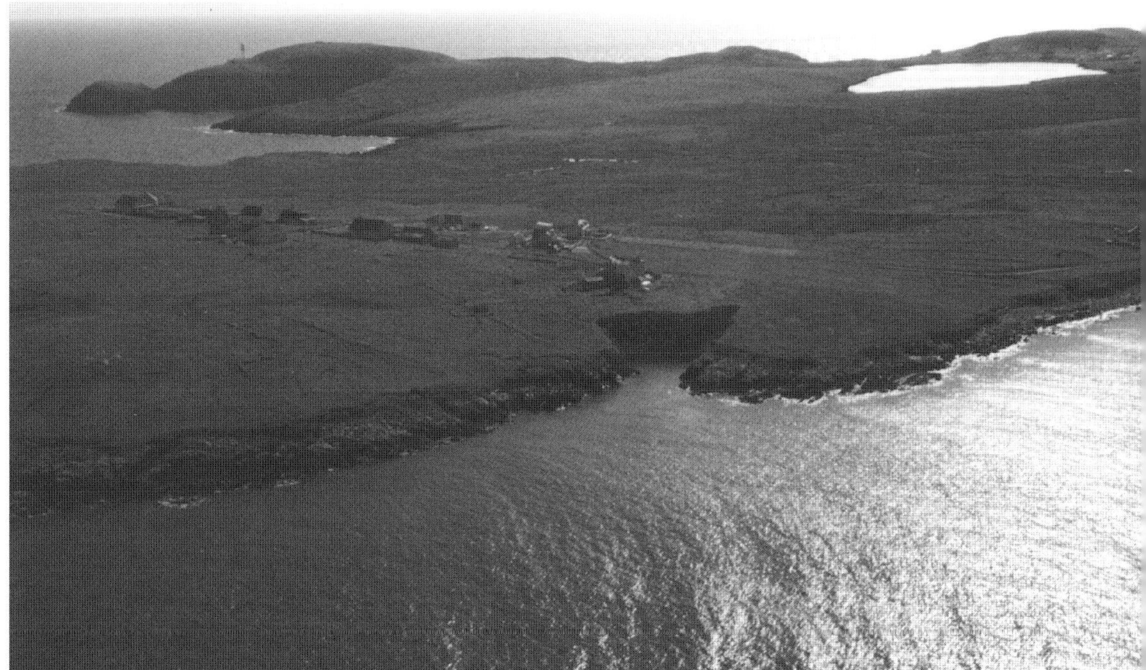

Looking east towards Port Mholair, An Ceann Beag with Geodha 'ic Sheòrais, centre picture

of the Cock's Comb) is **An Cìrean**, a long narrow partition of serrated rock.

Sgeir a' Bhreabadair The Weaver's Rock: G. 'breabadair' – a weaver.

Toll an t-Séididh The Blow-hole: G. 'an t-séididh', gen. sing. of 'an séideadh' – the blowing.

Geodha nan Luch The Gully of the Mice: G. 'nan luch', gen. plur. of 'an luchainn' – the mice.

Sgeir Dhearg The Red Rock: G. 'dearg' – red.

Giotra Mhic Shiamais, a name difficult to interpret. It may represent 'geodha' prefixed to Tràigh Mhic Shiamais – James's Son's Shore. However, this interpretation is uncertain: G. 'tràigh' – a shore; 'Siamas', a variant of 'Seumas'.

Sgeir Flinne The Sleet Rock: G. 'flinne' – sleet; or possibly 'Flinne' was a personal name.

Sgeir Spuaicein The rock associated with 'Spuaicean', a man's byname.

Geodha nan Calman The Rock-doves' Gully: G. see similar p. 229.

An Rubha Meadhanach The Middle Headland: G. 'meadhanach' – middle.

Sgeir na Starraig The Crow's Rock: G. 'na starraig', gen. sing. of 'an starrag' – the crow.

Geodha an Fhithich The Raven's Rock: G. 'an fhithich', gen. sing. of 'am fitheach' – a raven. **Leacan Geodha an Fhithich** The Flat Stones of Geodha an Fhithich: G. 'leacan' – flat stones.

Toll nan Ceàrdan The Tinkers' Cave: G. 'toll' – a cave; 'nan ceàrdan', gen. plur. of 'na ceàrdan' – the tinkers. Tinkers are said to have lodged there periodically in olden times.

Leac an Eòlaindich The Hollander's Flagstone: G. 'an Eòlaindich', gen. sing. of 'An Eòlaindeach' – the Dutchman.

Camas Uinn The Surf Bay; noted for its thunderous breakers, a broad shallow bay between An Grianan and An Rubha Meadhanach. This was probably a Norse name, with G. 'camas' (bay) added later; N. 'unn' – waves breaking on rocks.

Feille The Sheep Shelter: N. 'fé' – sheep; 'hlé' – shelter; a gully in which sheep shelter.

Sgeir an Uillt The Stream Rock (a large rock at the estuary): G. 'an uillt' – gen. sing. of 'an allt' – the stream.

Cnap Beag Sgeir an Uillt The Little Lump of Sgeir an Uillt, a 'satellite' of the former: G. 'cnap' – a lump.

Na Leacan Gorma The Blue Flagstones: G. 'leac' – a flagstone; 'gorm' – blue.

A' Gheodha Dhorch The Dark Gully: G. 'dorch' – dark.

Geodha a' Pheile The Pail Gully: G. 'peile' – a pail. The name may be a corruption of Geodha na Feille; see 'Feille' p. 238. Certainly, sheep use part of the gully as a shelter during foul weather.

Geodha an t-Sealap The Hut Gully: N. 'sel' – a shed; 'sel-lopt' – a shed on legs, likely to have been used by fishermen. The centuries-old ruined shielings of Druim Airigh an t-Siùmpain are about 300 metres away.

Port nan Giuran Hinterland

An Ceann Beag The Small End, a hamlet at the outer end of Port nan Giùran: G. 'ceann' – an end; beag – small.

Blàr nan Eun The Bird Moor: G. 'blàr' – a moor; 'nan eun', gen. plur. of 'na h-eòin' – the birds.

Tom nan Eun Bird Knoll: G. 'tom' – a knoll.

Tom Barabal Barabal Phàdraig, celebrated in song, lived in a house on this knoll.

Thunderous breakers in Camas Suinn

Port Mholair

Prior to the nineteenth century exploitation of the Loch a Tuath fishery, the two beaches on opposite sides of Ceann an t-Siùmpain may have been known simply as the 'Mol an Ear' – The East Beach and the 'Mol an Iar' – The West Beach. After 1824, when the so-called 'ports' were developed with oil-extraction facilities and salting houses, the Mol an Ear became known as 'Port a' Mhol Ear' (though 'Port a' Mhuil an Ear' might have been a grammarian's choice!); hence, Port Mholair: G. 'mol' – shingle (beach); 'an ear' – east; 'an iar' – west.

Sgràd A low cliff-face, topped by a broad ledge and capable of accommodating three or four fishermen or several dozen seabirds! The meaning is uncertain but possibly The Young Seabirds' Bank: N. 'skàra' – young seabirds; 'röth' – a low cliff or bank.

Geodha nan Calman Rock-doves' Gully; see similar, p. 229.

An t-Sròn Léith The Greyish Point; G. 'sròn' – a point/ness; 'léith' – grey, an oblique form of 'liath' – grey; cp. Stac Lì, St Kilda, which has been made greyish-yellow by centuries of gannet droppings.

A' Gheodha Bhàn The Light-coloured Gully: G. 'bàn' – fair, light in colour.

Geodha na Bà The Cow's Gully, so named perhaps, to commemorate the loss of a cow: G. 'na bà', gen. sing. of 'a' bhó' – the cow.

Geodha Mhurchaidh Bhàin The Gully of Murchadh (Bàn) MacDonald, first tenant of No. 1: 19th cent.

A' Gheodha Ruadh The Reddish Gully: G. 'ruadh' – reddish.

Aidigeadh The Gully with the Neck of Land; within the chasm of the Geodha Ruadh, a minor cleft flanked by a small rocky promontory popular with fishermen: N. 'eith – a neck of land; 'gjá' – a gully.

An Siùmpan, a corruption of **An Sìthean Bàn** – The Light-coloured Hill: G. 'sìthean' – 'a big rounded hill' (DW); 'bàn' – light-coloured. The name fits this hill perfectly.

Cnap Cìleag Cìleag's Lump, a rounded extension of Siùmpan sandwiched between the main hill and the peninsula of An Grianan: G. 'cnap' – a lump; 'Cìleag' – perhaps a woman's byname; see p. 59.

An Grianan The Green Meadow of Ceann an t-Siùmpain; the meadow so called because the varieties of short green grass growing there on guano contrast with the peatland deer-grass, and sphagnum of nearby Cnap Cìleag and An

Siùmpan: N. 'groen' – green; 'vin' – a meadow.

Caolas a' Ghrianan The Grianan Narrows, two gullies on either side of the isthmus that joins An Grianan to Cnap Cìleag: G. 'caolas' – a narrows.

An t-Sloc Ghorm The Blue Pit, immediately north-west of the lighthouse station perimeter: G. 'sloc' – a pit; 'gorm' – blue/green.

MacIlle Dhuilich A corrupt G. form of an original N. name that included 'bakki' – a cliff, and 'gilja' – a chasm. It is a steep and slippery cliff at the foot of the lighthouse. Irrespective of the N. meaning, it seems fitting that the G. word 'duilich' (difficult) should be associated with this cliff! It is a difficult rock-face to climb, affording only one ledge on which a fisherman might sit or stand – a dangerous place on which to relax. A few foolhardy fishermen occasionally ventured there, all prior to WW2. The name reminds one of the phrase 'duine duilich' used to describe a feckless young man who, against sound advice, engages in some hazardous activity. It is sometimes said jokingly of such a person that he is 'of the ilk of Mac Ille Dhuilich' – Son of the Difficult Fellow.

Sròn Neacail Daraich Nicol Darach's Point, a fishing-rock named after a person unknown: G. 'sròn' – a point.

An Sgeir Righe The Extended Rock, a minor promontory jutting into the sea from the cliff above which, the Tiumpanhead lighthouse stands: G. 'righe' – extended.

Geodha nan Crùbag The Gully of the Edible Crabs: G. 'nan crùbag', gen. plur. of 'na crùbagan' – the edible crabs.

An Sgeir Aid The Point with the Skerry on the End; situated some 200 metres south-east of Tiumpanhead Lighthouse. It consists of a long, narrow stretch of bare rock which has a skerry at its outmost tip: N. 'sker-eith' – the isthmus with an end skerry.

Caolas na Sgeire Faide The Ravine of the Sgeir Aid: G. 'caolas' – a narrows (but here a dry ravine), between the Sgeir Aid and the mainland; N. 'eith' mistaken for G. 'fada'

Fidigeadh The Driftwood Gully is a small shetlered horse-shoe of deep water which has a sandy bottom: N. 'vitha' – (drift)wood; 'gjá' – a gully.

Stacaichean an Taigh-Sholais The Lighthouse Steps; built around 1900 on the north rim of Fidigeadh and hardly ever used for their intended purpose, i.e. unloading supplies brought by a supply-ship: G. 'stacaichean', nom. plur. of 'staca' – a step.

Bogha Fhidigeadh The Fidegeadh Reef: visible only at low tide and almost closing off the entrance to Fidigeadh: G. 'bogha' – a reef.

Cnap Iain Ruaidh Iain Ruadh's Lump, a favourite fishing-rock of Iain 'Ruadh' MacLeod, No. 2 (19th cent.): G. 'cnap' – a rounded mass; 'ruadh' – red-haired.

Geodha na Sgalaig The Farm-worker's Gully: G. 'na sgalaig', gen. sing. of 'an sgalag' – the farm-worker or flunkey; from N. 'skalk' – a servant, slave, weapon-bearer.

An Toll Dubh The Black Hole. Nowadays, the name applies not to the small cave to be found at its landward end but to the sheer, blackish grey cliff-face, on the north-facing side of Goitealar: G. 'toll' – a hole/cave; 'dubh' – black.

Goitealar The Goat Sheds, one of the three hills of Port Mholair; the others being An Siùmpan and Foitealar. The number of hills and coastal features bearing Norse names suggests that

Sgeir Aid with Fidigeadh on the left and the twin gullies of Geodha nan Crùbag right

at one time a Norse-speaking people inhabited the district, living by animal husbandry and fishing: N. 'geita-seljar' – nanny-goat sheds.

Geodha na Bròig The Shoe Gully, a deep indent in the east side of Goitealar, shaped like the imprint of a shoe: G. 'na bròig', gen. sing. of 'a' bhròg' – the shoe.

An Clàr The Platter, a large shelf of bare rock between the east side of Goitealar and the sea: G. 'clàr' – a platter or plate.

Caolas Goitealair The Goitealar Ravine, a mainly dry ravine, separating An Clàr from the rest of the hill: G. 'caolas' – a narrow ravine. **Cnap Ard Goitealair** The High Lump of Goitealar; jutting south-westwards; a buttress between the main hill and the sea: G. 'cnap' – a lump; 'àrd' – high.

Geodha an Duilisg The Dulse Gully: G. 'an duilisg', gen. sing. of 'an duileasg' – the dulse (an edible seaweed). Separated from it by a small partition of rock is **Geodha Bheag an Duilisg** Little Dulse Gully.

Creag Mhurchaidh Mhoir Big Murdo's Rock, the favourite fishing-station of Murdo MacDonald, of No. 1 (19th cent.): 'Mhurchaidh Mhóir', gen. sing. of 'Murchadh Mór' – Big Murdo.

Geodha na Muic The Whale Gully; so-named because of a blow-hole which, at certain states of the tide, spouts like a whale: G. 'na muic', gen. sing. of 'a' mhuc' – a pig. Here, 'muc' is short for 'muc-mhara' – a whale.

Geodha Chùil na Muic The Gully behind Geodha na Muic: G. 'cùl' – posterior.

Foitealar The Fatness Hill, so-called on account of its excellent grazing: N. 'feita-hall' – fatness hill.

Geodha na h-Inghinn The Girl's Gully, said to be so named because of a fatal accident that occurred there early in the 19th cent.: G. 'na h-inghinn', gen. sing. of 'an nighean' – the girl.

Geodha Dealbh a' Chait The Gully of the Cat's Image: G. 'dealbh' – picture; 'a' chait', gen. sing. of 'an cat' – the cat.

Stac nan Sgarbh The Cormorant Rock: N. 'stak' – a stack; 'nan sgarbh' – gen. plur. of 'na sgairbh' – the cormorants.

Geodha nan Calman Rock-doves' Gully: see similar, p. 229.

Stac 'Ain 'ic Uilleim The Stack associated with Iain, son of William MacLeod. For rioting at Aiginis, 1888, father and son from were imprisoned in Edinburgh; see photos pp. 32, 145.

Geodha Chùil Foitealair The Aft Gully of Foitealair: G. 'cùl' – posterior.

Geodha Foitealair Foitealar Gully, a major gully, cutting into the south-east shoulder of Foitealar. **Sròn 'Ain Riabhaich** The Point of Iain Riabhach (MacLean) of Port nan Giùran, 19th cent. **Lorgan nam Bonnan Dubha** The Heel-marks; a small ledge on the south-facing rock-face so called because of impressions in the rock: G. 'lorgan' – indentations; 'nam bonnan dubha' gen. plur. of 'na buinn dubha' – the underside of the heels. This is the most sought after fishing-stance in Port Mholair.

Cnap Ard Foitealair The High Lump of Foitealar; see **Cnap Ard Goitealair**, which is similar in appearance and position relative to the hill, p. 243.

Bilidh Mhór The Great Fang, a low-lying, bare rock shelf measuring about one quarter acre. The word 'bilidh' is thought to be derived from 'biolaid', an Old Gaelic word related to 'beul' (a mouth) and meaning a lip or fang. DW gives 'bile na tràghad' – the rim of the shore.

Am Brillean The Spike: G. 'brillean' – a protrusion. This spike of rock situated to the left of the main fishing-station of Bilidh Mhór is permanently surrounded by the sea and is a metre high at high tide. **Bogha Bhilidh** The Reef of Bilidh lies a

The blow-hole of Geodha na Muic

stone's throw to the south of Bilidh Mhór: G. 'bogha' – a reef. **Caolas Bhilidh** The Bilidh Ravine, for the most part, is a dry fissure that almost cuts Bilidh Mhór from the land: G. 'caolas' – usually means a narrow channel between two land masses, but here means 'a ravine'.

Sgeir na Faing The Sheep-fank Rock: G. 'faing' – a sheep-fank.

Geodha a' Bhodaich The Old Man's Gully; a narrow gully at the foot of No. 3, at one time used by old men as an open-air toilet: G. 'a' bhodaich', gen. sing. of 'am bodach' – the old man.

A' Gheodha Bheag The Little Gully.

Bilidh Bheag A rock shelf less than half the size of **Bilidh Mhór** (p. 244).

Na Creagan Crèadha The Clay Cliffs, at the shore end of Crofts Nos 1 to 7, boulder-clay facades slowly retreating because of coastal erosion: G. 'crèadha', gen. sing. of 'crèadh' – clay.

Cladach Phort Mholair The Port Mholair Seashore. Here, at low tide, is revealed about a half acre of small rocky outcrops and rock-pools which is bisected by Cladhan a' Phuirt leading from a small pier to the open sea: G. 'cladach' – a seashore.

Stac 'Ain mac Uilleim in the distance

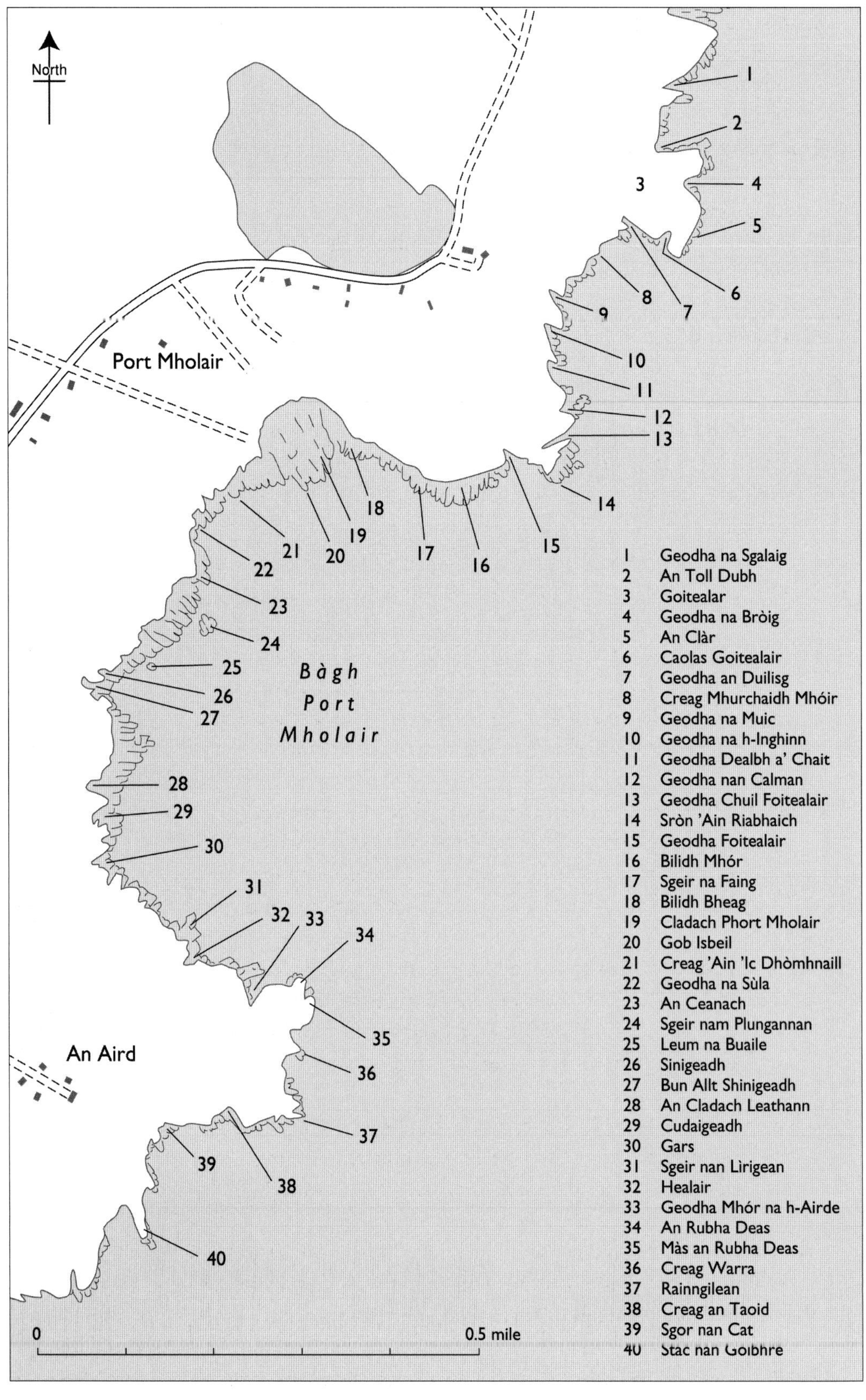
North
Port Mholair
Bàgh Port Mholair
An Aird
0
0.5 mile
1 Geodha na Sgalaig
2 An Toll Dubh
3 Goitealar
4 Geodha na Bròig
5 An Clàr
6 Caolas Goitealair
7 Geodha an Duilisg
8 Creag Mhurchaidh Mhóir
9 Geodha na Muic
10 Geodha na h-Inghinn
11 Geodha Dealbh a' Chait
12 Geodha nan Calman
13 Geodha Chuil Foitealair
14 Sròn 'Ain Riabhaich
15 Geodha Foitealair
16 Bilidh Mhór
17 Sgeir na Faing
18 Bilidh Bheag
19 Cladach Phort Mholair
20 Gob Isbeil
21 Creag 'Ain 'Ic Dhòmhnaill
22 Geodha na Sùla
23 An Ceanach
24 Sgeir nam Plungannan
25 Leum na Buaile
26 Sinigeadh
27 Bun Allt Shinigeadh
28 An Cladach Leathann
29 Cudaigeadh
30 Gars
31 Sgeir nan Lìrigean
32 Healair
33 Geodha Mhór na h-Airde
34 An Rubha Deas
35 Màs an Rubha Deas
36 Creag Warra
37 Rainngilean
38 Creag an Taoid
39 Sgor nan Cat
40 Stac nan Goibhre

Cladhan a' Phuirt The Port's Navigation Channel: G. 'cladhan' – a man-made channel, blasted out of the rock (partly conglomerate and partly gneiss) in the early 19th cent.; 'a' phuirt' – gen. sing. of 'am port' – the port.

Lòn Mór nam Partanan The Great Pool of the Green-crabs: G. 'lòn' – a pool; 'nam partannan' – gen. plur. of 'na partanan' – the green crabs.

Sgeir Balaich Shiadair The Rock of the Siadar Lads, a large boulder on which a Siadar boat came to grief in a storm early in the 20th cent.

An Carragh Bàn The Light-coloured Rock, a large outcrop, demarcating the eastern end of the Mol (Shingle) on which boats were berthed: G. 'carragh' – a large rock.

Na Carraichean Dubha The Black Rocks: G. 'na carraichean' – plur. of 'an carragh' – a rock.

An Carragh Dearg The Red Rock, at low tide, is an obstacle to navigation at the approach to the Cladhan: G. 'carragh' – a rock; 'dearg' – red. On the seaward side of this rock is a lobsters' lair accessible with the spring ebbtide, about a foot underwater.

A' Chlach Tholltach The Notched Stone, so named because of a notch in its side. It is a smooth, cow-sized, oval boulder, deposited at the end of the last Ice Age – a major feature of Cladach Phort Mholair: G. 'clach' – a stone; 'tolltach' – holed.

Giollaman The Boys' Stance, measuring about three metres square. This is low shelf of conglomerate rock on which children used to stand at half tide to welcome incoming boats: G. 'giullan' – a boy; 'giolaman' – a prattling child (DW).

Gob Isbeil Isabella's Point, named after 19th cent. Isabella Ferguson, No. 7. This point, some fifty metres long, consists of a jumble of large rocks which protects the south flank of the basin of Cladach Phort Mholair; Bilidh Bheag does likewise to the north.

Clach na Muilne The Millstone, an elephant-size, rounded rock at the southern end of Cladach Port Mholair; it is integral to Gob Isbeil: G. 'na muilne', gen. sing. of 'a' mhuileann' – a water-mill.

Croit an Rathaid The Road Bend, a sharp elbow at the shore terminus of 'Rathad an Rìgh' – the original main road to the Port: G. 'croit' – a bend; 'an rathaid', gen. sing. of 'an rathad' – the road.

Geodha Bheag na Sràide The Little Gully of the Street-folk; the

This map shows the rock names along the shore of Bàgh Phort Mholair

'Sràid' is a street of houses stretching from Crofts Nos 9 – 18. Soolivan lived at No. 11.

Creag 'Ain 'Ic Dhòmhnaill The Rock of Iain son of Donald (Martin), No. 9.

Geodha Leathann na Sràide The Street-folk's Broad Gully: G. 'leathann' – broad; 'na sràide', gen sing. of 'an t-sràid' – the street.

Geodha na Bà Ruaidhe The Gully of the Brown Cow: G. 'na bà ruaidhe', gen. sing. of 'a' bhò ruadh ' – the brown cow.

An t-Sùil The Eye, a large crater created by nature. Some ten metres deep, it is situated at the shore end of No. 9 and is connected to the sea by a narrow tunnel: G. 'sùil' – an eye.

Geodha na Sùla The Gully of the Sùil, from which the sea flows into the Sùil: G. 'na sùla', gen. sing. of 'an t-sùil'. **Sgeir na Sùla** – The Sùil Rock, at the entrance to the gully.

An Ceanach The End Field, a long, angled slab of greyish rock jutting south-eastwards from Geodha na Sùla. It takes its name from Ceann Achadh (The End Field), the most southerly field in the arc of arable land round the Port.

Lòn Mór a' Cheanaich The Great Pool of the Ceanach: G. 'lòn' – a pool.

Sgeir nam Plunganan The Pollack Rock: G. 'nam plunganan', gen. plur. of 'plung', a pollack; **Sgeir Bheag nam Plunganan** Lesser Pollack Rock, also known as **Sgeir a' Chlòcamain** The Clòcaman's Rock, a favourite fishing-place of 'An Clòcaman', the byname of Norman MacIver of No. 15, a well-known fisherman of the early 20th Cent.

Geodha an Tairbh The Bull Gully: G. 'an tairbh' – gen. sing. of 'an tarbh' – a bull.

Leum na Buaile The Leap (seaward of) the Cattle-enclosure: G. 'leum' – a leap. The 'Leum', in this instance, is a rock to which fishers of pollack used to leap at low tide.

Sinigeadh The Swimming Gully: N. 'synda' – swimming; 'gjá' – gully: see p. 231.

Bun Allt Shinigeadh The Estuary of the Sinigeadh Burn which separates the townships of Port Mholair and An Àird.

Names in the Hinterland of Port Mholair

Camas Creag Mhurchaidh Mhóir The Bay of Murchadh Mór's Rock: G. 'camas' – a bay.

Druim Airigh an t-Siùmpain The Ridge of the Siùmpan Shieling. G. àirigh – a shieling.

Tom an Fhithich Raven Hillock: G. 'tom' – a hillock; 'an fhitheach', gen. sing. of 'am fitheach' – the raven.

Tom nan Corra-Ghritheach The Herons' Knoll: G. 'tom' –a knoll; 'nan corra-ghritheach', gen. plur. of 'na corraichean-gritheach'.

An Leabaidh Laighe The Resting Bed, a broad hollow on the Common Grazing between Loch an t-Siùmpain and Creag Mhurchaidh Mhóir; here cattle were milked and rested overnight, during the summer and autumn. G. 'leabaidh' – a bed; 'laighe' – lying.

Geàrraidh Foitealair The Foitealar Summer Grazing used by people from the far side of the Loch a Tuath prior to the creation of the crofting community of Port Mholair in 1824: G. 'geàrraidh' – a summer-grazing.

Creagan Foitealair The Foitealar Outcrop, on the south-west side of the hill: G. 'creagan' – an imposing shoulder of rock showing through grass, heather, etc.

Tom nan Eun The Bird Knoll: G. 'tom' – a knoll; 'nan eun', gen. plur. of 'na h-eòin' – the birds.

Buaile a' Chnocain The Hillock Cattle-enclosure; MacDonald, No. 4: G. 'a' chnocain', gen. sing. of 'an cnocan' – the hillock; 'cnocan' is diminutive of 'cnoc' – a hill.

A' Chliath Dhubh The Black Slope, a fertile, heavily-cultivated slope in the upper reaches of Nos 8 and 9: G. 'cliath' – the side of a hill, DW.

Clitig – A narrow strip of land on the Minch side of the main road, opposite the churches. Originally, a measure of land one eighth of an old Scots shilling.

An Àird The Headland: G. 'àird' – a headland or promontory.

Sgeir Bhàn a' Ghàrraidh – The Light-coloured Rock; at the terminus of the boundary wall (of the old village). On the north side of this rock and beneath it is a productive lobster's lair. G. 'a' ghàrraidh' – see p. 233.

An Cladach Leathann The Broad Shore, an area of large white boulders: G. 'cladach' – shore; 'leathann' – broad.

Cudaigeadh The Cuddies' Gully in which the *cudaig* (young saithe) is plentiful in the late autumn: N. 'kútha' – cuddies/fish fry; 'gjá' – gully.

Gars Ghorm The Grassy Gars, the first of three adjacent gullies, known as Gars, and presumed to take their name from a wall or fence constructed to prevent stock from venturing on to the grassy cliff: N. 'garth'– a wall, as, for example, in 'geila-garth' – a wall along a ravine; G. 'gorm' –blue/green; here refers to the green grass.

Gars The Cliff Wall Gully, the second of the three. **Gars Chaol** The Narrow Cliff-wall Gully: G. 'caol' – narrow.

Sgeir nan Lìrigean The Lea-rigs' Rock: G. 'sgeir' – rock; 'nan lìrigean', gen. plur. of 'na lìrigean' – the lea-rigs. The G. 'lìrig' is a borrowing from Eng.

Creag 'Ain 'ic Eachainn The Rock of John, son of Hector: G. ''Ain 'ic Eachainn', gen. sing. of 'Iain mac Eachainn'.

Healair The Fishing Huts; reminiscent of the bothies at Port nam Bothagan in Tolastadh, used seasonally by fishermen from the Rubha: N. 'sel' – a fishing-hut; plur. 'seljar'. Healair continues to be a favourite fishing-point near the end of An Àird headland.

Geodha Mhór na h-Àirde The Àird's Great Gully: G. 'na h-àirde', gen. sing' of 'an àird' – the promontory.

An Rubha Deas The Southern Headland, known in Seisiadar to the south as Rubha na h-Àirde: G. 'deas' – south.

Màs an Rubha Deas The Backside of the Southern Headland: G. 'màs' – a backside.

Creag Warra The Rock of 'Warra': 'Warra', a byname for Angus MacLeod, No. 2 Àird, 19th cent.

Leabaidh Aileach The Stone Bed: G. 'leabaidh' – a bed; 'aileach' from obsolete G. 'ail' – a rock. The upper reaches of this gully, in which sheep take shelter during wild weather, is deep in sheep dung; compare Feille, p. 238.

Sgeir Hogs The Rock of 'Hogs': G. 'Hogs' – byname of a person unknown.

Rainngilean The Crooked Ravine: N. 'rang' – crooked; 'gilja' – a ravine. The name may have acquired a terminal 'n' through Gaels confusing the N. 'gilja' with 'gillean' – lads. A less likely alternative is that the name is a corruption of Rinn Ghillean – the Lads' Point: G. 'rinn' – a point; 'ghillean', gen. plur. of 'gillean' – lads.

Creag an Taoid The Cable Rock: G. 'an taoid', gen. sing. of 'taod' – a cable, chain or rope.

Brata-bilidh The Steep Bilidh, a name suggesting that the Gaelic word 'bilidh' has been substitutued for an earlier Norse name: N. 'bratt'– steep; for 'bilidh' see p. 244.

Sgor nan Cat The (Feral) Cats' Crevice: G. 'sgor'– a crevice; 'nan cat', gen. plur. of 'na cait'– the cats.

Leaca Héibheal The Stone Slab of Héibheal: G. 'leaca', local for 'leac' – a stone slab. **Héibheal** The Crag of the Stone Slab: N. 'hellu' – a slab; 'fjall' – a crag/rocky hill.

Stac nan Goibhre The Goats' Stack: G. 'nan goibhre', gen. plur. of 'na gobhair' – the goats.

Nead nan Curran, a corrupt form of **Nead nan Gurrag** The Rock-dove's Nest: G. 'nead' – a nest; 'nan gurrag', gen. plur. of 'na gurragan' – the rock-doves. The gully is also known as **Geodha Muinntir Gharraboist** Gully of the Garrabost Folk: G. 'muinntir' – folk.

Sròn an t-Searraich The Colt's Ness: G. 'sròn' – a point/ness; 'an t-searraich', gen. sing. of 'an searrach' – the colt.

Dóbhraidh The Sea Fortress, a large rock set like a buttress against the cliff-face: G. 'dobhar' – sea; 'rath' – fortress.

Creag Mhurchaidh Màrtainn Rock of Murdo Martin: Murdo Martin of 11 Port Mholair, late 19th cent.

Eilligeadh The Flat Stone Gully, a small inlet: N. 'hellu' – a flat stone; 'gjá' – a gully.

Sgeir Dhubh Eilligeadh The Black Rock of Eilligeadh. Close by, **Stac Eilligeadh** – The Stack of Eilligeadh

Geodha nam Faochag The Winkle Gully: G. 'nam faochag' – gen. plur. of 'na faochagan' – the winkles.

Bun a' Ghlinne The Foot of the Glen: G. 'a' ghlinne', gen. sing. of 'an gleann' – the glen.

Bun Allt Dìobadail The Estuary of the Dìobadail Burn; see similar, p. 227.

Geodha Mhór na h-Airde left of centre; Rubha Chùdainis in the distance

Hinterland placenames

An Tom Léibh The Brood-based knoll, in croftland, overlooking Na Lìrigean: G. 'léibh', an oblique of 'liamh' – broad-based.

Cnoc an Smodain At the foot of No. 5, a hillock on which potato-shaws and other croft refuse was burned: G. 'smodan' – smoke.

Druim Healair Healair Ridge overlooking Healair: G. 'druim' – a ridge. Interestingly, it is claimed that the town of Drumheller, Alberta (famed for its dinosaur fossils), was named after a local farmer called Samuel Drumheller. Perhaps the town was, in fact, named by Soolivan or other homesick Rubhach itinerant who, being depressed by the dour scenery of the Albertan Badlands, yearned for the beauty of Druim Healair of An Àird!

Roisilin Horse-field, on Nos 5/6, close to the main road: N. 'hrossa-land' – horses' field.

Druim Oidealar The Ridge of the Triangle of Fields: G. 'druim' – a ridge; N. 'odda' – a triangle; 'vellir' – fields. Assuming that this interpretation of the N. is correct, one wonders what the 'triangle of fields' means: perhaps a triangular area cleared of peat to allow planting. Sgoil na h-Àirde was built on Druim Oidealar in 1878.

Seisiadar

The Seaside Grazing: N. 'sja' – sea; 'saetr' – sheiling.

Geodha Mhór Sheisiadar The Great Gully of Seisiadar.

Dìobadal Deep Glen: N. 'djúp' – deep; 'dal' – a glen. **Bun Allt Dìobadal** The Estuary of the Dìobadal Burn: G. 'allt' – a burn.

Ròigeadh The Gully of the Crevice: N. 'rauf' – a crevice; 'gjá' – gully. **Leac Ròigeadh** The Rock Slab of Ròigeadh; and **Stac Ròigeadh**, also known as **Stac Mhurchaidh 'ic 'Ain Luaithre** The Stack of Murdo, the son of Iain Luaithre.

A' Chùl-Chreag The Back Rock: G. 'cùl' – back.

Sgor nan Calman The Rock-dove Cave: G. 'sgor' – a crevice/cave.

Stiùir na Luinge The Ship's Rudder (so named because of the shape of a rock formation): G. 'stiùir' – a rudder; 'na luinge' gen. sing. of 'an long' – a ship. The G. nouns are derived from N. 'styri' – a rudder, and 'lung' – a warship.

Rubha Chùdanais The White Headland (which is, in fact, light grey): N. 'hvit' – white; 'nes' – a headland. G. 'rubha' is superfluous. BMK suggests The Smolts' Headland: N. 'kútha' – cuddies or salmon smolt.

Geodha an Rainich Mhór The Great Bracken Gully: G. 'an rainich', gen. sing. of 'an raineach' – bracken; and **Geodha an Rainich Bheag** The Little Bracken Gully.

An Sguinnean Bhàn The Light-coloured Stone Block. G. 'sguinnean' – a stone block; 'bàn' – light-coloured. MacI. has 'Sgonnan Bhàn'. On this flat rock, salted fish was spread for drying in the spring, 19th cent.

Bun an Uillt Mhóir The Great Stream Estuary: G. 'an uillt mhóir', gen. sing. of 'an t-allt mór' – the big stream.

Geodha an Uillt The Gully of the Stream; also **Stac Geodha an Uillt.**

Geodha an Ucais The Gully of the Coalfish: G. 'an ucais', gen. sing. of 'an ucas' – a coalfish (large saithe).

Geodha an t-Sìonna The Phosphorescence Gully: G. 'sionn' – phosphorescence; also, **Stac Geodha an t-Sìonna.**

Geodha an Tuill The Cave Gully: G. 'an tuill' – gen. of 'an toll' – the cave/hole; near its entrance, **Stac Geodha an Tuill.**

Geodha an Àradh The Ladder Gully: G. 'àradh' – a ladder. Close by, two stacks, **Stac Geodha an Àradh** and **Stac nam Bodach** The Old Men's Stack.

Geodha Na Lice Duibhe The Black Slab Gully: G. 'na lice duibhe' – gen. sing. of 'an leac dhubh'; 'leac' – a flat stone; 'dubh' – black.

Creag Nìos Nios's Rock: G. 'Nios' – a person's byname, perhaps.

Geodha na Sgotha Deirg The Red Boat's Gully: G. 'na sgotha deirg', gen. sing. of 'an sgoth dhearg' – the red boat.

An Sgeir Mhaol The Smooth Rock: G. 'maol' – smooth/rounded.

Cailleach a' Phuirt The Old Woman of the Port, a rock at the entrance to the port was removed with explosives towards the end of the 20th cent.: G. 'cailleach' – an old woman; 'a' phuirt', gen. sing. of 'am port' – the port. Close by, **Sgeir Bheag a' Phuirt** The Little Rock of the Port.

Geodha Bheag a' Phuirt The Little Gully of the Port.

Beul Allt na h-Àthadh The Mouth of the Kiln Burn: G. 'beul' – a mouth; 'na h-àthadh', gen. sing. of 'an àth' – the kiln.

Am Port The Port; during the 19th and early 20th cent. up to eight fishing-boats were based here.

An Coire Mór The Great Kettle: G. 'coire' – a kettle; an area where fishermen dried their nets after barking them in a big iron pot; bark (G. 'cairt') was the preservative used.

Stac Seònaid Janet's Stack: G. 'Seònaid' – Janet.

Geodha Mhic 'Ain Chéir The Gully of Iain Ciar's Son: G. ''Ain Chéir', gen. sing. of Iain Ciar. The gully is also called **Geodha Nighean 'Ain Ruaidh** The Gully of the Daughter of Iain Ruadh; so called, in remembrance of the drowning of a girl who overbalanced while trying to bring ashore a *tàbh* laden with bream: G. 'nighean' – daughter (of Iain Ruadh). The *tàbh* is a fish-trap consisting of a wide metal ring from which is suspended a net bag. Ropes attach the ring to a stout pole which is held over the sea by one person. When the ring is lowered to about a foot under the suface, bait is spread over the net area so as to attract fish

Stac nan Starrag: The Crows' Stack: G. 'starrag' – a crow.

Sailgeadh A-staigh The Near Fishing-hut Gully: N. 'sel'– a fishing-hut; 'gjá' – a gully. Another possible interpretation is The Near Seal Gully: N. 'sel-gjá' – seal-gully. G. 'a staigh' – in, or near. The next gully is **Sailgeadh A-muigh**: G. 'a muigh' – out/further away.

Na Tollan Brèagha The Beautiful Caves: G. 'tollan', plur. of 'toll' – a cave; 'brèagha' – beautiful.

Stac Sheumais James's Stack: G. Seumas – thought to be Seumas 'Ain Bhàin (James MacLeod), cottar, who died in the 1950s; ''Ain Bhàin', gen. sing. of 'Iain Bàn'.

Ceann a' Ghàrraidh The Dyke End, i.e. the boundary dyke of the old village: 'ceann' – a head/terminus; 'a' ghàrraidh', gen. sing. of 'an gàrradh'. **Sgeirean Dubha Ceann a' Ghàrraidh** The Black Rocks of the Dyke End: G. 'sgeirean dubha' – black rock.

Geodha nan Sòrnaichan The Gully of The Boulder Heaps: G. 'nan sòrnaichean', gen. plur. of 'na sòrnaichean' – a heap of boulders at the foot of a cliff.

An t-Uta-Sgeir The Out Rock, a small rock, easily accessible at low tide: N 'út-sker' – the outskerry.

An Sgeir Léith The Grey Rock: G. 'léith', an oblique form of 'liath' – grey.

A' Chreag Dhorch The Dark Rock: G. 'dorch' – dark.

Bun na h-Abhainn The River Estuary: G. 'na h-abhainn'(more commonly, 'na h-aibhne'), gen. sing. of 'an abhainn' – the river. Close by, **Eilean Bun na h-Abhainn** The Isle of the River Estuary: G. 'eilean' – an isle.

Geodha nam Botal The Bottle Gully, where household refuse was discarded, 20th cent. G. 'nam botal', gen. plur. of 'na botail' the bottles.

Na Drochaidean The Bridges: G. 'drochaid' – a bridge.

Stac Alasdair: Alasdair's Stack.
Sloc na h-Eubhachd The Hollow of the Shouting; presumably, noted for its echo: G. 'sloc' – a hollow; 'na h-eubhachd', gen. sing. of 'an eubhachd' – the shouting.
Siofainn Bheag The Little Sea Finger, one of two narrow points jutting into the sea: N. 'sja' – sea; 'fingr' – a finger; close by, **Siofainn Mhór** The Great Sea Finger.
A' Gheur-Chreag The Sharp Rock, like a knife-edge: G. 'geur' – sharp.
An t-Sròn Ghathach The Barbed Point: G. 'sròn' – a point/ness; 'gathach' – barbed.
Na Séithrichean The Chairs: G. 'na séithrichean', plur. of Eng. loan word 'séithir' – a chair; so called because of rock formations which suggest seating.
An Grianan The Green Meadow: 'grianan', see p. 241.
Magairlean a' Ghrianan The Grianan Testicles: smooth rounded rocks: G. 'magairle' – a testicle.
Cìrean a' Ghrianan The Grianan Comb: G. 'cìrean' – a row of serrated rocks; a cock's comb. **Geodha a' Chìrein** The Gully of the Serrated Rocks. **Camas Geodha Chìrein** The Bay of Geodha a' Chìrein.
Sròn Tuath a' Ghrianan The North Point of the Grianan: G. 'tuath' – north.
Cluasan a' Choin The Dog-ears, which appear at low tide at the north point of the Grianan: G. 'cluasan', nom. plur. of 'cluas' – an ear; 'a' choin', gen. sing. of 'an cù' – the dog.
Creag 'Ain Mhic Shomhairle The Rock of Iain, son of Somerled MacDonald, No. 7: G. 'Somhairle' – Somerled.
Stac Dubh Màs a' Ghrianain The Black Stack of the Grianan's Rear: G. 'màs' – a rear.
A' Chùl-Chreag The Back Rock: G. 'cùl' – back.
Stac a' Ghutha The Voice Stack; so called, presumably, because of an echo: G. 'a' gutha', gen. sing. of 'an guth' – a voice.
An Leac Dhubh The Black Rock.
Sròn 'Ain Chailein The Stack of Iain, son of Colin: G. 'sròn' – a point.
Ùrlar na Glaic The Floor of the Hollow (i.e. the isthmus leading to the tall peninsula of the Grianan): G. 'ùrlar – a floor; 'na glaic', gen. sing. of 'a' ghlaic' – the hollow.
An Caolas A-muigh The Out Narrows: G. 'caolas' – a narrows; 'a muigh' – out.
An Sgiath Bhàn The Light-coloured Wing: G. 'sgiath' – a wing; bàn' – light-coloured.
Sloc Bòit The Bòit Hollow, a fishing rock in the south-west

corner of the Grianan peninsula: G. 'sloc' – a hollow; 'bòid' may be a variant of G. 'baoit' – 'bait'. At the little promontory of Sloc Bòit, there is a perfectly shaped hollow about the size of a kitchen bowl, which appears to have been carved out of the rock. For generations, fishermen pulverised raw limpets or boiled green-crabs in this *sloc* and used the resulting pulp as bait. Similar 'bait-bowls' are found in rocks further south.

Geodha an Tairbh: The Bull Gully: G. 'an tairbh', gen. sing. of 'an tarbh' – the bull.

Na Riasanan The Streaks: G. 'rias' – a streak.

Sròn Màiri Iain The Point of Màiri, Daughter of Iain; so named in remembrance of a woman who drowned while gathering limpets for bait.

Geodha nan Calman Rock-doves' Gully (see similar, p. 229).

Ligh-bilidh Bilidh of the Wide Gap: N. 'hlith'– a wide gap; for G. 'bilidh' see p. 244. The name suggests that the Old Gaelic word 'bilidh' has been substituted for an earlier N. name. (See **Creag** an Daill, p. 28). Close by, **Stac Ligh-bilidh.**

An t-Eilean Glas The Grey Island: G. 'glas' – grey or green. **Caolas an Eilein Ghlais** Grey Island Narrows: G. 'caolas' – a narrows: G. 'an eilein ghlais', gen. sing. of 'an t-eilean glas'.

Sgaoilteach an Eilein Ghlais The Spreading-place of the Eilean Glas, i.e. where nets were spread out to dry.

Seisiadar headlands: An Grianan, nearest and An Dùn Dubh in the distance

Geodha Bheag nan Calman The Rock-doves' Little Gully: similar on p. 229.

Creag na Faing Sheep-fank Rock: G. 'faing' – a sheep-fank.

Stac Mhurchaidh Fhionnlaigh The stack associated with Murdo, son of Finlay.

An Stangan Dubh The Black Pool: G. 'stangan' – a pool; 'dubh' – black.

Geodha a' Mhairt The Cattle-beast Gully: G. 'a' mhart', gen. sing. of 'am mart' – the cattle-beast.

Geodha an Fhuarain The Spring Gully: G. 'an fuarain', gen. sing. of 'am fuaran' – a spring.

Na Taighean-Saillidh The Salting-houses: G. 'sailleadh' – salting; 'taighean', nom. plur. of 'taigh' – a house.

Geodha Chaol nan Taighean Saillidh The Narrow Gully of the Salting-houses: G. 'caol' – narrow; 'nan taighean-saillidh', gen. plur. of 'na taighean saillidh' – the salting-houses (in which fish such as cod was salted for export in the 19th and early 20th cent.).

An t-Sloc Ghorm G. The Green Hollow; 'sloc' – a hollow; 'gorm' – green, but sometimes used to mean blue.

Norabhaig The North Bay: N. 'north' – north; 'vík' – a bay; **Sròn Norabhaig** Norabhaig Point/ness: G. 'sròn' – a point/ness; **Toll Norabhaig** – Norabhaig Cave.

Geodha a' Bhùirn The Water Gully: G. 'bùrn' – water. **Stac Geodha a' Bhùirn** The Stack of the Water Gully.

Brata-bilidh The Steep Bilidh: N. 'bratt' – steep; for 'bilidh', see p. 244. **Sgeirean Dubha Bhrata-bilidh** The Black Rocks of Brata-bilidh.

Sròn Sheumais James's Point: G. 'Seumas' – James.

Gàrradh na Caillich The Old Woman's Dyke: G. 'cailleach' – an old woman.

Geodha Bun a' Ghàrraidh The Gully at the Terminus of the Wall: G. 'gàrradh' – a dyke. See **Sgeir a' Ghàrraidh,** p. 233.

Geodha a' Chlèibh The Creel Gully: G. 'a' chlèibh' – gen. sing. of 'an cliabh' – the creel. Close by, **Sròn Geodha a' Chlèibh** The Point of Creel Gully: G. 'sròn – a point.

An Caolas A-muigh The Out Narrows: G. 'caolas' – a narrows; 'a muigh' – out.

Geodha an Daimh The Bullock Gully: G. 'an daimh', gen. sing. of 'an damh' – the bullock.

Geodha nan Sgarbh The Cormorants' Gully: G. 'nan sgarbh', gen. plur. of 'na sgairbh' – the cormorants.

Am Balla a Thràigh The (Gully of the) Wall that Ebbed: G. 'balla' – a wall; 'a thràigh' – past tense of 'tràighadh' –

ebbing. The gully is so called because of a wall more than a metre high that begins to appear when the tide is on the ebb. Nearby are two associated features: the Stac (stack) and the Sloc (hollow) of the Balla a Thràigh.

Creag an Tobair The Well Rock: G. 'tobair' – a well.

An Stac Dubh The Black Stack: G. 'dubh' – black.

Sròn Leitch 'Leitch's' Point: G. 'Leitch', byname for Donald MacLeod, No. 16, 20th cent.

Sròn Chnugs 'Cnugs's' Point: G. 'Cnugs' – a person's byname.

An Ordag A-muigh The Out Thumb; 'òrdag' – a thumb. Close by, **An Ordag A-staigh** The In Thumb; and **Stac na h-Ordaig.**

Ionacair (pron. 'een-akir') In the past, this narrow point was a popular fishing-rock. The origin of the name is unclear. **Surrag na h-Ionacair** – The Ionacair Gap, a grassy hollow leading down to the rock: G. 'surrag' – a gap, as in a mountain profile.

Geodha nan Daoine The Gully of the Men: G. 'nan daoine' gen. plur. of 'na daoine' – the men.

An Caolas A-staigh The Inner Narrows: G. 'a-staigh' – in, inner.

An Dùn Dubh The Black Fort/Pile: G. 'dùn' – a fort/pile; 'dubh' – black. Large boulders on top of this headland suggest there may have been some form of fortification.

Geodha a' Mhinidh The Gully of the Owl: G. 'minidh', an owl; ('meanaidh' is better, DW). Close by, **Stac Geodha a' Mhinidh** The Stack of Geodha Mhinidh.

A' Chalg The Barb: G. 'calg' – a barb or spear.

Cudaigeadh 'This word could be N. "kutha-vík-gjá" – the gully of the bay of the young salmon. The word "kutha" occurs in a surprising number of N. place-names' (BMK). **Sròn Chudaigeadh** Cudaigeadh Point.

Sròn nan Robaid Rabbit Point: G. 'robaid' – rabbit.

Geodha Mhór an Leathad Rainich The Great Gully of the Bracken Brae: G. 'leathad' – a slope or brae; 'an rainich', gen. sing. of 'an raineach' – the bracken.

Aodann 'Ain 'Ic an Lighiche The Cliff-face of Iain, Son of the Healer: G. 'aodann' – a face; 'lighiche' – a healer.

Geodha Mille Gruaman The Gully with the Big Room. 'In most places where there is a name with Grum- or Gruam- in it, you find ancient burial mounds or cairns and a tradition of supernatural presence of some kind. Here presumably, you would need two caves with a gjá in between, as it certainly looks like a Norse *milli* name. I wonder if it might be a corrupt form of *mikill rúm* (big space) with the final – an added when it became a Gaelic "geodha" name. Was the cave reputed to be haunted, I wonder? If so, some might well assume that *gruamain* (spirits) were present' (BMK).

Excerpt from McI's book, pub. in 1900: 'There are marks of fireplaces in the cave as if people have been using it as a refuge in the past.'

Osabhaig The Bay of Estuary: N. 'ós'– an estuary; 'vík' a small bay; Rubha Osabhaig The Osabhaig Headland: G. 'rubha' – a headland.

Am Bàgh Dubh The Black Bay: G. 'bàgh' – bay; 'dubh' – black.

A' Gheodha Bhàn The Light-coloured Gully.

Hinterland Placenames

Cnoc an Lighiche The Healer's Hill: G. 'lighiche' – the healer. The hill is also known as Cnoc an Fhithich The Raven's Hill: G. 'an fhithich', gen. sing. of 'am fitheach' – the raven.

Gàrradh nan Cailleachan The Old Women's Dyke: G. 'nan cailleachan' – gen. plur. of 'na cailleachan' – the old women.

Glaic nan Cuaran The Shoes' Hollow: G. 'glaic' – a hollow; 'nan cuaran', gen. plur. of 'na cuarain' – the homemade shoes (usually of 'peilid' – sheepskin).

Creagan Chulpaig Culpag's Outcrop: G. 'Culpag' – a person's byname.

An Daras Beag The Little Door: G. 'daras' – a door. This old name applies to a small group of houses at the south end of Seisiadar but may, originally, have applied to a gully (unidentified) used for beaching a boat. That minor berthing-place might have earned the description 'little' as it would have been only a short distance from Port Sheisiadair. Alternatively, the name may be **An t-Aros Beag** – The Little House: G. 'aros' – a house.

Pabail Uarach

According to Oftedal, the name Pabail 'must be identical to "papyli" in Iceland and "Papull" in Orkney which is mentioned in the Orkneyinga Saga'. According to Marwick, it is 'a contraction of N. "papa-byli" – home of a settlement of Papae', i.e. early Celtic clergy. Pabail is divided in two: G. 'uarach' – upper and 'iarach' – lower.

A' Gheodha Bhàn The Light-coloured Gully: G. 'bàn' – light-coloured or fair.

Geodha a' Chalmain The Rock-dove Gully: G. 'a' chalmain', gen. sing. of 'an calman' – a rock-dove/pigeon.

Creag an Leuma The Jump Rock: G. 'an leuma', gen. sing. of 'an leum' – a jump.

Creag Knox Knox's Rock: 'Knox' – a person's byname, presumably the father of Alasdair 'Knox'; see p. 80.

Rubha Iodh-nis (pron. 'eenish') The Inner Headland: N 'inn' further in; 'nes' – a headland; the G. 'rubha' is superfluous; also known as Rubha nam Bàirneach – Limpets Headland: G. 'nam bàirneach', gen. plur. of 'na bàirnich' – the limpets/shellfish. Close by, Geodha nam Bàirneach – The Limpets' Gully.

Creag Chaluim Calum' s Rock: G. 'creag' – rock.

Creag Choinnich Kenneth's Rock: G. 'Coinneach' – Kenneth.

Rubha an t-Searraich – The Colt's Gully: G. 'an t-searraich', gen. sing. of 'an searrach' – the colt.

Bun Sruthan Iodh-nis The Estuary of the Iodh-nis Burn: G. 'bun' – estuary.

Creag Fhionnlaigh Finlay's Rock: G. 'creag' – a rock; 'Fionnlagh' – Finlay.

Stob Phaileis Phaileis's Pillar: G. 'stob' – a pillar; 'phaileas' from Gr. 'phallus'.

Nead nam Faoileag The Seagulls' Nest: G. 'nead' – a nest; 'nam faoileag', gen. plur. of 'na faoileagan' – the seagulls.

An t-Eilean Glas The Green Island: G. 'eilean' – an island; 'glas' – green/grey.

Geodha nan Cnuimhean The Worm Gully: G. 'nan cnuimhean', gen. plur. of 'na cnuimhean' – the worms.

Rubha na Bantraich The Widow's Headland, where a widow is said to have waited for days, hoping that her husband had survived a local shipwreck: G. 'na bantraich'/'a' bhantrach' – a widow; the name of the headland is associated with **Sgeir an Atran**, below.

Am Braga The Braga Cliff: G. 'braga' – growing seaweed such as tangle; however, in this instance, the name is used of the high cliff-face overlooking an extensive reef clad with seaweed.

Uamh a' Bhraga – The Braga Cave: G. 'uamh' – a cave. **Leac a' Bhraga** The Braga Flag-stone: G. 'leac' – a flat stone/flag. **Sròn a' Bhraga** Braga Point: G. 'sròn' – a point/ness.

Beul na Geodhadh The Gully Entrance: G. 'beul' – entrance/mouth; 'na geodhadh', gen. sing. of 'a' gheodha'.

Sgeir an Atran The Atran Rock: G. 'atran' a corruption of 'atrach' or 'àrd-ràmhach' – an eight-oared galley (DW).

According to folklore, an 'olden days ship' was wrecked here, an event supposedly associated with the tragic story of **Rubha na Bantraich** (above).

Geodha na Bantraich The Widow's Gully: see **Rubha na Bantraich** above.

Striat'sial The Landslip Hill, consisting of a long slope with a scree at its foot: N. 'skritha' – a scree; 'fjall' – a precipitous rock-face.

Geodha Cràthainn The Wound Gully; buried by a landslip in 1937, the gully no longer exists; however, the exposed cliff is red in colour; G. 'crà' – blood.

Bun an Uillt The Burn Estuary: G. 'an uillt', gen. sing. of 'an t-allt' – the burn.

Bàire na Luinge Boat Path: G. 'bàire'– a path; 'na luinge', gen. sing. of 'an long' – a ship. This gently shelving shingle beach is said to have been used for beaching large wooden vessels as far back as Norse times; crews replenished their water-casks from the stream close by. According to DW, 'bàire' is 'a beaten path, commonly, one opened through deep snow, hence *fear brisidh bàire*, applied to a leader in an arduous enterprise'.

Rubha na Bantraich with Pabail Uarach houses in the distance

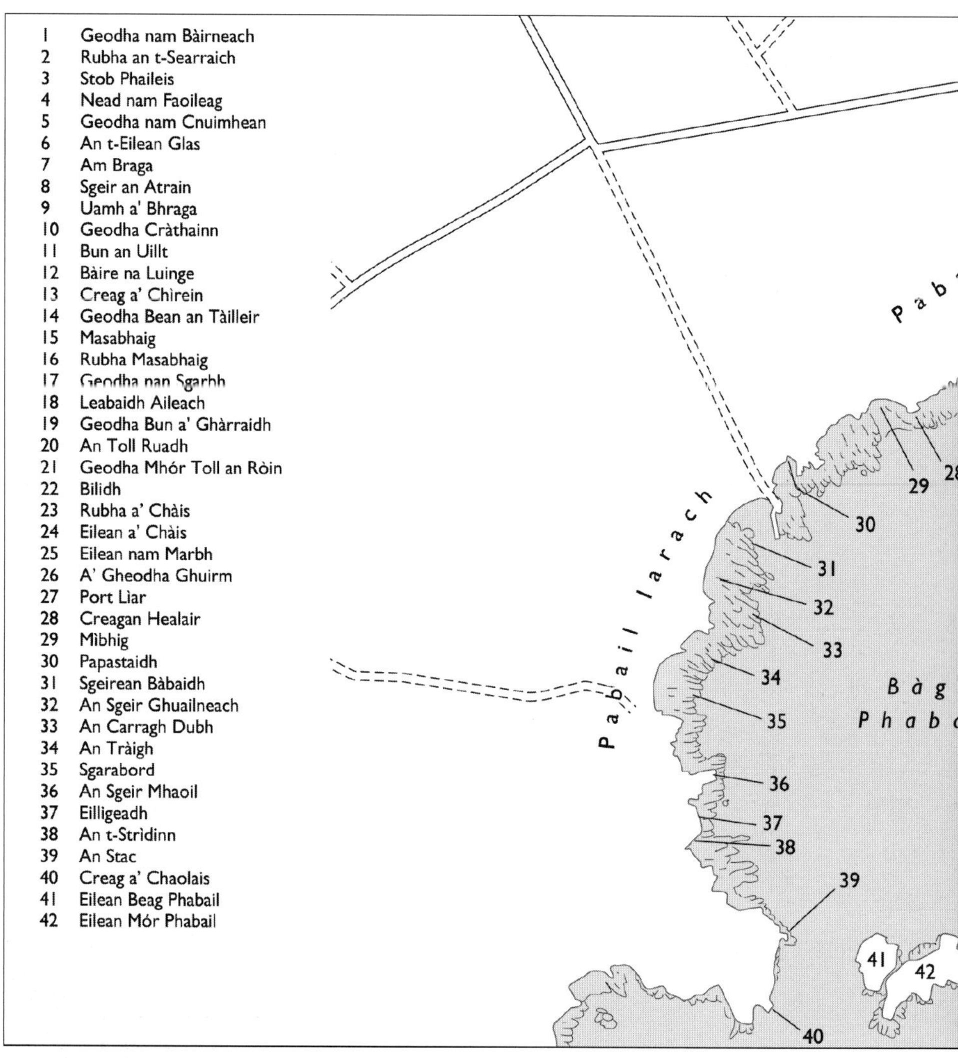

Map showing the rock names along the shore of Pabail Uarach

Sloc Alasdair Alasdair's Pit: G. 'sloc' – a hollow.

Creag a' Chìrein The Cock's Comb Rock: G. 'creag' – a rock.

Geodha Bean an Tàilleir The Gully of the Tailor's Wife: G. 'bean' – a wife; 'tàillear' – a tailor.

Masabhaig The Mossy Bay: N. 'mosa-vík' – moss-grown bay.

Rubha Masabhaig The Masabhaig Headland.

Geodha nan Sgarbh The Cormorants' Gully.

Leabaidh Aileach The Stony Bed; see similar, p. 250.

Geodha Bun a' Ghàrraidh The Gully at the Estuary of the Boundary Wall; see **Sgeir Bun a' Ghàrraidh** p. 233.

An Toll Ruadh The Reddish Hole: G. 'toll' – hole; 'ruadh' – reddish. This deep crater at the foot of No. 1 is connected to the sea by a tunnel.

Also known as **Toll an Ròin** The Seal's Cave: G. 'ròn' – a seal. **Geodha Mhór Toll an Ròin** The Great Gully of the Seal Cave.

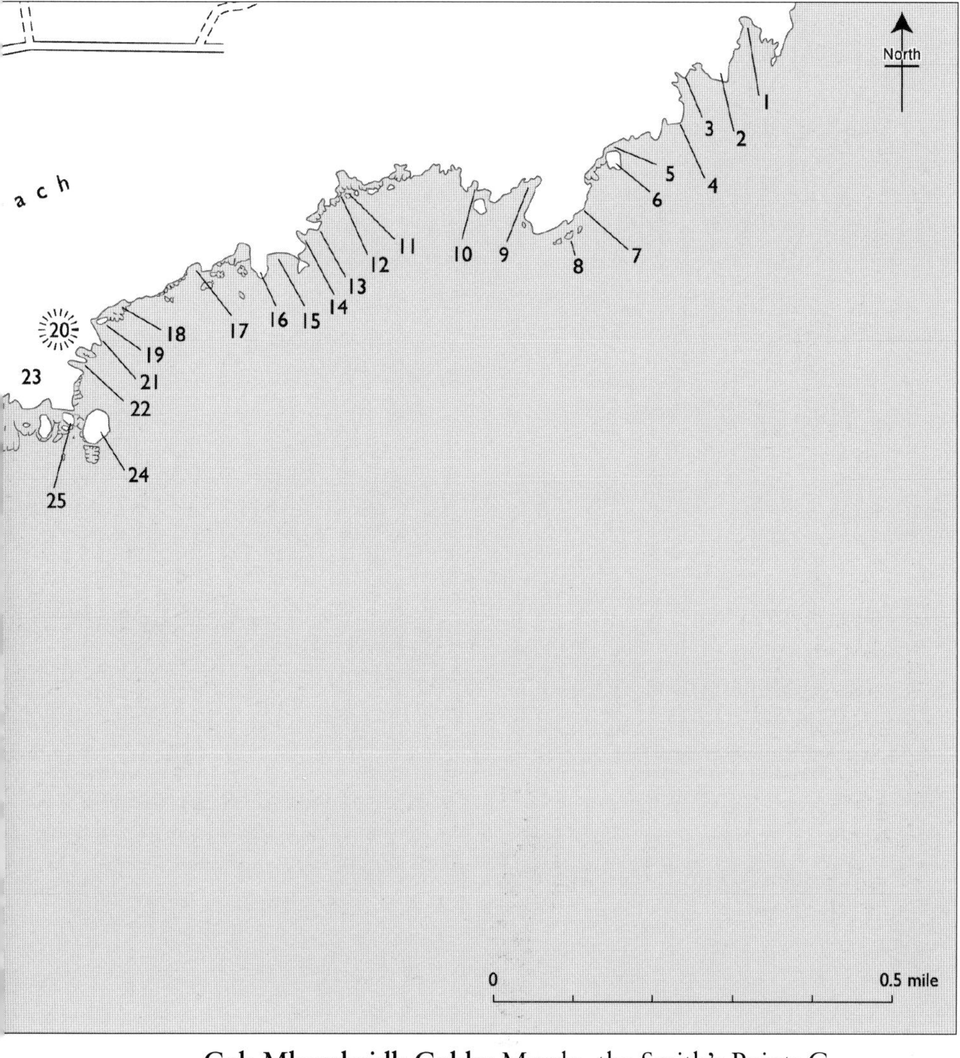

Gob Mhurchaidh Gobha Murdo, the Smith's Point: G. 'Murchadh' – Murdo; 'gobha' – a smith (also the surname).

Bilidh The Fang, a low-lying point of rock, good for fishing. See similar on p. 244.

Càrn an Eisg G. The Fish Cairn: G. 'càrn' – a cairn; 'an èisg' – gen. sing. of 'an t-iasg' – the fish.

Rubha a' Chàis The Sorrow Headland: G. 'a' chàis', gen. sing. of 'an càs' – the sorrow. The meaning of the word 'càs' in this context is uncertain. According to folklore, bodies were interred here; see **Eilean nam Marbh**, below. Eilean a'Chàis The Isle of Sorrow: G. 'eilean' – an island.

Eilean nam Marbh The Isle of the Dead, at the south-east corner of Rubha a Chàis: G. 'nam marbh', gen. plur. of 'na mairbh' – the dead persons. Also **Sgeir Dubh a' Chàis** and **Sgeir a' Chàis,** which are bare-rock satellites of the said isle.

Sgeir Léith Mhór The Great Greyish Rock: G. 'léith', an oblique form of 'liath' – greyish; also **Sgeir Léith Mheadhanach** – The Middle Sgeir Léith; and **Sgeir Léith Bheag** – The Little Sgeir Léith.

Caolas nan Sgeirean The Narrows of the Rocks; i.e. between the rocks and the mainland: G. 'caolas' – a strait; 'nan sgeirean', gen. plur. of 'na sgeirean' – the rocks.

A' Gheodha Ghuirm The Blue Gully: G. 'guirm', an oblique form of 'gorm'

Port Lìar Lìar's Port, a very small beach; G. 'Lìar' (pron. 'lee-ur'), perhaps a person's byname.

Geodha na Sgalaig The Farm-worker's Gully; see similar, p. 242.

Creag Healair The Rock of the Stone Slabs: G. 'créag' – rock; N. 'hellur' – stone slabs.

Mìbhig The Middle Bay: N. 'mìth' – middle; 'vík' – a bay; a minor cove between Port Lìar and Papastaidh. In the spring, huge quantities of seaweed come ashore in this bay.

Stiogha nan Cliabh The Creel Path; see similar, p. 228.

Bun na h-Aibhne The River Estuary: G. 'na h-aibhne', gen sing. of 'an abhainn' – the river.

Papastaidh The Monk's Place: N. 'papi' – a monk; 'stath' – a place, spot. A beach of rough shingle where, in recent centuries, the Cléid boats were sometimes beached; evidently a place with a very long history.

Na Taighean-Saillidh The Salting-houses: G. 'taigh-saillidh' – salting-house; 19th Cent.

Abhainn Mhór Phabail The Great River of Pabail, forming the boundary between Pabail Uarach and Pabail Iarach; enters the sea close to Port Phabail.

Pabail Iarach

Sgeirean Bàbaidh MacKenzie's Rocks: G. 'Bàbaidh', a byname of the MacKenzies of Lewis.

An Sgeir Ghuailneach The Shouldered Rock: fem. form of 'guailneach' from G. 'guailneach' – a shoulder. By the level of the tide on this tall hunched rock to the south of the Port entrance, fishermen bringing heavily-laden boats in to the beach were able to judge the depth of the sea under the keel.

An Sgeir Dhearg The Red Rock; G. 'dearg' – red.

Cladach nan Sgait The Skate Beach: G. 'nan sgait', gen. plur. of 'na sgaitean' – the skates; N. 'skatta'.

An Carragh Dubh The Black Rock: G. 'carragh' rock; 'dubh' black.

An Tràigh The Shore. A large area of the shore exposed with the ebb-tide and productive of limpets and winkles: G. 'tràigh' – an ebb.

Sgarabord The Cormorants' Shore: N. 'skarfa' – of cormorant; 'borth' – the strip between high and low water, BMK: G. equivalent, 'Cladach nan Sgarbh'.

Sgeir na Buaile The Rock at the Cattle-enclosure; G. 'na buaile', gen. sing. of 'a' bhuaile' – the cattle-enclosure.

Sgeir an Tuill The Cave Rock; G. 'an tuill', gen. sing. of 'an toll' – the cave; also known as **Carragh Choinnich** Kenneth's Rock: G. 'carragh' – a rock; 'Coinneach' – Kenneth.

An Sgeir Mhaoil The Bare Rock: G. 'maol' – bare; i.e. without a covering of seaweed.

Geodha nan Calman The Rock-doves' Gully; see similar, p. 229.

Sinidh-geodha The Swimming Gully: N 'synda-gja' – swimming – gully: see p. 231.

Eilligeadh The Flat Stones Gully: N. 'hellur' – flat stones; 'gjá' – a gully.

An t-Strìdinn The Brindled (Rock): G. 'strìdeach' – brindled, i.e tawny with streaks of darker hue.

Stac nan Rionnach Mackerel Stack: G. 'nan rionnach', gen. plur. of 'na rionnaich' – the mackerels.

Na Tuill Dhubha The Black Caves: G. 'tuill', plur. of 'toll' – a cave/hole.

An Stac The Stack: N. 'stak' – a stack.

Creag a' Chaolais The Narrows Rock: G. 'caolas' – a strait.

Eilean Mór Phabail G. Great Pabail Island

An Tang The Tongue: N. 'tangi' – a tongue of land jutting into the sea; G. 'teanga' (a N. loan-word) – a tongue.

Sròn a' Chinn a Tuath The North-end Point. G. 'tuath' – north; 'a' cinn', gen. sing. of 'an ceann' – the head.

An Fhaing, a fishing point but named thus because of an old sheep-fank nearby.

Creag Alasdair Rois (also known as Creag A. Ross); so-named after Alasdair Ross who, generations ago, used to visit Eilean Mór Phabail to conduct academic research.

Eilean Beag Phabail Little Pabail Island.

Ursainn an Eilein Bhig The Doorpost (at the north-west corner) of the Eilean Beag: G. 'ursainn' – a doorpost or side pillar; 'an eilein bhig', gen. sing. of 'an eilean beag'.

An Tanalach The Shoal: G. 'tanalach' – a place of shallow water.

Bogha a' Chùirn The Cairn Reef: G. 'bogha' – a reef; 'a' chùirn', gen. sing. of 'an càrn' – a cairn.

Hangada Fada The Long Overhanging Cliff: N. 'hangandi' –

hanging (pres. part. of 'hanga'); G. 'fada' – long.

Leac Raghnailt Rachel's flagstone: G. 'Raghnailt' – Rachel.

Creag Thùr The Rock of Towers: G. 'tùr' – a tower.

Geodha Iomhair Ivor's Gully: G. 'Iomhar' – Ivor or Evander

Creag Dhòmhnaill Daoithean Dòmhnall Daoithean's Rock: 'Daoithean' a person's byname: G. 'daoithean' – a kind of edible seaweed; see p. 5.

An Rubha Liath The Grey Headland: G. 'liath' – grey.

Toll nan Calman Rock-doves' Hole/Cave: G. see similar, p. 229.

Sròn na Saorach The Liberty Point; perhaps the point at which farm animals were released after the harvest was complete: G. 'saorachadh' – the act of liberating.

Liathghal Greyish Rock: G. 'liath' – grey; 'gall' a rock.

Geodha a' Ghàrraidh Geodha of the Boundary Dyke; see **Sgeir a' Ghàraidh**, p. 233.

Gars The Fence (Gully); see similar, p.250.

Geodha Bheag an Fhraoich The Little Heathery Gully: G. 'fraoch' – heather.

Faing nam Fiadh The Deer Fank: G. 'nam fiadh', gen. plur. of 'na féidh' – the deer. There aren't any deer here! The word 'fiadh' was used locally for sheep that were difficult to access, due to their grazing on cliffs or seashore: G. 'fiadhaich' – wild.

Grod The Stones: N. 'grjót' – stones.

Geodha nan Cuiseag The Dockens' Gully: G. 'nan cuiseag', gen. plur. of 'na cuiseagan' – the dockens.

Leac Dhubh Adaim Adam's Black flagstone: G. 'Adam', a byname from Eng.; the G. form is 'Adhamh'.

In the distance, Eilean Mór and Eilean Beag Phabail which appear as one island

A' Chrotach The Hunchback Female; a high stack, about 100 metres from the Pabail Iarach cliffs: G. 'crotach' – having a hunched back.

Geodha a' Bheileis Chaim The Gully of the Crooked Mouth: G. 'beileis', archaic for 'beul' – a mouth; 'cam' – crooked.

Geodha na Sgalaig The Farm-worker's Gully: see similar, p. 240.

Geodha nam Faochag The Gully of the Winkles: G. 'nam faochag', gen. plur. of 'na faochagan' – the winkles.

A' Gheodha Ruadh The Reddish Gully: see similar, p. 240.

Surrag Bheag an Teampaill The Temple Gap: G. 'surrag' – a gap or cavity, the word often being used to name cavities in mountain-tops; 'an teampaill', gen. sing. of 'an teampaill' – the temple. **Surrag Mhór an Teampaill** The Great Gap of the Temple. Near here, are the ruins of an ancient building.

A' Churachd The Plantation: G. 'curachd' – a place in which plants or crops are growing; alternatively G.'currach' – a burial-place, DW.

An Coileach The Cockerel: G. 'coileach' – a cockerel. This stack, on the Pabail Iarach side of Gob na Circe and some forty metres from the shore; is shaped rather like a crowing cockerel.

Suardail

The Grassy Glen: N. 'svarth' – grass; 'dal' – a glen. Alternatively, it may derive from 'suthr' – southern. With Pabail to the north, this would make Suardail 'The Southern Glen'.

Uaigh Nighean an t-Sagairt The Grave of the Priest's Daughter: G. 'uaigh' – a grave; 'nighean' – a girl or daughter; 'an t-sagairt', gen. sing. of 'an sagart' – the priest. Clergy of the early Celtic Church were allowed to marry.

Geodha Mhór an Teampaill Great Temple Gully: G. 'an teampaill', gen. sing. of 'an teampaill' – the temple. **Geodha Bheag an Teampaill** The Small Temple Gully.

Rubha an Teampaill The Temple Headland; also known as **Rubha 'n Iar-dheas** – The South-west Headland: G. 'an Iar-dheas' – south-west.

Leacan Mhic 'Ain 'ic Greumainn The Flagstones of the son of Iain son of Graham, said to be the place where Iain was killed in olden times. G. 'leac' – a flat stone.

Toll Mhòr Gaoth 'n-Iar-dheas The Great Hole of the South-west Wind: G. 'toll' – hole; 'gaoth' – wind; 'an iar-dheas' – south-west.

Circe-sgeir The Church Rock: N. 'kirkja' – a church; 'sker' – a rock.

Bà-Ciaraidh, a notoriously dangerous cliff which has claimed the lives of many animals. At one point on the rim there is an inviting downward slope, at the foot of which is a steep step leading on to a grassy breast that becomes increasingly steep. Once on the slope, an animal cannot escape. The name may not be G. ('bà' – cattle, etc.), but N. and comprised two words, the first of which is 'bakki' – a cliff.

Stac Creag na Caraidh The Stack of the Unstable Rock; severe erosion here: G. 'na caraidh', gen. plur. of 'a' charadh' – evidence of erosion.

Gob na Creige The Point of the Rock, i.e., the headland nearest to the Chicken Rock: G. 'na creige', gen. sing. of 'creag' – a rock. The headland is also known as **Gob na Circe,** literally, The Hen's Beak: G. 'na circe', gen. sing. of 'a' chearc' – the hen.

A' Chearc The Chicken Rock (lit. The Hen) is a low stack situated about 200 metres seaward of Chicken Head, the most southerly headland of An Rubha. Centuries ago, there was a Celtic church, with an associated community, on the headland of **Àird Chirc.** Cartographers and others confused the N. 'kirkja' (cf. Scots 'kirk') with G. 'cearc' – a hen.

An t-Isean The Chick: G. 'isean' a chick; a small stack close to the Chicken Rock.

Stac nan Caorach The Sheep Stack: G. 'nan caorach', gen. sing. of 'na caoraich' – the sheep.

Rubha a' Ghuilbnich The Curlew Headland: G. 'guilbneach' – a curlew.

Geodha an Làir or **Geodha na Làrach** The Mare Gully: G. 'làir' – a mare.

Leabaidh a' Phearsain or **Leabaidh a' Mhinisteir** The Parson's or Minister's Bed: G. 'pearsan'/'ministear' – a clergyman; 'leabaidh' – a bed/resting place.

Sròn Chreag Nó The Point of Nó's Rock; 'Nó', a person's byname.

Leabaidh na Bà Bàine The White Cow's Bed: G. 'leabaidh' – a bed; 'na bà bàine', gen. sing. of 'a' bhò bhàn' – a white cow. It is also known as Leabaidh na Bà-bainne The Dairy-cow's Bed: G. 'na bà-bainne', gen. sing. of 'a' bhó-bhainne' – the dairy cow.

Geodha nan Coineanach The Rabbits' Gully: G. 'nan coineanach', gen. plur. of 'na coineanaich' – the rabbits.

An Rubha Dearg The Red Headland: G. 'rubha' – a promomtory; 'dearg' – red.

Sgaraisgeir The Cormorant Rock: N. 'skarf' – a cormorant; 'sker' – a rock.

Bugha nam Bodach – The Old Men's Green: G. 'bugha' or 'bogha' – an arc of green grass found, for example, round the bend of a river. Here, it is an arc of grass half way down the cliff, which has become known by the above name.

Bun an Uillt Bhig The Estuary of the Allt Beag: G. 'an uillt bhig', gen. sing. of 'an t-allt beag' – the little burn.

Bun an Uillt Dhruisich The Estuary of the Druiseach Burn: G. 'an Uillt Dhruisich', gen. sing. of 'an t-Allt Druiseach'; 'druis' (local for 'dris') – gorse.

Am Murtair The Killer, a stretch of high cliffs, notorious for the number of animals killed there: G. 'murtair' – a killer/ murderer.

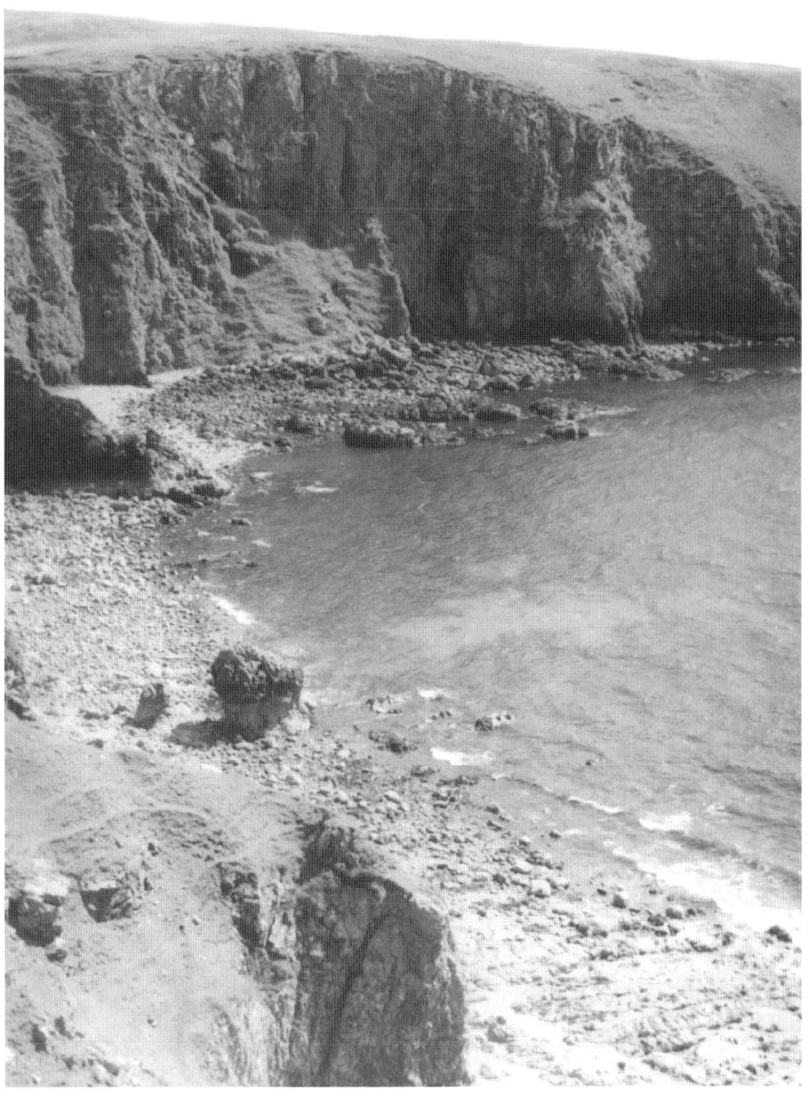

Bugha nam Bodach with the 'old men's green' in the cliff-face left of centre

An Carragh Gorm The Blue Rock: G. 'gorm' – blue.

An Carragh Sgreabach The Scabbed Rock: G. 'sgreab' – a scab.

A' Gheodha Mheadhanach The Middle Gully: G. 'meadhanach' – middle.

Stiogha Mhic Ille Chaim It is likely that the name (excluding G. 'stiogha' – a path) consisted of three words: N. 'bakka-hlithe-kamb' – The Crest of the Slope of the Cliff. Gaels mistook the N. 'bakka' for G. 'mac' – a son, hence 'mhic', gen. sing. of 'mac'.

Bun Allt Bhòsdaidh The Estuary of the Bòsdaidh Burn: G. Bòstaidh, from N. 'bolstath' – a farm.

Bun na Gile The Foot of the Gil: G. 'gil' (a N. loan-word) – a ravine; 'bun'- a terminus.

Geodha an Tairbh The Bull Gully: G. 'an tairbh' – gen. sing. of 'an tarbh' – the bull.

Frata-sgeir The Steep-sided Rock: N. 'bratt' – steep; 'sker' – a rock.

Geodha a' Chuibhrig The Concealment Gully: G. 'a' chuibhrig', 'an cuibhrig' – a covering or concealment.

Grèinigeadh The Green Gully; one side is entirely covered with grass: N. 'groen' – green; 'gjá'. According to contemporaneous reports, the mutineers of the *Jane* landed with their haul of silver in this gully in 1821. Locals claim that in fact the mutineers were arrested while attempting to conceal their loot in the adjacent Geodha a' Chuibhrig. See p. 62.

Cluas Creag Tharmoid The Bulge of Norman's Rock: G. 'cluas' – an ear. 'Tarmod' – Norman. The word 'cluas' included in the names of rocks and reefs may mean an extention or, as in this case, a bulge.

Sailigeadh The Fishing Huts Gully; alternatively, The Seals' Gully; see similar on p. 254.

Creag nan Eun The Birds' Rock: G. 'nan eun' gen. plur. of 'eun' – a bird.

Geodha na h-Inghinn The Girl's Gully, a name usually indicating that a girl perished at this place; see similar on p. 244.

Cràbhaig Crab Bay: N. 'krabba' – edible crabs; 'vík' – a bay.

Clach Chràbhaig The Stone of Cravig: G. 'clach' – a stone.

Creag Mhic Ghille Phàraig The Rock of the Son of St Patrick's devotee: G. 'gille' – a lad, servant, follower, etc.

Stac Shuardail The Stack of Swordale: G. form of N. 'stak' – a stack. **Caol na Stac** The Stack Narrows: G. 'caol' – narrows.

Bòit: a short tip of rock pointing into the Minch; see Slochd Bòit, p. 255.

A' Gheodha Fhada The Long Gully: G. 'fada' – long.

Geodha nan Sgait Skate Gully: G. 'nan sgait', gen. plur. of 'na sgaitean' – the skates; also **Piotar nan Sgait** The Skate Pool; loanwords from N. 'pyttr' – a pool; 'skata' – a skate.

Bun Allt na Faing The Estuary of the Fank Burn.

Rubha nan Caorach Sheep Headland: G. 'nan caorach', gen. plur. of 'na caoraich' – the sheep.

Geodha nan Caorach The Sheep Gully.

Geodha a' Mhairt Gully of the Cattle-beast: G. 'a' mhart', gen. sing. of 'am mart' – a cattle-beast.

Geodha Bun a' Ghàrraidh The Gully at the Foot of the Boundary Dyke.

An Sgonnan The Stone Block – a flattish reef of irregular surface, accessible at low tide and covered with seaweed: G. 'sgonnan' – a stone block; also called **An Sgòrnan** The Throat: G. 'sgòrnan' – a throat.

Creag nan Ceumannan The Steps' Rock: G. 'nan ceumannan' – gen. plur. of 'na ceumannan' – the steps.

Am Port Caol The Narrow Port: G. 'caol' – narrow.

An Carragh Beag and **An Carragh Mór** – The Big Rock and the Little Rock: G. 'carragh' – a rock.

An Stiogha The term here is applied, not only to the cliff-path, but also includes the opening into which boats were hauled and berthed: G. 'stiogha' – a path.

Frataisgeir (centre picture) with Bugha nam Bodach behind

Port Shuardail Suardail Port, the beach on which fishing-boats were berthed during the fishing season.

An Cnoc

The Hill: G. 'cnoc' – a hill.

Ramadal Ravens' Glen: N. 'hrafna-dal' ravens' – glen. Hrafni may have been a personal name, making Ramadal Hrafni's Glen. (BMK)

Tràigh Ramadail Ramadal Shore: G. 'tràigh' – a seashore; the area exposed at low tide is productive of shellfish and/or seaweed. Gob Ramadail Ramadal Point.

Geodha nan Calman The Rock-doves' Gully; see similar, p. 190.

Geodha na Cairteach The Cart Gully, so named at a time when seaweed used for fertilizer was transported by horse and cart to the crofts: G. 'na cairteach', gen. sing. of 'a' chairt' (pron. carst) – a cart.

Grioga The Landings Gully; a little cove on the Bràigh side of Ramadail, used for embarking and disembarking crewmen and their gear: N. 'greith' – free from obstacles; 'gjá' – a gully.

Oitir a' Bhràighe The Bràigh Sandbank; stretching offshore for about quarter of a mile: G. 'oitir' – a sandbank: for 'bràigh', see p. 226.

Glossary

air bhiod on tenterhooks
amadan a fool
aran bread
aran-coirc oaten bread
arbhar a cereal crop such as oats or barley, standing or in sheaf

bantrach a widow
balach a boy; plur. balaich
being/an bench/es
bodach an old man; plur. – *bodaich*
bothag a bothy or small hut
bothag-chearc a hen-coop
brà a quern
brogach a lad; an urchin
buidhe yellow
buntàta a potato or potato crop
bunag-slait the butt-end of a bamboo fishing-rod

cailleach/an old woman/women
caithris na h-oidhche – night-time courtship
caithtean a worn-through area of fabric
calaboose jail
caraid a friend or blood relation
ceàrd/an tinker/s
céilidh a social gathering
clach a stone
clann children
co-dhiù anyway
coileach a cockrel
còinneachan a moorland bee
conastapal a constable
cràic a stack of hair
criothnachd wheat
crodh cattle
croman a kind of hoe
cruach a stack;
cruach-mhònach a peat-stack
cuip whip, a birch, i.e. an instrument for applying corporal punishment
cùlaist a bedroom

Cruthaighear The Creator

deoch n. drink/ alcoholic drink
Diabhal The Devil
diathad the main afternoon meal
dìg a ditch; plur. – *dìgean*
dìomhain idle/ futile/ doomed to failure
dosan in hairstyle, a frontal tuft
druimeag a backpack or knapsack
duilich difficult/sorry

eathar a boat
eathar-rothaid a road-boat
eòrna barley

fàd a block of peat dried by wind and sun
faoileag a seagull
feòil meat; gen. – *feòla*
feòil-réisgt' smoked pickled meat
fliuch wet
fireann male, adj.
Gàidhealtachd a Gaelic region
galair a disease
galair nan cearc fowl-pest
gealach a moon
giomach a lobster
gràdh n. love
gun fhiosd in secret/ involuntarily

Hearach a man from Harris; (Na Hearadh – Harris)

iodhlann a small garden or yard
iodhlann-chàil a cabbage nursery
ionmhainn beloved

Leódhasach a Lewis-man
luinneag a ditty

mac a son
Mac an Diabhail Devil's Son
manachan a buttock

muc a pig
muc-mhara a whale
muc-bhreac a killer whale

oileag/an fist-sized stone/s
òr gold

peic a crumb/ sliver
(am) piocas (the) chickenpox
piullag/an rag/s
poit a pot
poit-dhubh a still
poit-mhùin a chamber-pot
pollag/an peat-bank/s

rabhd a rhyme
riasg raw peat
Rubhach n. – an inhabitant of An Rubha; adj. – belonging to An Rubha
rusbadaich n. – rustling

seall look
seanair a grandfather
sgoth an open-decked boat used for inshore fishing
sgumair an instrument used for trapping dead herring escaped from a drift-net
sitig mire/ mud
slugan a mouthful of liquid
smodal refuse
somag a cosy little nest
spealtrag/an fried filleted herring/s
sràid a street
stiùireag a drink of water fortified with oatmeal and seasoning
strùpag a cup of tea, etc.
suathaid disreputable, ridiculous
sùbhag a strawberry

taigh-dubh a blackhouse
taobh a side;
taois dough
tàrnach a resounding blow
teine-dé shingles
tighearna a lord
tocasaid a hogshead (a very large barrel)
tòin backside
treas-tarraig thrice distilled whisky
troimhe a chéile – upset/miffed
trustar a disreputable person; a villain
trusgan attire/ uniform
Tursachan Standing Stones (Calanais)

Uibhisteach a man from Uist
Uill! Well!
uisge water
uisge-beatha whisky; lit. 'water of life'

Phrases and Exclamations

The following phrases and exclamations are devices used by the storyteller to reinforce the truth, to emphasise the dramatic content of his story, or to show contempt or rejection of another's.

Ach seo ort . . . But then . . .
Ach a ghràidh ort, But, oh, beloved one, . . . (followed by an account of a set-back)
Gu sealladh Dia ort! May God look upon thee!
A bhalaich ort! Oh, boy!
Aig Dia tha fios! God only knows!
A Dhia gléidh mi! Oh, God save me!
Gu sealladh Dia ort! Goodness Gracious! (lit. May God attend to thee!)
A charaid ort! . . . Boy, O Boy! (lit. Oh dear, friend!)
A chiall, gléidh mi! Oh, sanity, preserve me!
A dhuine bhochd! Oh, Man alive!
A Thighearna Oh Lord
An Taobh Siar The West Side
'San cac A likely story! (a dismissive exclamation)
Seadh, a bhalaich! Yes, lad!

Cù gun urra A stray dog, i.e. one without a master
Cuan nan Orc The Whales' Ocean – between the Isle of Lewis and Sutherland
Cuidich an Rìgh Help the King: motto of Clan MacKenzie and of the Seaforth
Cuidich v. help: rìgh – a king
Sin thu fhéin, a bhalaich! That's the way, my lad!